IMAGES
of America

THE CRUISER *HOUSTON*

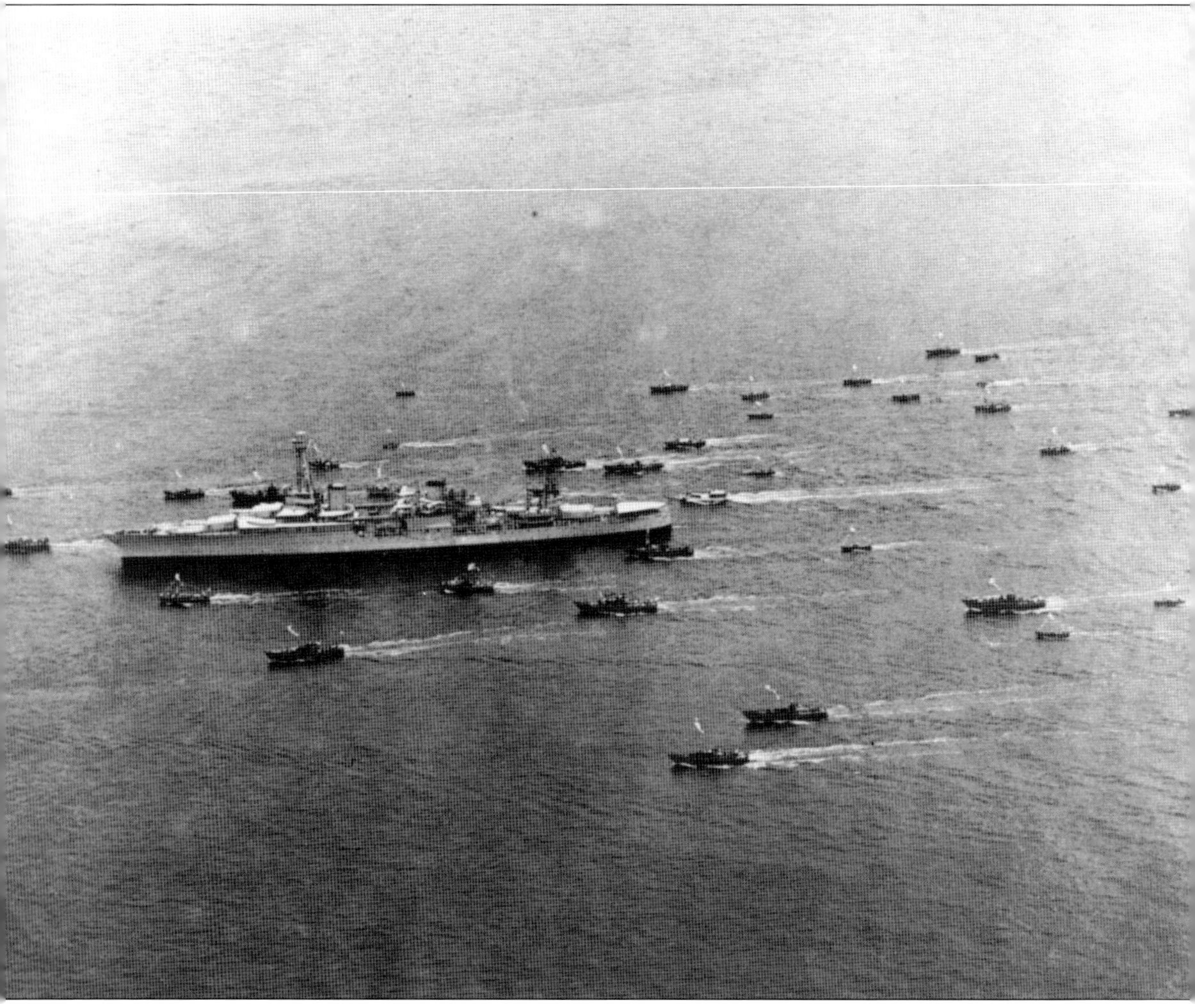

The cruiser *Houston*, with Pres. Franklin D. Roosevelt aboard, steams into Honolulu escorted by a flotilla of smaller vessels during Roosevelt's 1934 voyage aboard the vessel. (US Navy Heritage and History Command.)

On the Cover: *Houston's* colors are at half-mast awaiting the return of its funeral party ashore at Tjilatjap, Java, for the burial of 48 men killed when a bomb exploded above *Houston's* aft eight-inch turret during the Battle of the Makassar Strait. This photograph was taken from the light cruiser USS *Marblehead*, also heavily damaged during the battle. (US Navy Heritage and History Command.)

IMAGES
of America

THE CRUISER *HOUSTON*

Mark Lardas

ARCADIA
PUBLISHING

ISBN 978-1-4671-2742-4

Published by Arcadia Publishing
Charleston, South Carolina

Printed in the United States of America

Library of Congress Control Number: 2017939397

For all general information, please contact Arcadia Publishing:
Telephone 843-853-2070
Fax 843-853-0044
E-mail sales@arcadiapublishing.com
For customer service and orders:
Toll-Free 1-888-313-2665

Visit us on the Internet at www.arcadiapublishing.com

To Janet, my wife—40 years and counting.

Contents

ACKNOWLEDGMENTS

No book is the product of a single author. Many folks helped me as I wrote and assembled this book. Those I especially would like to note include my son, William Lardas, for accompanying me on many of my trips and doing the photography; all the wonderful folks at the Houston Maritime Museum, including, but not limited to, Leslie Bowlin (museum director), Nathan Kyllonen (curatorial assistant), Caitlin Avinger (outreach and education coordinator), and Lucia Cerritos (former administrative manager); and Christian Kelleher, head of special collections for the University of Houston Libraries, for all his help with their collection.

I would also like to thank Mike Kinsella and Caitrin Cunningham, my editors at Arcadia Publishing, for their assistance. Lastly, I thank my wife, Janet, for her support during this project.

The following list indicates the sources of the illustrations used in this volume:

AC	Author's collection
HMM	Houston Maritime Museum
LOC	Library of Congress
NARA	National Archives
RNDM	Royal Netherlands Defense Ministry
TPWD	Texas Parks and Wildlife Department
UHDL	University of Houston Digital Archive Library
USNHHC	US Navy Heritage and History Command
USN	US Navy
WL	Photograph by William Lardas

Introduction

It was the pride of Houston. A warship of an entirely new class, the cruiser *Houston* was born because of the Washington Naval Treaty of 1923 and was shaped by the London Naval Treaty of 1930. The Washington treaty was intended to stop a battleship construction race started during World War I. It throttled back battleship building and limited numbers retained. Old battleships and battleships currently being built were scrapped, and a 10-year moratorium on building new ones was instituted. The treaty did not limit cruiser numbers, however, only their maximum size and armament.

A cruiser-building race began. Before the Washington treaty, cruisers typically displaced 5,000 tons and were armed with six-inch guns. The treaty permitted cruisers to displace no more than 10,000 tons and to carry guns up to eight inches. Suddenly, every nation with a navy was designing and building 10,000-ton cruisers with main batteries of eight-inch guns.

The US Navy jumped into this race, getting congressional authorization to build eight new "treaty" cruisers. In 1925, the Navy approved construction of two cruisers. These became the *Pensacola* class. However, the Navy did not want all its cruiser eggs in one design basket. In 1926, when funds for three new cruisers appeared, the Navy went to a new design. Longer than the first treaty cruiser, with nine 8-inch guns in three triple turrets, the first ship in this new class was eventually named *Northampton*. Six were ultimately built.

Meanwhile, the city of Houston learned about the new cruisers planned by the Navy. The Bayou City was emerging as one of the principal cities of the Gulf Coast. The Port of Houston opened in 1914, supercharging growth. In 1920, *Houston's* population exceeded 138,000. By 1930, its population more than doubled. Houston wanted recognition.

Cruisers were traditionally named for cities. The only Navy ship named for Houston was a transport seized from Germany during World War I and renamed *Houston*. It was sold after the war's end. Houston wanted a more martial ship representing it. A brand-new cruiser sounded right.

The Cruiser Houston Committee emerged in January 1927 with the goal of getting the Navy to name one of its new cruisers for Houston. Prominent Texas citizens and politicians lobbied the Navy. Schoolchildren, prompted by the committee, sent letters. The Navy yielded to these appeals. On September 1, 1927, Curtis D. Wilbur, secretary of the Navy, announced the fifth *Northampton*-class ship would be named *Houston*.

The ship would be 600 feet, 3 inches long, with a beam of 66 feet, 1 inch. Its maximum draft was 23 feet. It had four propellers. Eight boilers fed four steam turbines producing 107,000 shaft horsepower. On trials, it reached 32.7 knots. With a full load of fuel, it could travel 12,000 nautical miles at 15 knots.

The fourth, fifth, and sixth *Northampton*-class ships were special in another way. They were built as fleet flagships. The forecastle was extended aft almost to the forward funnel, creating cabin space for an admiral commanding a fleet and his staff.

Houston was armed with nine 8-inch guns, four 5-inch/25-caliber antiaircraft guns, and six torpedo tubes in two triple mounts, and carried four floatplanes in a blast-proof hangar. The floatplanes were launched from two catapults, one on each side of the ship. *Houston's* only weakness was its thin armor, just 3–3 ¾ inches maximum for its belt, 1–2 inches for its deck, and 2–2 ½ inches maximum on its turrets. As a result, the Navy initially classified it as a light cruiser. As the 30th light cruiser built for the Navy, its identifying number was CL-30 (CL for cruiser, light).

Construction began May 1, 1928, when its keel was laid at Newport News Shipbuilding & Dry Dock Company in Newport News, Virginia. *Houston* was launched September 7, 1939. Over 2,000 Texans attended the launching. A delegation from the Cruiser Houston Committee participated in the launch ceremony. The sponsor was Elisabeth Holcombe, daughter of former Houston mayor Oscar Holcombe. He had spearheaded the letter-writing campaign. On September 9, the committee ordered a silver service for the cruiser. It was over a year before the City of Houston presented the silver service to its namesake cruiser.

It took another nine months to finish *Houston*. It was commissioned as a US Navy warship on June 17, 1930. Capt. Jesse B. Gay was *Houston's* plank-owning commander, the first of nine men who served as *Houston's* captain. By then, it had been re-rated as a heavy cruiser. The London treaty created this new category for cruisers with eight-inch guns, and the United States signed the treaty a month before *Houston's* commissioning. The only thing it changed was *Houston's* hull number, which became CA-30. Once commissioned, *Houston* made a shakedown cruise, sailing to Europe and back, before visiting its namesake city in October 1930.

Between *Houston's* launch and its arrival in Houston, the Roaring Twenties were replaced by the Great Depression. The Black Tuesday stock market crash occurred October 29, 1929. Good-looking *Houston* seemed to Houstonians symbolic of earlier, better days. The visit started a love affair between cruiser and city that outlived the ship.

The visit ended, and *Houston* left to complete its final runs and trials. *Houston* visited Houston twice more, once in 1934 and again in 1939. The city showered the cruiser with gifts as varied as a piano and Christmas fruitcakes and attention, which the crew cherished.

Meanwhile, *Houston*, then commanded by Capt. Robert A. Dawes, departed on January 14, 1931, for the Asiatic station, its first duty station. *Houston* arrived in Manila on February 22, and Adm. Charles B. McVay Jr. broke his flag on *Houston's* mast. He was the first of 23 flag officers and officials who used *Houston* as a flagship. Fourteen different admirals, one assistant secretary of the Navy, one secretary of the Navy, and the president of the United States flew their flags over *Houston*. The cruiser spent most of its career as a flagship.

Houston spent three years as flagship of the Asiatic Fleet, serving three admirals. Longest serving was Montgomery M. Taylor, aboard for nearly two years. China was in a tumult during the cruiser's tour. Japan picked a fight with China at Shanghai, and *Houston* witnessed the fighting.

Houston left the Asiatic Fleet for the United States on November 17, 1933, for a well-earned refit. Shortly after finishing the refit, *Houston* gained another important admirer, Pres. Franklin D. Roosevelt. He boarded *Houston* on July 1, 1934, for an "inspection tour." Really a vacation trip for the president, he spent over a month aboard. Roosevelt enjoyed it so much he would return to *Houston* for three more multiweek inspection tours in 1935, 1938, and 1939.

Houston split the rest of the 1930s between the Atlantic Fleet and the Pacific Fleet, spending most of its time in the Pacific. *Houston* was usually part of the Scouting Force, often its flagship. The Battle Force contained the Navy's modern battleships, a cruiser division, and covering destroyers. The Scouting Force was everything else. Its mission was finding enemy naval forces for the Battle Force.

As the decade ended, war clouds gathered. In 1937, Japan invaded China, starting the Second Sino-Japanese War. In September 1939, Germany invaded Poland, starting World War II. The United States stayed neutral for the first two years, but war with Japan or Germany seemed likely.

Houston had a substantial refit in 1940, preparing it for a war that loomed ahead, but which the United States was not yet in. Reflecting the increasing importance of aircraft since *Houston's* launch, its antiaircraft capabilities were improved. The five-inch guns were doubled, and many light antiaircraft guns were added. More importantly, better antiaircraft fire control systems were added.

In 1940, *Houston* was again assigned to the Asiatic Fleet, becoming its flagship on November 22 after arriving in Manila. It was a different Asiatic Fleet than the one *Houston* left earlier. Its commander was now the prescient Adm. Thomas Hart. As 1940 became 1941, Hart prepared for war with Japan. The fleet's ships, including *Houston*, were painted a dull gray. Hart withdrew US Navy river gunboats in China to the Philippines. He scattered the fleet's surface ships to ports safely out of range of Japanese warplanes stationed in Formosa and, later, French Indo-China.

On December 8, 1941 (or December 7 in Hawaii, on the other side of the International Date Line), Hart's fears were realized. Japan attacked Pearl Harbor, crippling the Navy's Pacific battleships in Hawaii. Later that day, the Japanese bombed Clark Field in the Philippines, surprising the US Army Air Corps on the ground, destroying the aircraft there, and gaining air superiority. The next day, Japan bombed Cavite Navy Yard, devastating it. On December 11, they sank the British battleship *Prince of Wales* and battle cruiser *Repulse*, the only Allied capital ships in the Far East. *Houston* was now the region's most powerful Allied warship.

The Philippines proved indefensible. Hart sent the fleet's auxiliaries to the Dutch East Indies. On December 15, *Houston* sailed to Surabaya, Java, to escort these ships to Darwin, Australia. *Houston* made two round trips between Java and Darwin over the next month. On January 31, 1942, *Houston* left Surabaya to stop a Japanese invasion of Borneo. The Allied fleet was discovered by Japanese aircraft on February 3 and attacked the next day by bombers.

In the Battle of Makassar Strait, *Houston* learned that three-fourths of its five-inch antiaircraft ammunition was defective. Despite this, due to excellent ship handling, only one bomb hit *Houston*. That one exploded above the aft turret. Shrapnel punched through the turret's thin top armor, disabling the turret and killing its crew.

Houston steamed to Tjilatjap, unloaded its wounded, and buried its dead. Even with only six working eight-inch guns, *Houston* remained the area's most powerful Allied surface warship. All other US cruisers had been sent home, damaged. If *Houston* left too, the effect on the Allies' morale would be devastating. Despite *Houston's* injury, its captain, Albert H. Rooks, opted to keep it in the fight.

Throughout February, the Allies fought a rearguard action against a Japanese juggernaut. Borneo fell, Sumatra fell, and the Japanese threatened Java. On February 27, the Allied fleet sailed from Surabaya to stop the Japanese invasion force. That day, the largest surface ship battle since Jutland was fought, the Battle of the Java Sea.

It was a disaster for the Allies. Two cruisers and three destroyers were sunk, and one cruiser badly damaged. *Houston* was one of two cruisers to escape undamaged. At battle's end, the Dutch admiral commanding ordered the surviving ships to retire.

The next day, February 28, *Houston* and Australian cruiser *Perth* attempted to escape the Java Sea through the Sunda Strait. Approaching it near midnight, the two warships discovered a Japanese invasion fleet. Realizing escape was impossible, the two cruisers attacked the troop transports. In a battle lasting two hours against a vastly superior force, first *Perth* and then *Houston* were sunk. On March 1, 1942, *Houston's* favorite warship died heroically.

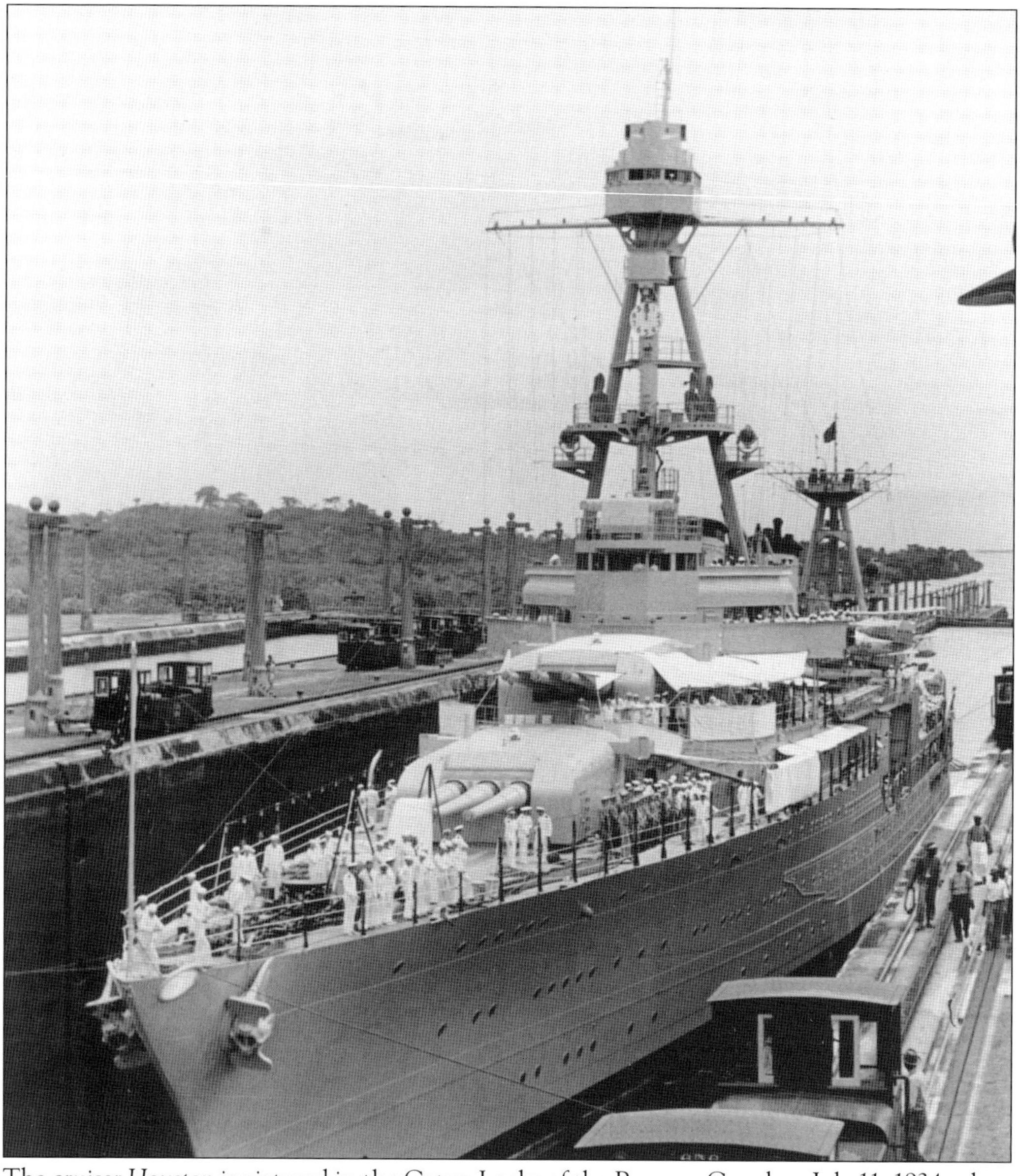

The cruiser *Houston* is pictured in the Gatun Locks of the Panama Canal on July 11, 1934, when Pres. Franklin D. Roosevelt was embarked on his first presidential cruise. (USNHHC.)

One

A Treaty Cruiser

Houston was a commissioned warship of the US Navy for just under 12 years, from June 1930 to March 1942, yet its history is longer. *Houston* took four years to plan and two years to build—18 years from conception to death. Although made from steel, like a living creature, *Houston* evolved and changed over its lifetime.

It was one of a new class of warships in the US Navy—armed like an armored cruiser but with the speed of a scout cruiser and protected like one. It carried eight-inch guns but had armor a five-inch gun could penetrate. This novel design sprang from the 1923 Washington Naval Treaty, intended to limit warship size and construction. Instead, it resulted in increasing the size and number of cruisers built worldwide.

Houston's design yielded the biggest warship permitted by the treaty, which was a displacement of 10,000 tons and guns no larger than eight inches. The Navy added smaller guns to protect *Houston* from destroyers, torpedo tubes for close combat, aircraft for reconnaissance, and powerful engines for speed. The added weapons and larger engines meant something had to go to keep it within 10,000 tons, so the designers went easy on the armor. *Houston* and its sisters were dubbed "tinclads" and called "eggshells armed with hammers."

Intended as a flagship, *Houston* had a long forecastle to provide cabin space for an admiral and his staff. The resulting ship was a beauty. It was long, lean, bristling with guns, and a pleasure to look at, especially in early 1930s white paint.

When the City of Houston learned the Navy was building a new set of cruisers, it lobbied to get one named for the city. When the Navy yielded to the campaign, Houston fell in love with its namesake cruiser, even though *Houston* the cruiser visited Houston the city only occasionally.

As time passed, *Houston* changed. The torpedoes were removed. The secondary battery was increased, and more small antiaircraft guns were added to protect *Houston* from the growing aerial threat. Yet, its basic beauty remained. This chapter tells the story of *Houston's* creation, its evolution, and its capabilities.

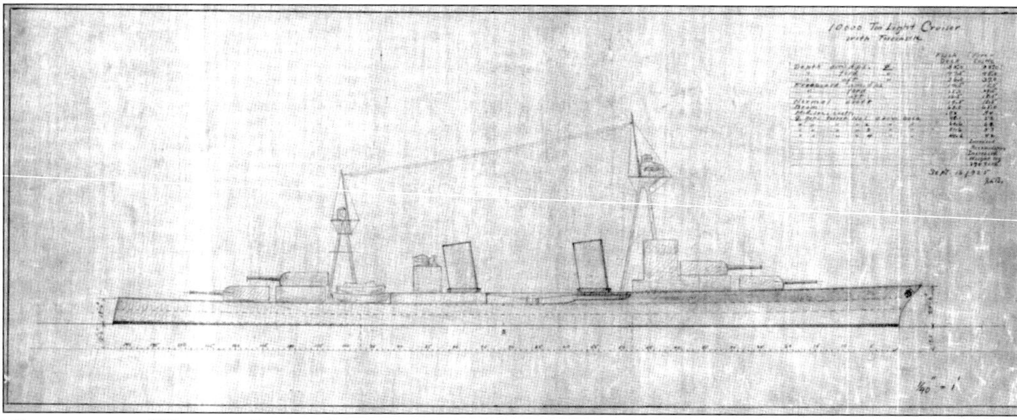

The genesis of *Houston* lay in this 1925 design for a light or scout cruiser, which displaced 10,000 tons and mounted a battery of 12 eight-inch guns in four triple turrets. This kept the ship within the constraints of the 1922 Washington Naval Treaty while providing the most powerful ship possible under its terms. (USNHHC.)

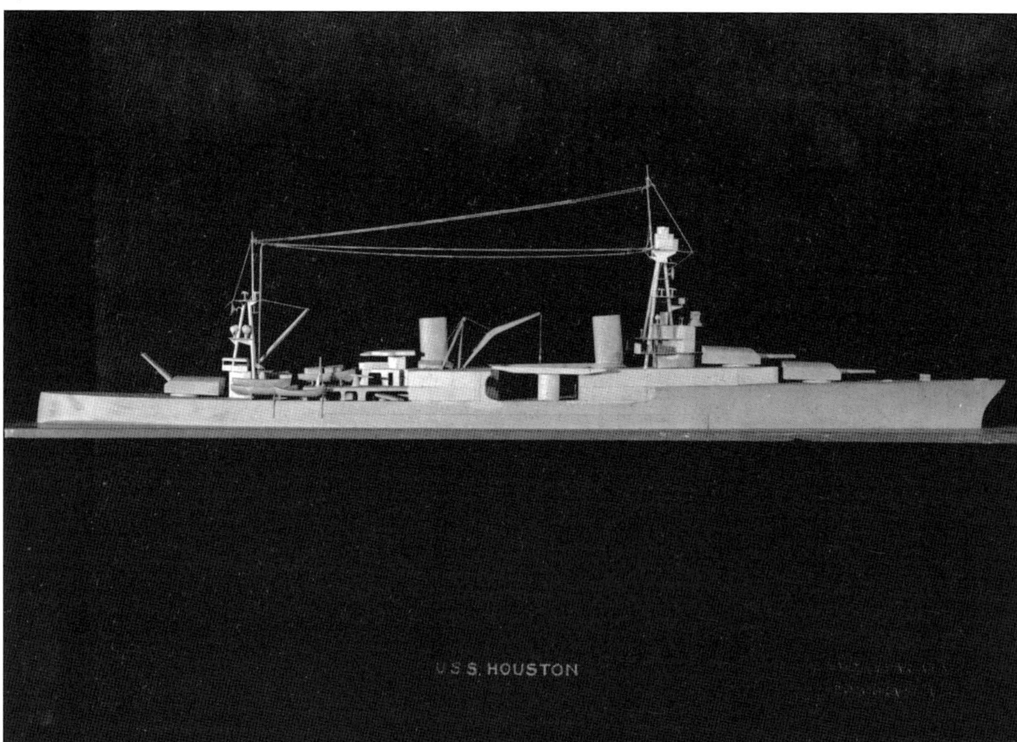

This model shows the design finally adopted for *Houston*. It had nine 8-inch guns in triple turrets, six torpedo tubes in triple mounts, and provision to carry four aircraft (launched off catapults amidships). It was originally a light cruiser due to its thin armor, designed to keep its weight under the 10,000-ton treaty limit. (USN.)

In 1927, when Houston heard the Navy was building a new batch of cruisers, the city formed the Cruiser Houston Committee to get the Navy to name one for the Bayou City. The committee was originally chaired by Thomas F. Ball. The governor of Texas, Daniel Moody (pictured here), was a supporter of the effort. (LOC.)

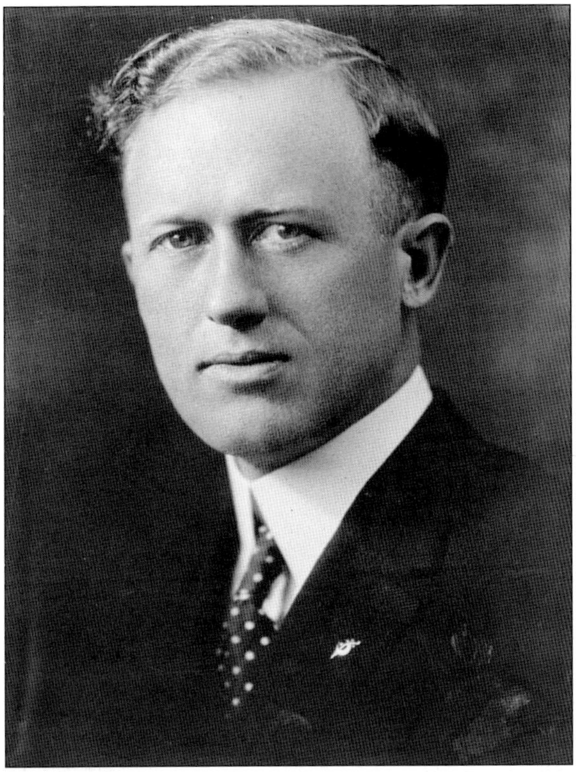

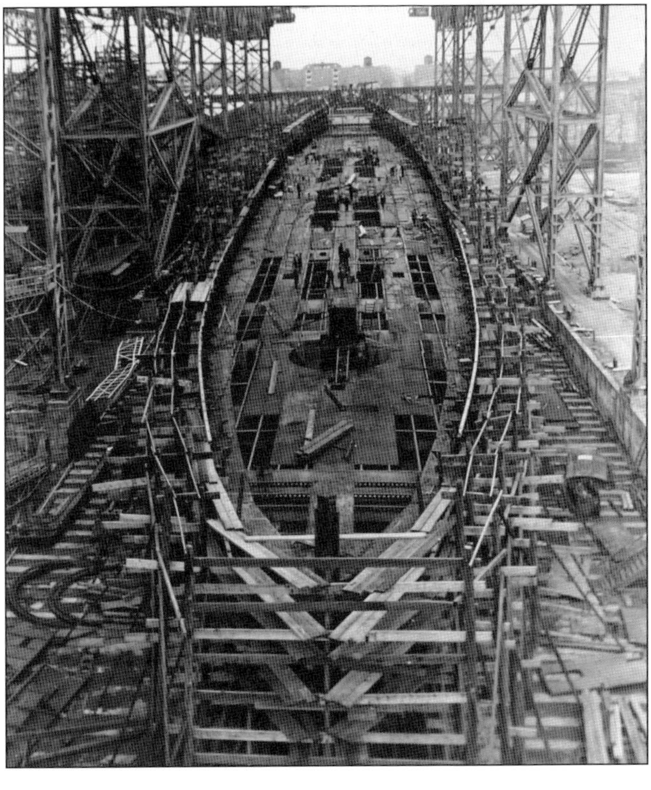

Construction of *Houston* started on May 1, 1928, when its keel was laid at Newport News Shipbuilding & Dry Dock Company in Newport News, Virginia. By the time of this photograph on January 2, 1929, construction was well along, with the hull taking shape. (NARA.)

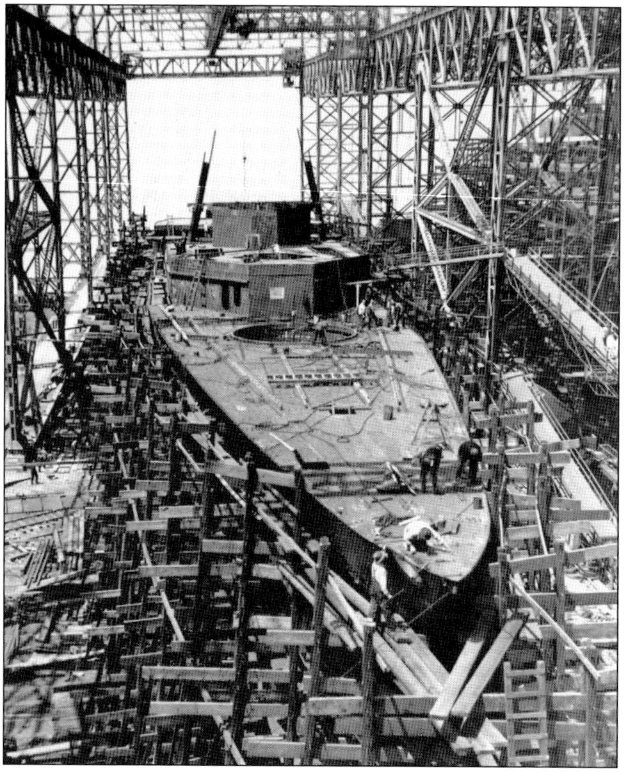

Six months later, on July 1, 1929, work on the hull was complete and progress on the superstructure was being made. Note the circular holes in the forecastle and forward superstructure. This was where two of *Houston's* three main turrets would go. (NARA.)

By September 1929, *Houston* was ready to be launched. Its namesake city sent a delegation to participate in the launching. The delegates stopped off at Washington, DC, to meet with Pres. Herbert Hoover, as seen here. To Hoover's right is Judge W.O. Huggins, representing Governor Moody of Texas. To Hoover's left is Houston mayor Walter Monteith. The woman at far left is Mary Ellen Bute, maid of honor for the christening, and next to her is Elisabeth Holcombe, the ship's sponsor. (LOC.)

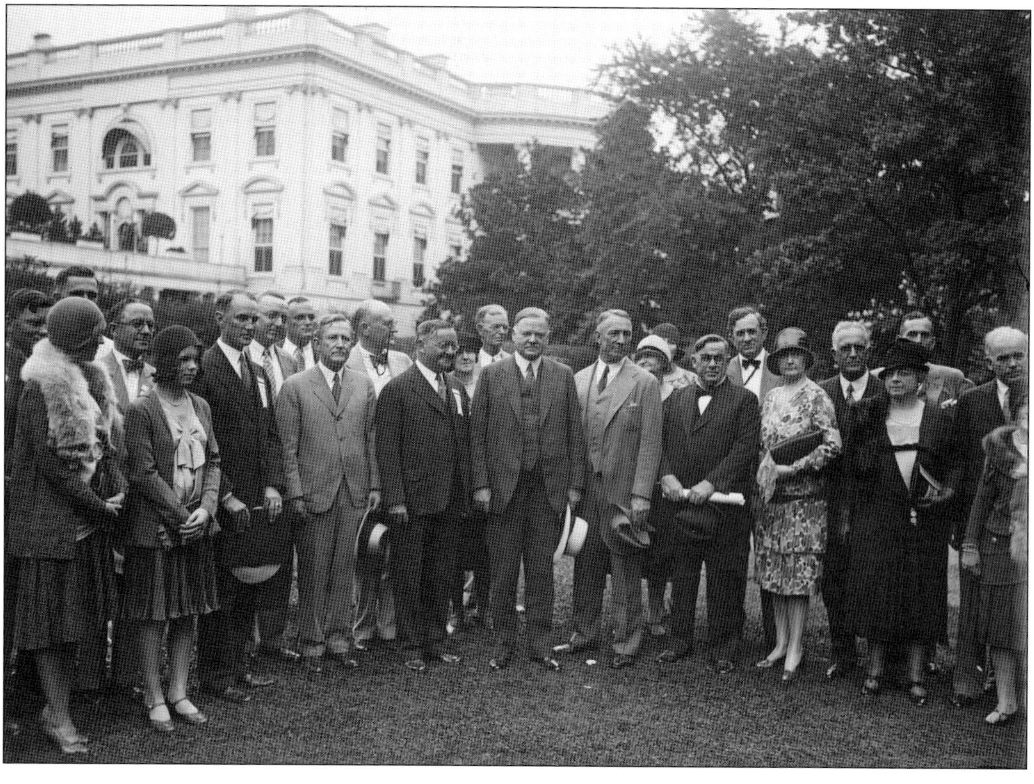

Here is *Houston* on its launch day, September 9, 1929. It was still rated as a light cruiser. Note the absence of the No. 3 turret. The turrets would be installed after launch. (NARA.)

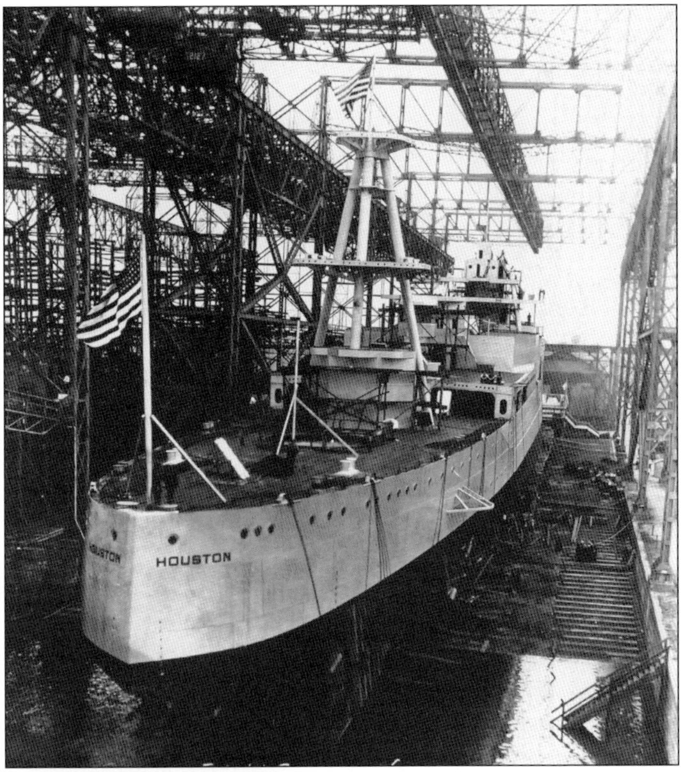

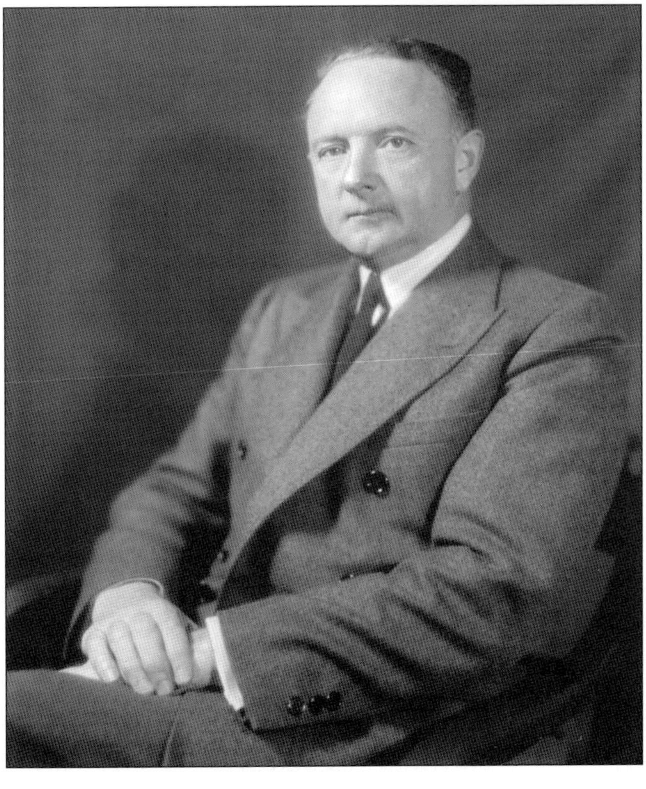

Master of ceremonies at the launch was Harry F. Byrd, the governor of Virginia, the state where *Houston* was built. (LOC.)

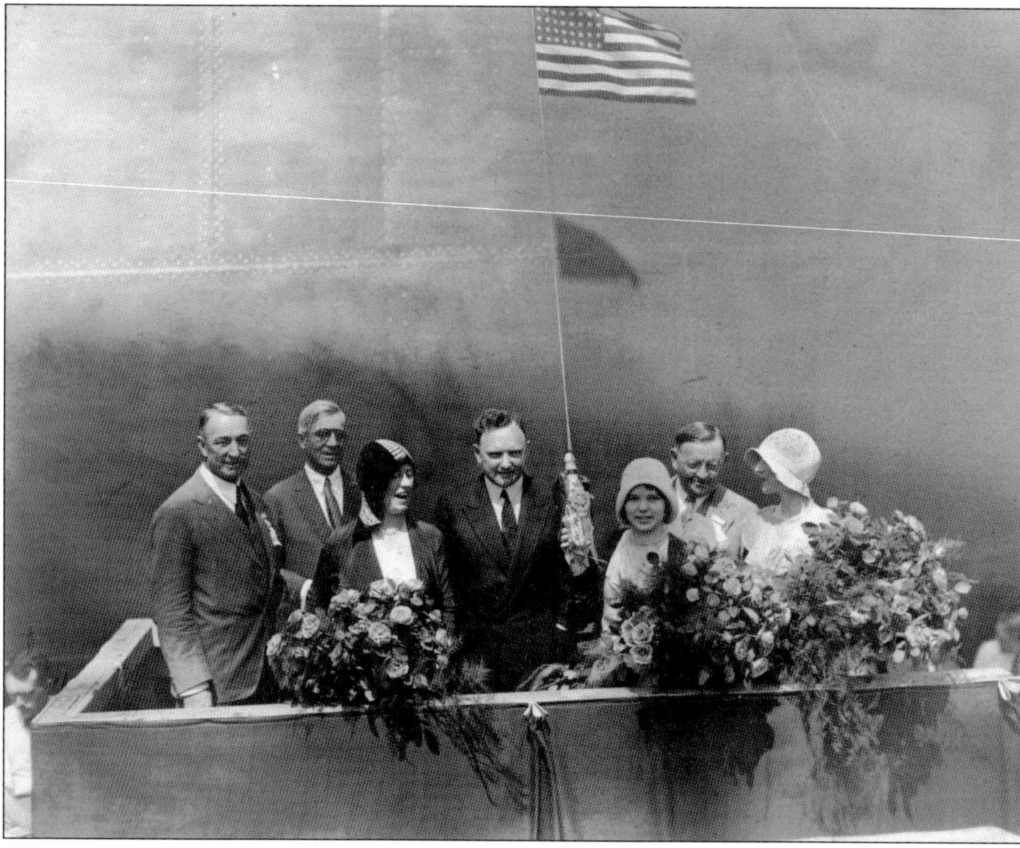

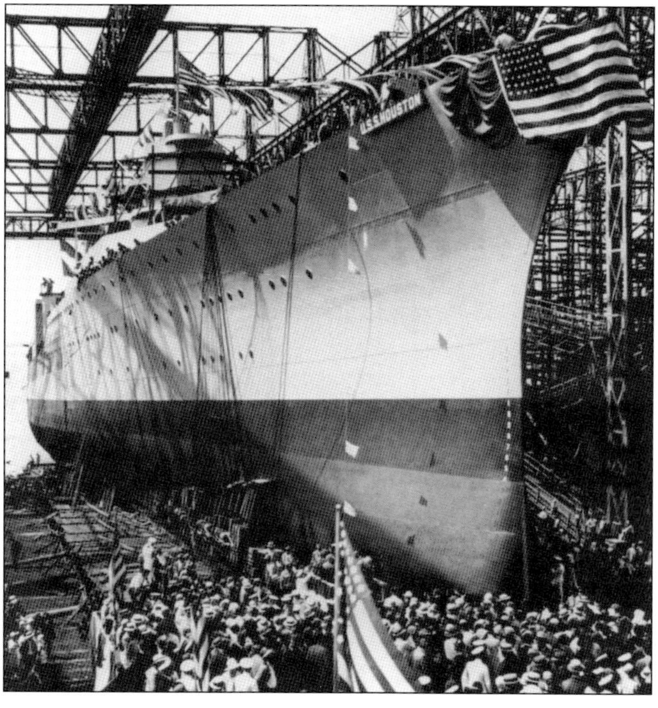

The christening party includes, from left to right, Mayor Monteith, unidentified, Mary Ellen Bute, Governor Byrd, Elisabeth Holcombe, Judge Huggins, and Charlotte Williams. Elisabeth Holcombe is holding a bottle filled with water from Houston's Buffalo Bayou. Bute became a noted filmmaker. Williams was a great-granddaughter of Gen. Sam Houston. (USN.)

Here, Holcombe is about to break the bottle against *Houston*, followed by the ship sliding down the launching ways. The 1920s were still roaring. Six days earlier, on September 3, 1929, the stock market hit a record high; however, Black Tuesday and the start of the Great Depression were seven weeks away. (USN.)

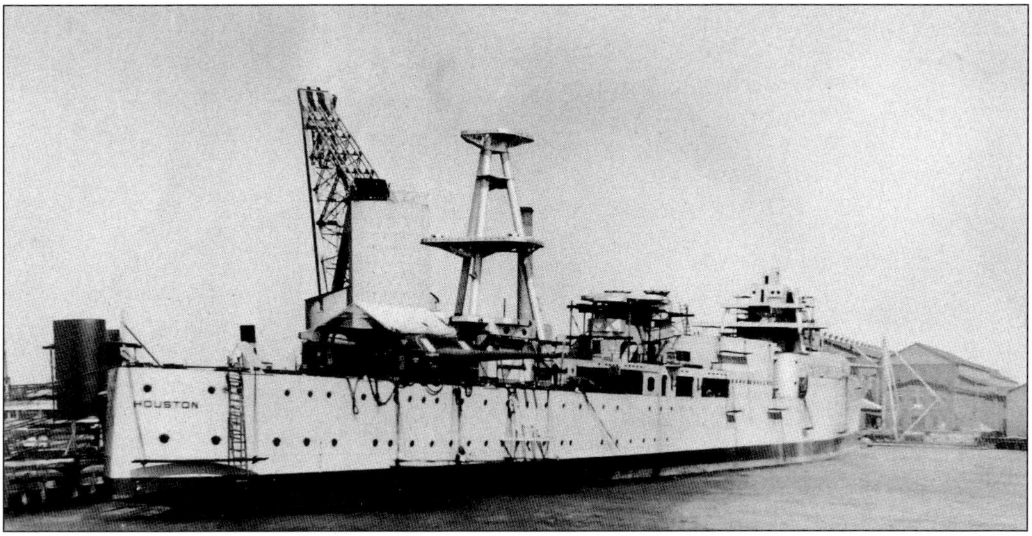

Three weeks later, *Houston's* main gun turrets had been added at a fitting-out dock at Newport News Shipbuilding & Dry Dock Company. The mainmast was also installed. The torpedo tubes, aircraft catapults, and much else remained to be added on October 1, 1929, when this photograph was taken. (NARA.)

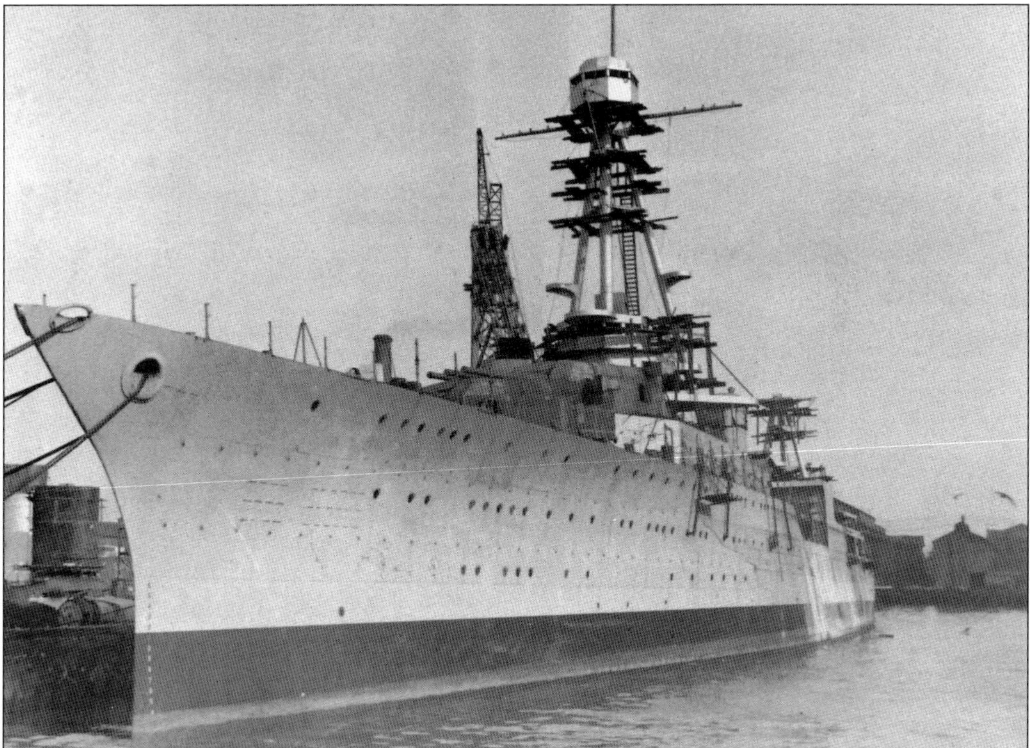

By January 1, 1930, *Houston* was much closer to completion, with both masts installed. It was still rated as a light cruiser. The London Naval Treaty of 1930, which redefined ships carrying eight-inch guns as heavy cruisers, would not be signed until April 22. On January 1, *Houston* was still nearly six months from joining the Navy as a commissioned ship. (NARA.)

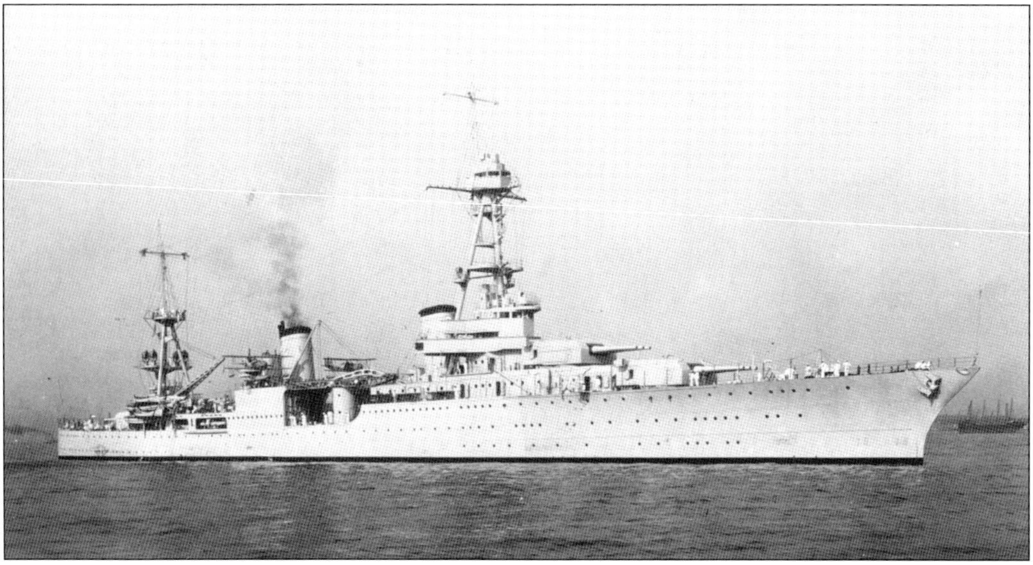

By the time *Houston* was commissioned on June 17, 1930, it had been reclassified as a heavy cruiser. It kept its hull number, changing from CL-30 to CA-30. After the commissioning ceremony, *Houston* started a shakedown cruise, which took it to England, the Netherlands, and France before returning to the United States. (USNHHC.)

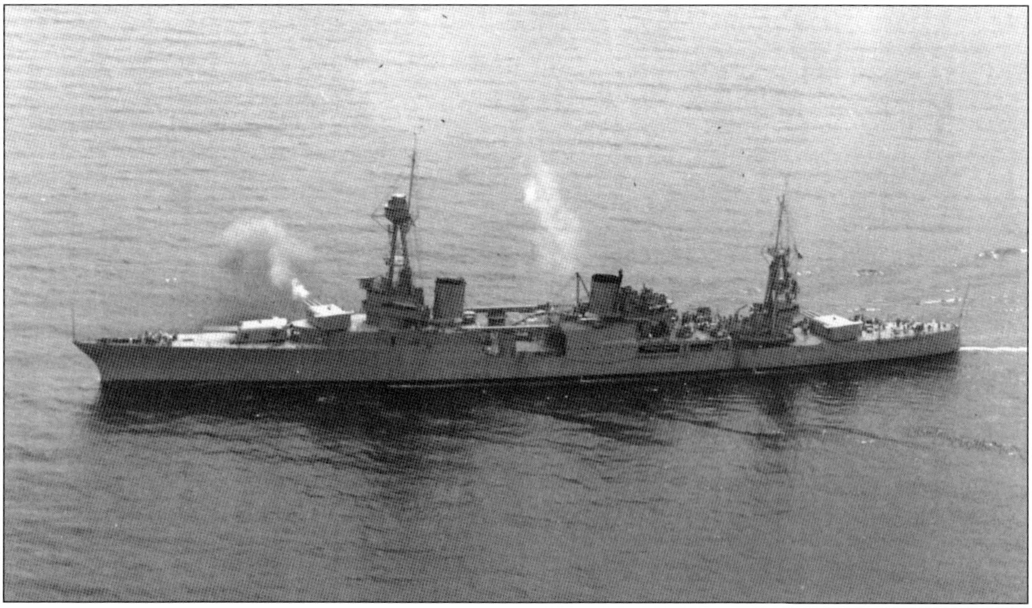

Houston's main armament was its nine 8-inch guns. They were placed in three lightly armored triple turrets. To save weight, and differing from then-standard practice, the guns in a turret could not elevate individually but were raised or lowered together. (NARA.)

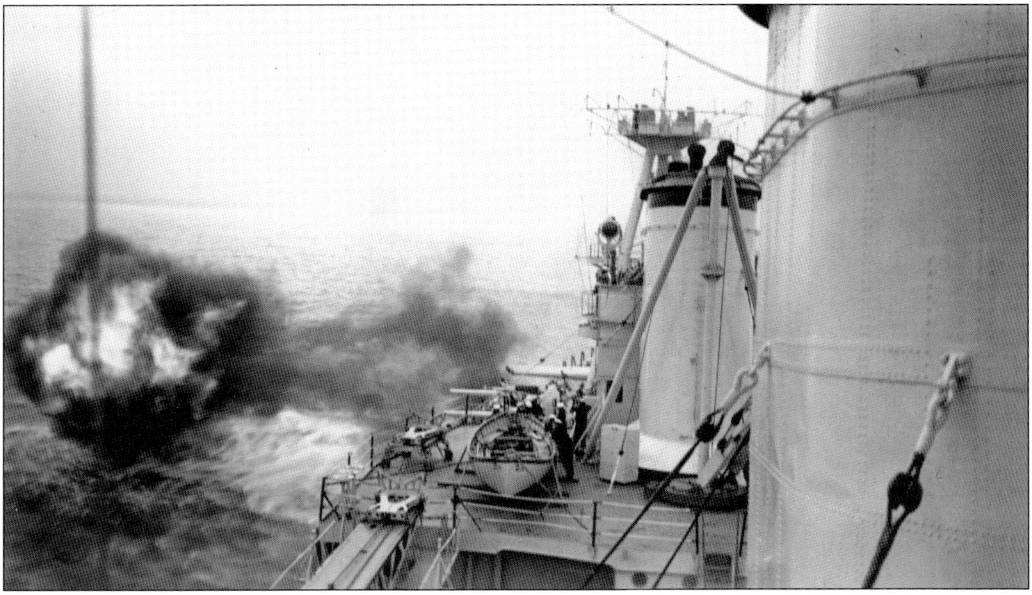

Each eight-inch gun fired a 260-pound shell. Using two 45-pound bags of propellant for each shot, each gun could send the shell 31,860 yards, or over 15 nautical miles. (HMM.)

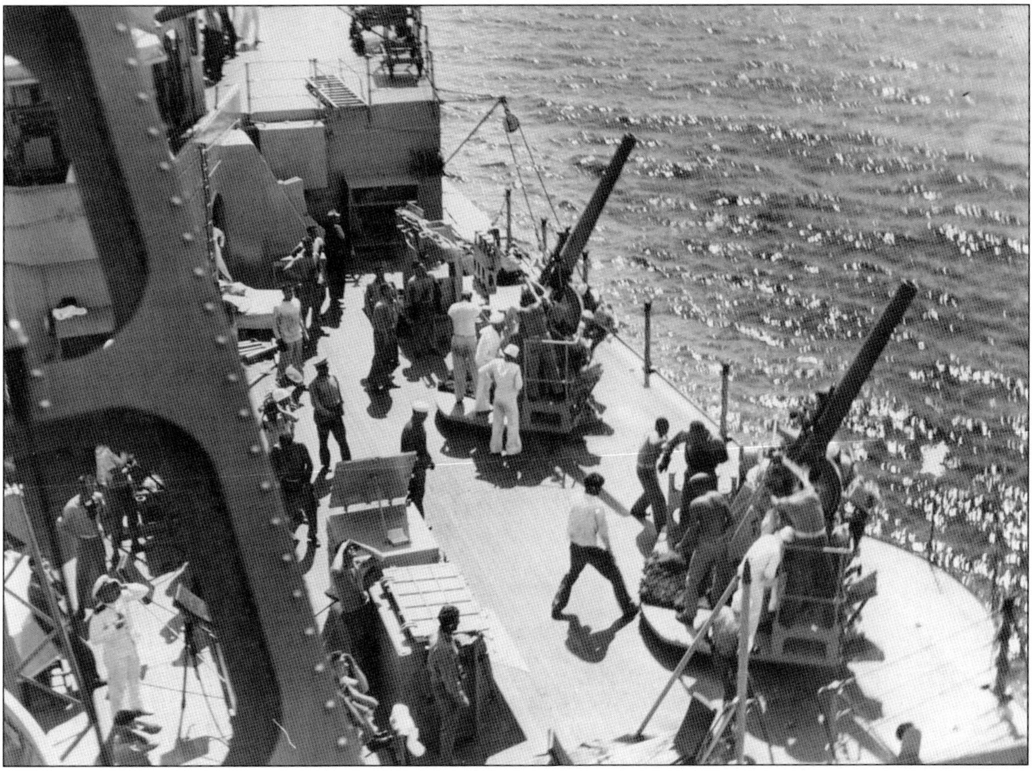

Houston also carried four 5-inch/25-caliber dual-purpose guns, which could be used against either aircraft or surface targets. When *Houston* was designed, these guns were seen primarily as protection from enemy destroyers. Over *Houston's* lifetime, aircraft grew more dangerous and threatening. The guns were not only seen in more of an antiaircraft role, but more were also added. (USNHHC.)

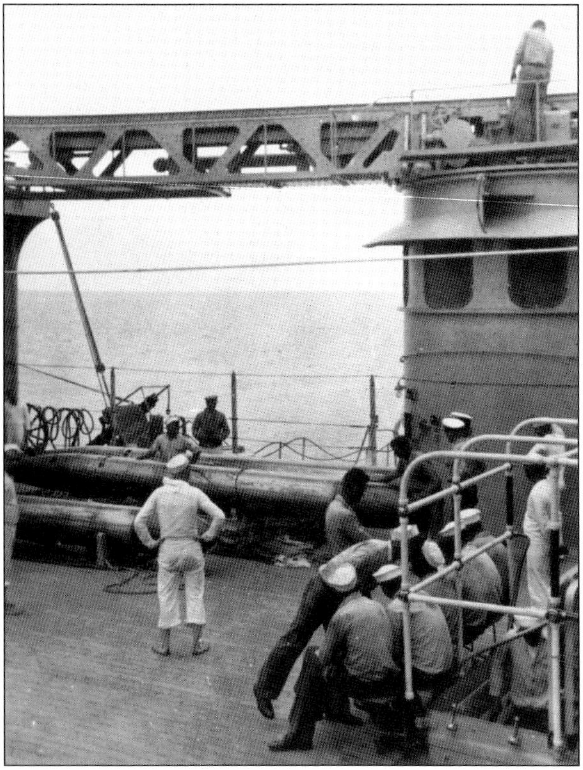

As launched, *Houston* also carried two sets of triple torpedo tubes, one on each side, behind the aft funnel. While *Houston* mounted torpedoes during its first tour as flagship of the Asiatic Fleet, they were removed shortly after its return to the United States. (USNHHC.)

Finally, *Houston* carried four aircraft. They were floatplanes, which were launched off its two catapults. These aircraft were used to assist *Houston* in its scouting role. They could see farther and move faster than the cruiser. They were also intended as gunnery spotters. *Houston* carried two types of floatplanes: the Vought Corsair (shown launching) and later, the Curtiss SOC Seagull. (USNHHC.)

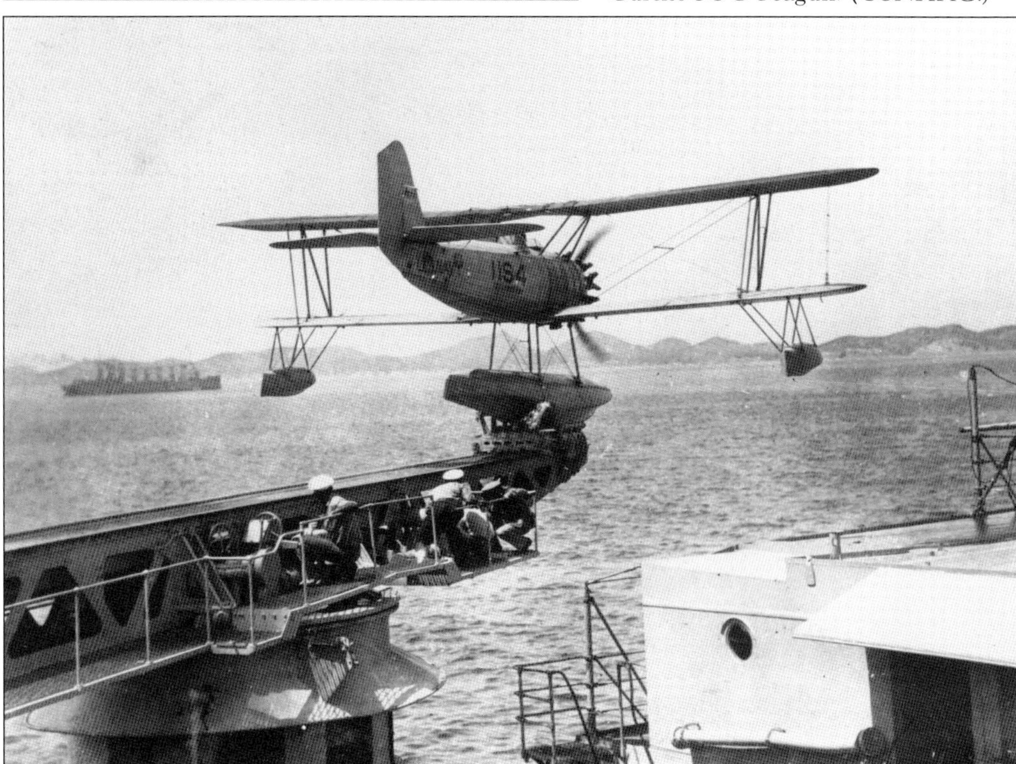

Capt. Jesse B. Gay was *Houston's* first commander. He served in that role through November 1930, when Capt. Robert A. Dawes took over. Gay superintended the ship's fitting out and oversaw its shakedown. (USNHHC.)

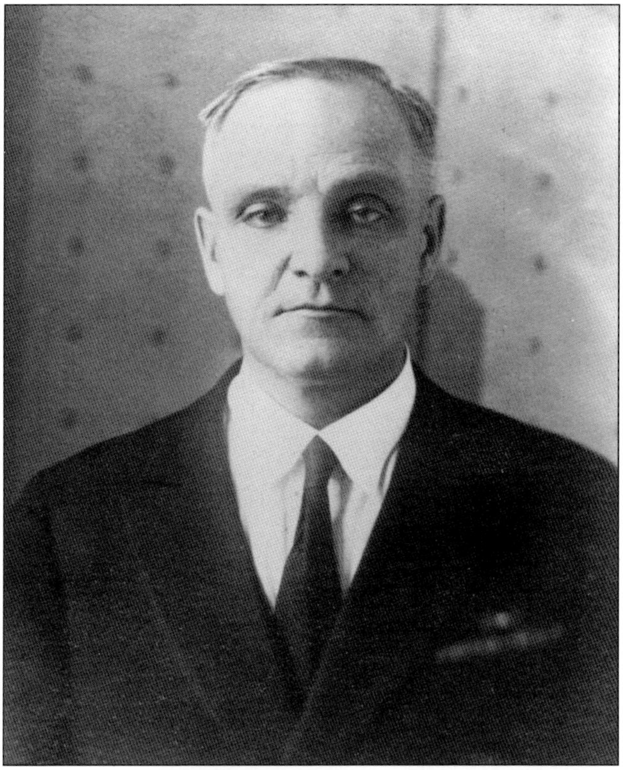

Houston ended its shakedown cruise with a visit to the city of Houston. It is seen here sailing down the Houston Ship Channel on its way to the Turning Basin and then the main terminal for the port. (USNHHC.)

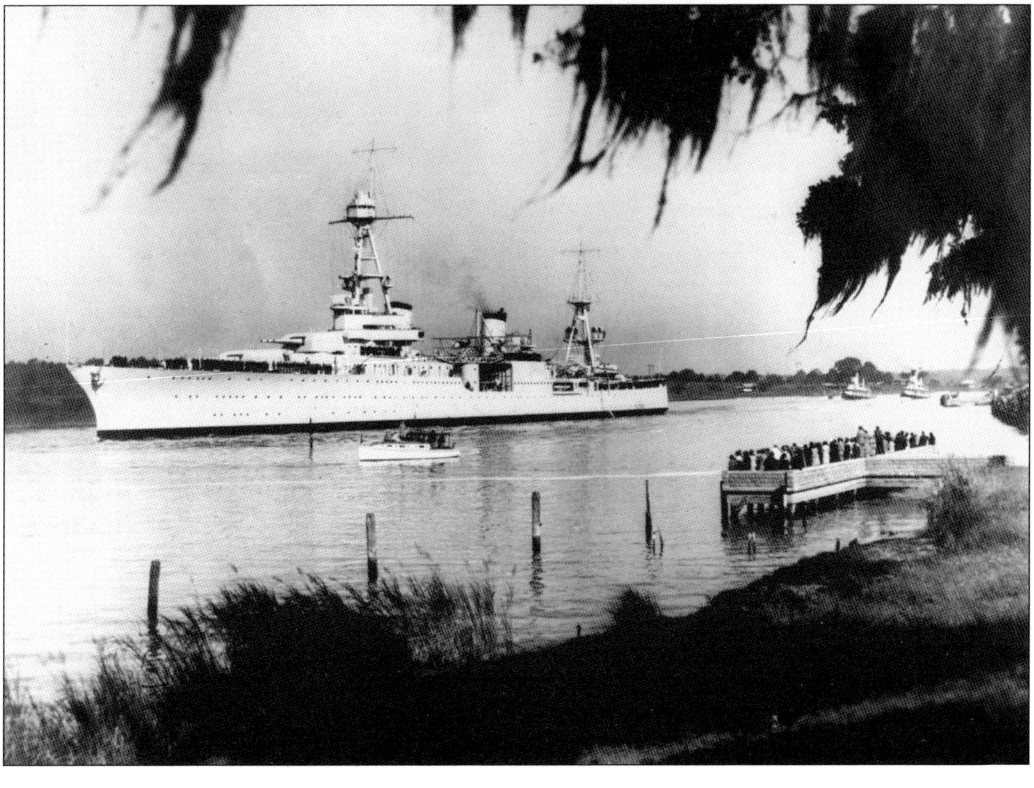

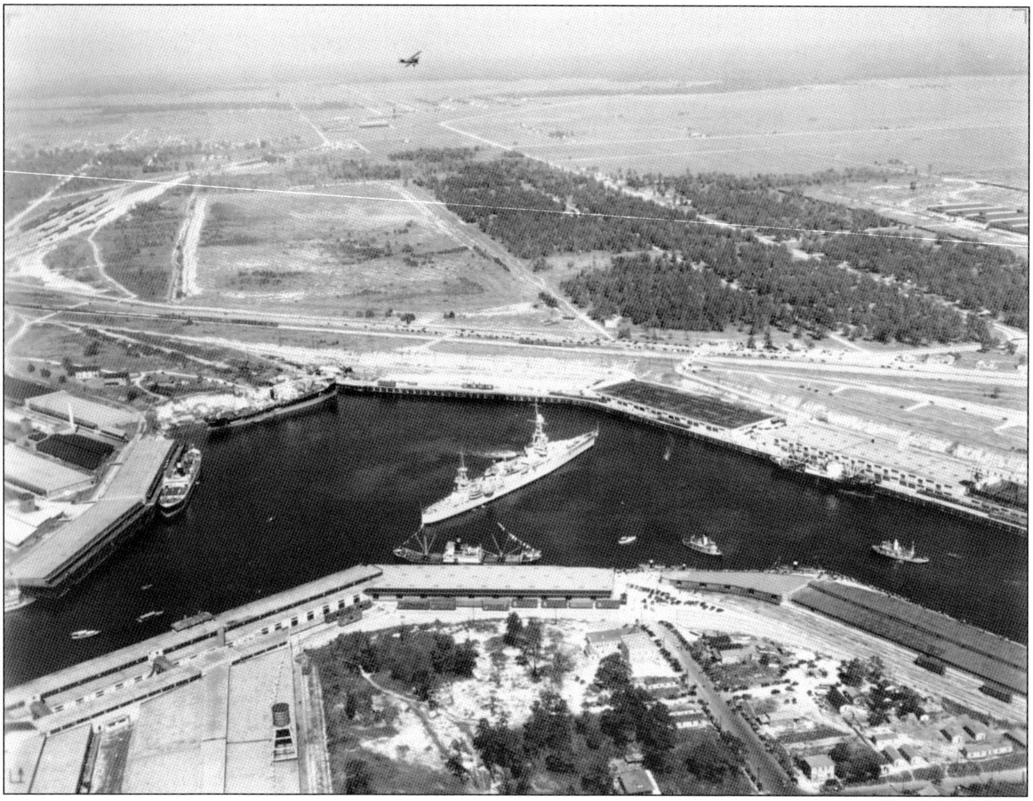

While *Houston* was at the Turning Basin, it was opened to the public. The public responded to its namesake cruiser enthusiastically. Over 100,000 people visited, theoretically every person who lived in Houston at the time. (USNHHC.)

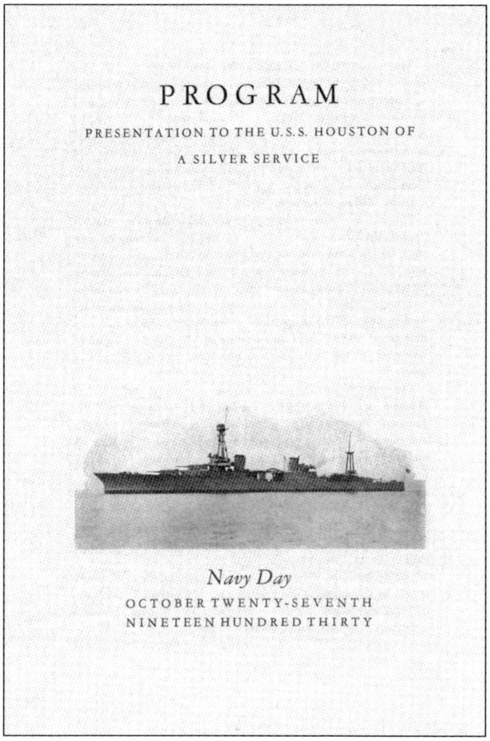

PROGRAM

PRESENTATION TO THE U.S.S. HOUSTON OF A SILVER SERVICE

Navy Day

OCTOBER TWENTY-SEVENTH NINETEEN HUNDRED THIRTY

A high point of the visit was the presentation of a silver service to the cruiser *Houston* by the City of Houston. It was the first of many gifts presented by the city to "its" cruiser, ranging from a piano to fruitcakes at Christmas. (HMM.)

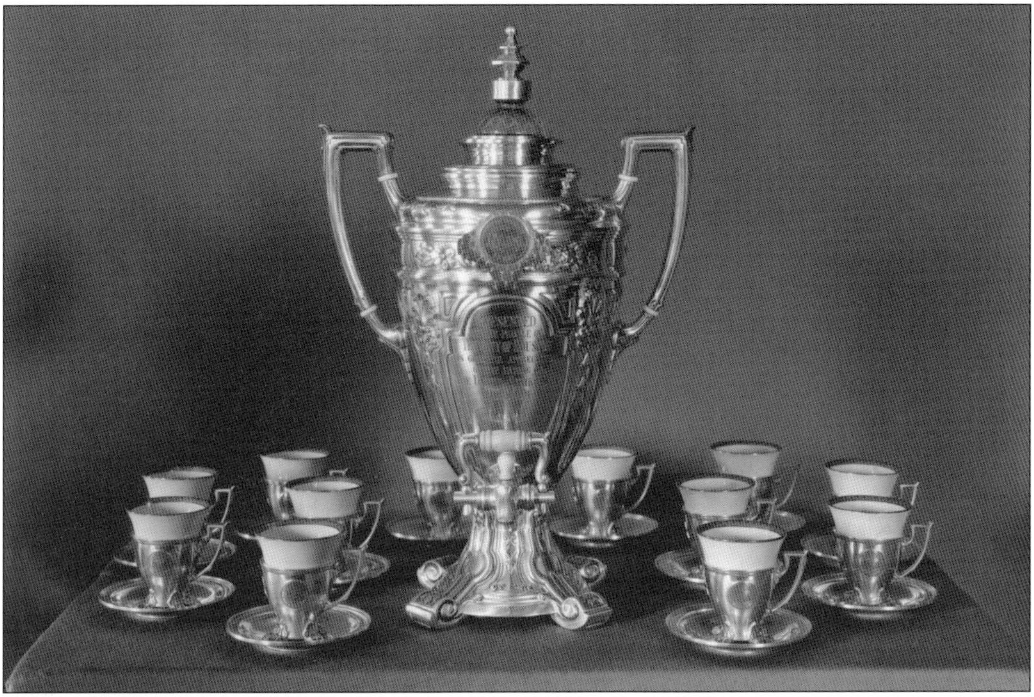

The silver service served the cruiser for over a decade. It was still aboard when World War II started and was unloaded at Cavite Naval Base for safekeeping. It disappeared at some point during the Japanese occupation of the Philippines during World War II. (HMM.)

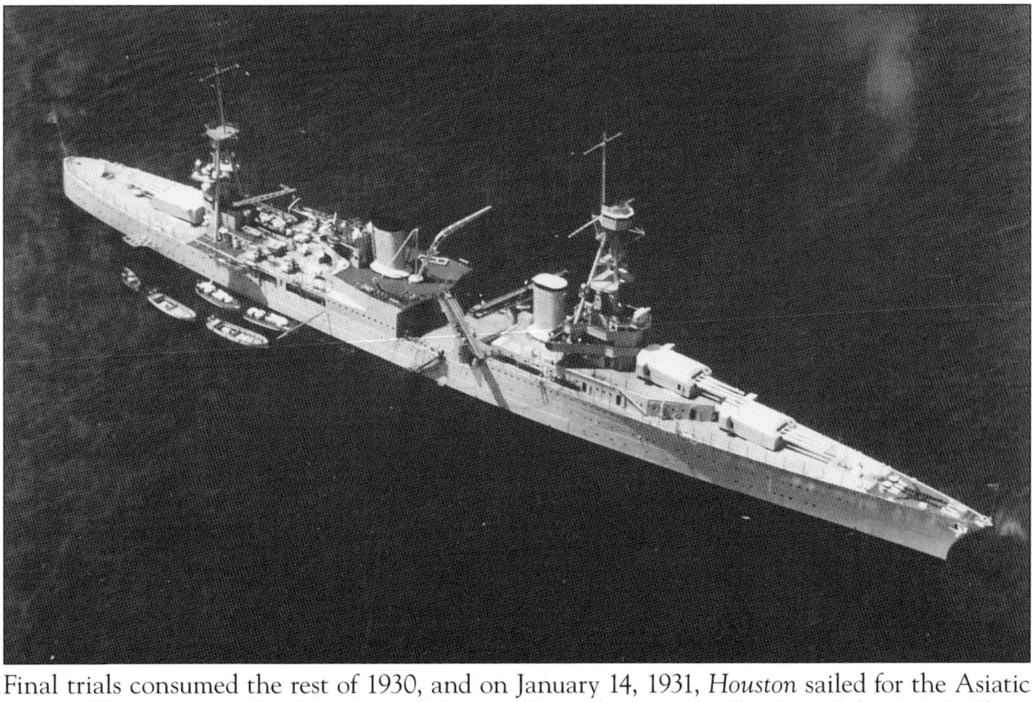

Final trials consumed the rest of 1930, and on January 14, 1931, *Houston* sailed for the Asiatic station. *Houston* arrived in Manila on February 22 and became the flagship of the Asiatic Fleet. Note the opening for the torpedo tubes above the boat by the boom. (NARA.)

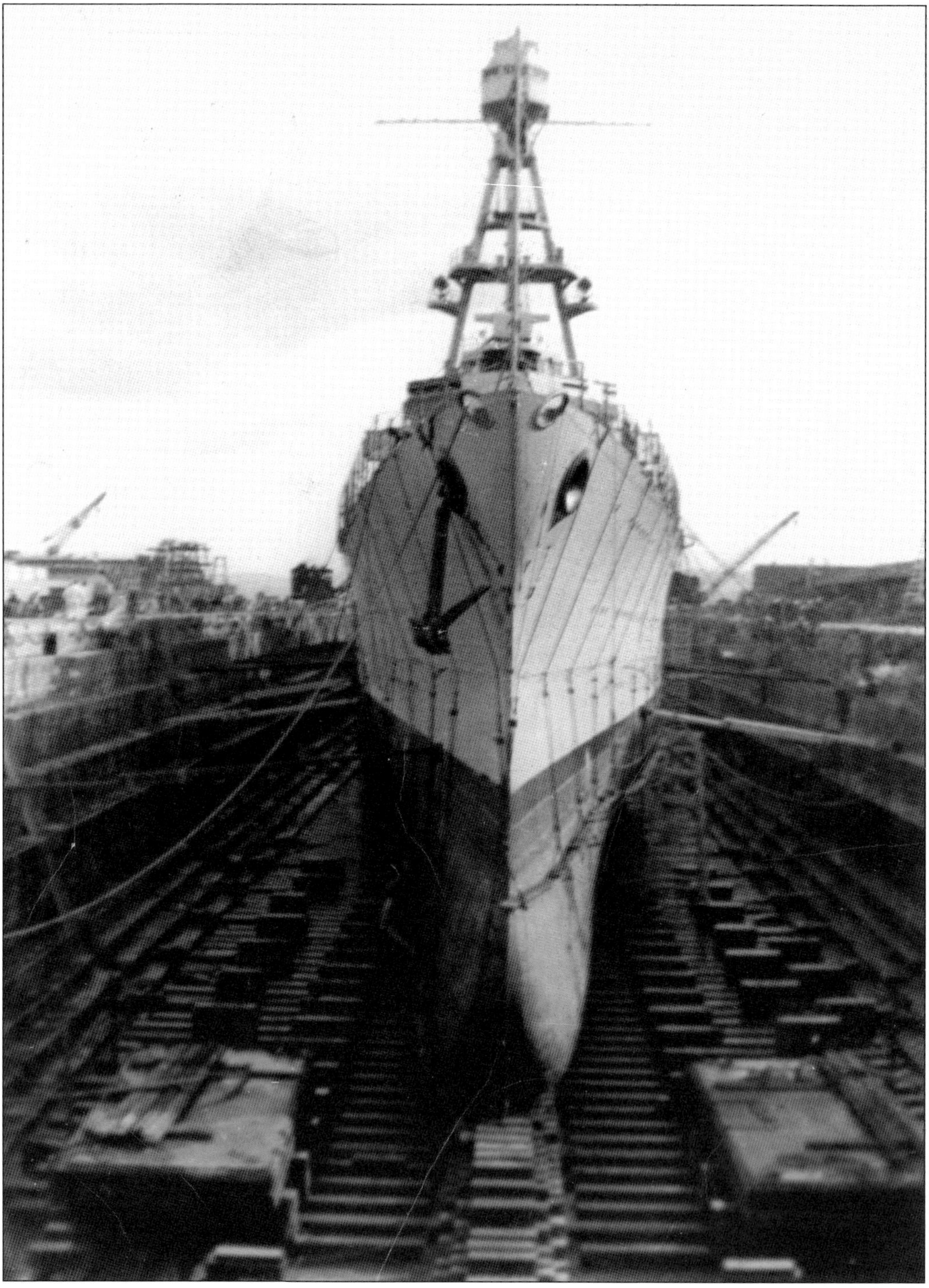

Overhauls and refits were part of life for any US Navy warship. Sometimes major changes were made. At a minimum, *Houston* would be dry-docked at least annually to check the hull and repair problems. In this picture, stages are laid out so *Houston's* bottom could be cleaned and painted. (USNHHC.)

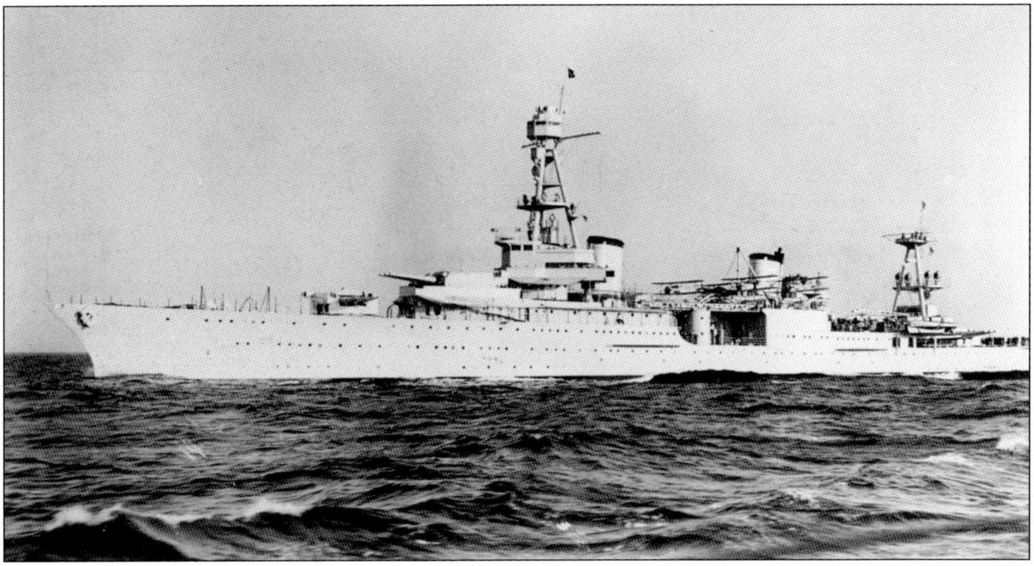

By 1934, the torpedo tubes were gone, and the openings plated over. The change was probably made at *Houston's* overhaul in the Puget Sound Navy Yard after returning from the China station. (HMM.)

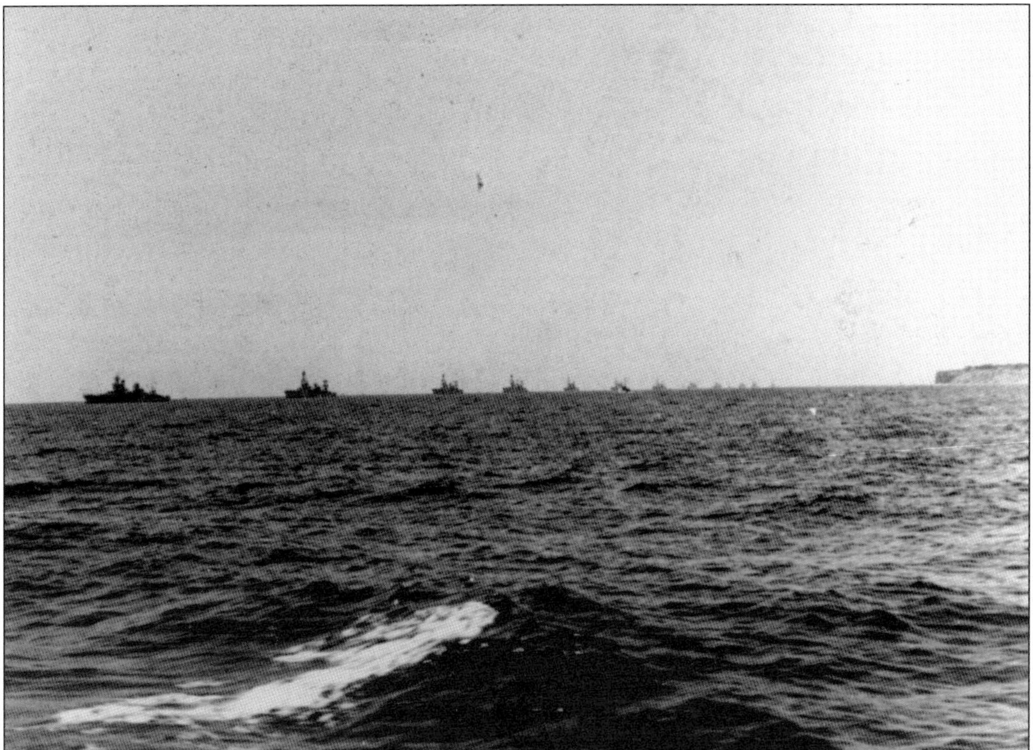

Houston spent time in the Scouting Force, sometimes as a flagship and sometimes not. In the peacetime 1930s, that meant long intervals spent in squadron and division exercises. Here, *Indianapolis* leads a column of 12 Scouting Force cruisers back to Long Beach, California, after an exercise. *Houston* is second in line. This picture was probably taken in early 1934. (USNHHC.)

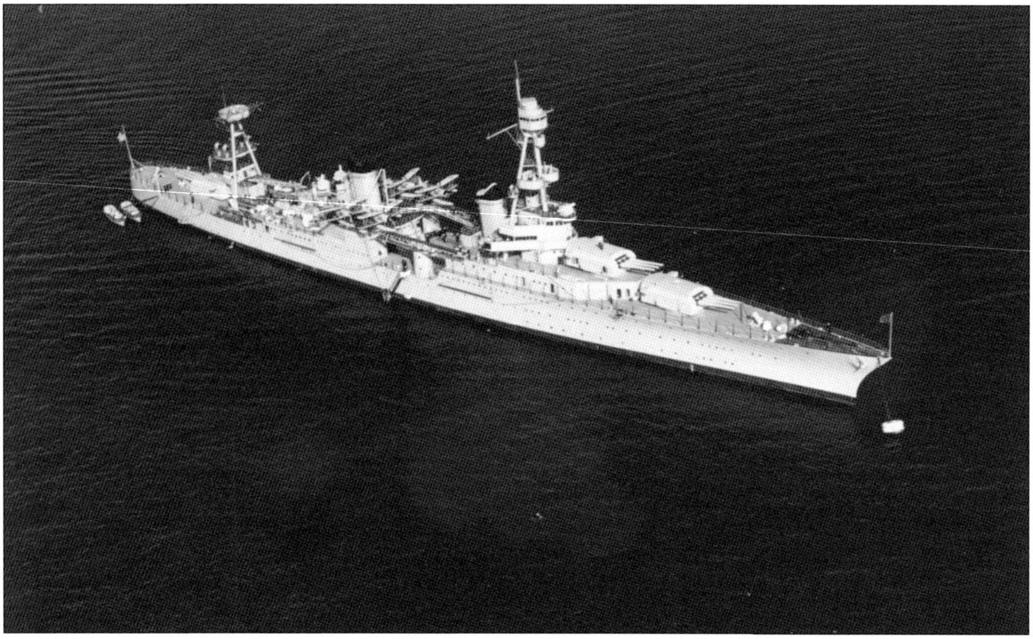

This March 1937 photograph shows *Houston* moored off San Diego. Not much had changed since 1934, when the torpedoes were removed. The aircraft are more modern Curtiss SOC floatplanes, which replaced the Vought O2U Corsairs carried in the early 1930s. (USNHHC.)

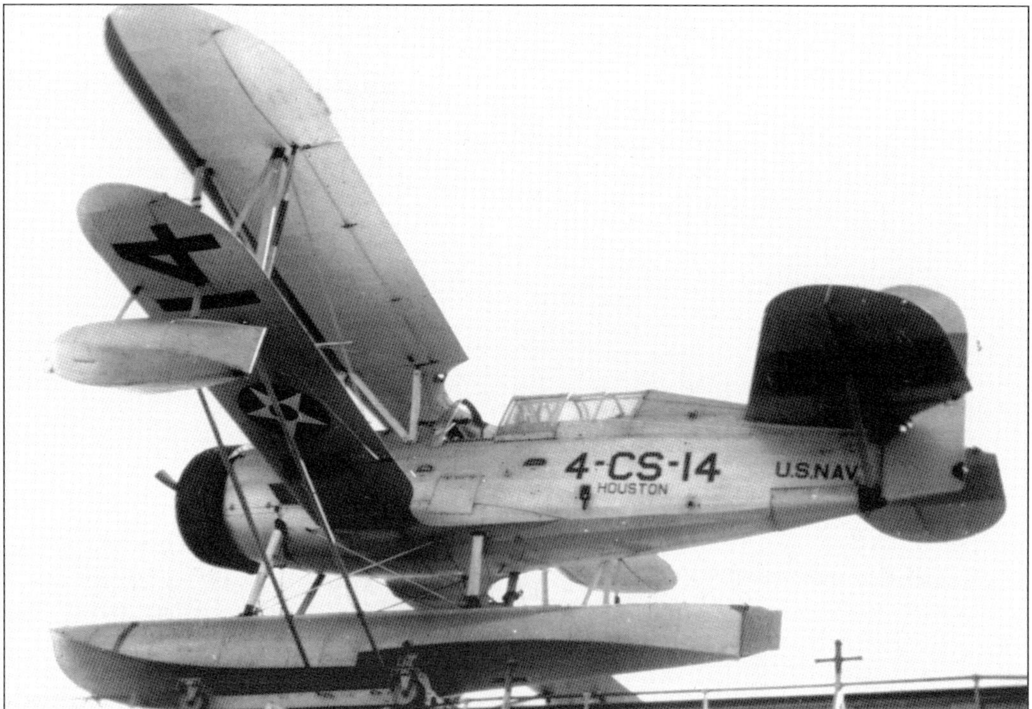

While the SOC had the same range and top speed of the Vought O2U, it had an enclosed cockpit, was sturdier, and could carry a bigger payload. It was named the Seagull in 1941 but was known only by the SOC designation until then. (HMM.)

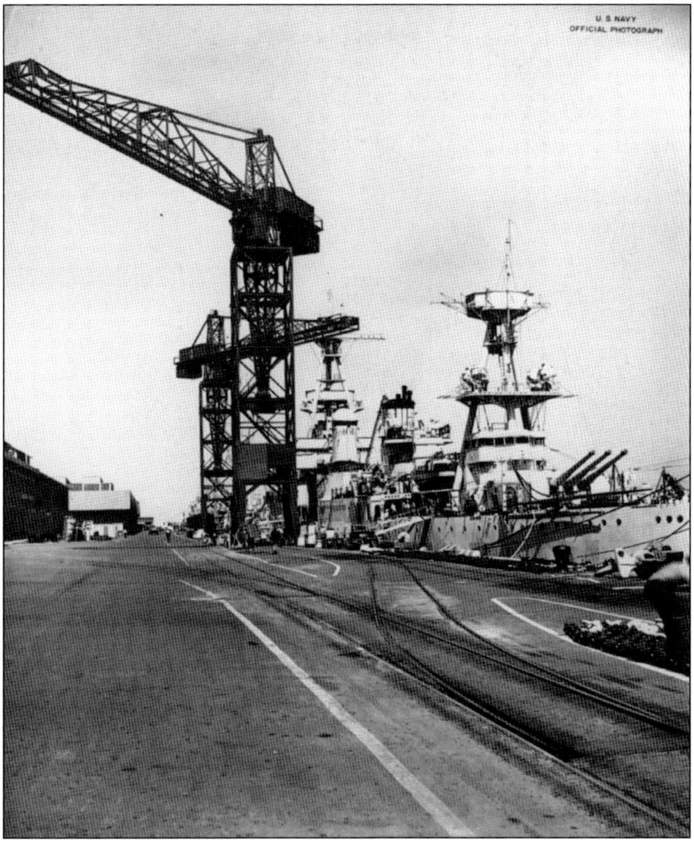

In 1938, *Houston* went through another maintenance overhaul at Mare Island Navy Yard in California. It went through a number of alterations to prepare it for the third presidential cruise aboard *Houston*. It started almost as soon as *Houston* left the shipyard. (USNHHC.)

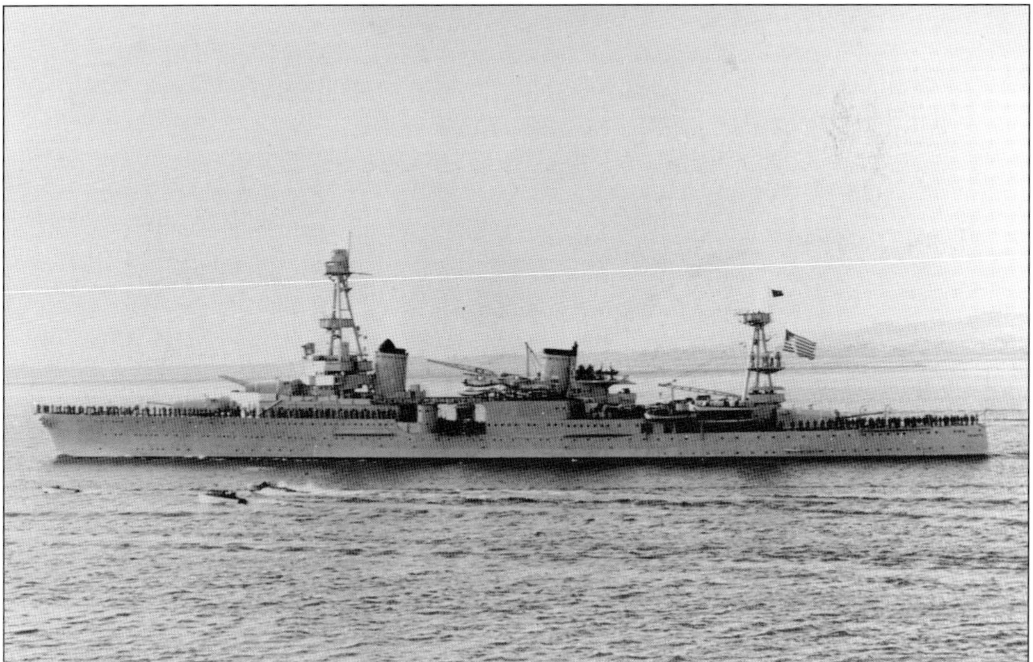

Houston's crew is seen manning the rails on July 15, 1938, as the ship is departing San Diego. President Roosevelt boarded the previous day. (USNHHC.)

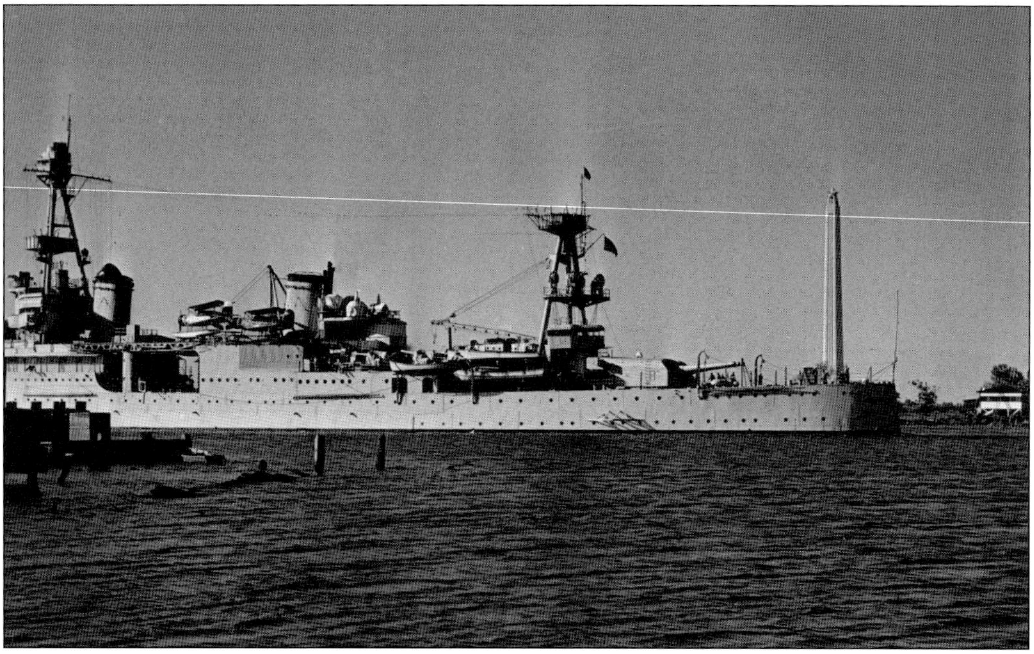

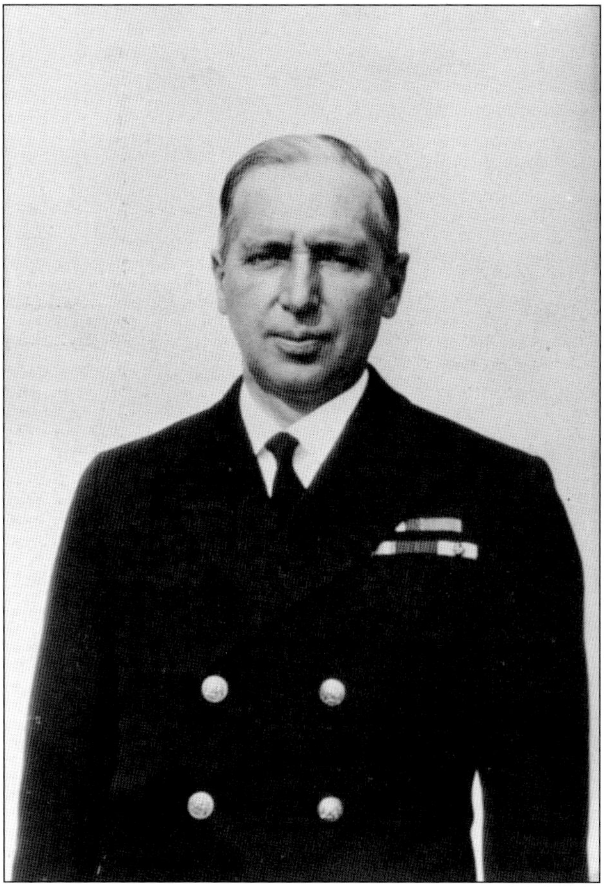

On April 7, *Houston* steamed up the Houston Ship Channel for its final visit to the city for which it had been named. Since the last time *Houston* visited, something new had been added, the San Jacinto Monument, built between 1936 and 1939. The cruiser spent 10 days in the port and enjoyed an enthusiastic welcome by the city's citizens. (USNHHC.)

Houston had nine captains. Francis Cogswell was the seventh. He took command in May 1939 and held command for a shorter period than any other captain, dying in a naval hospital when *Houston* was at Puget Sound on September 22, 1939. (USNHHC.)

Cogswell was replaced by Capt. Jesse B. Oldendorf, who commanded *Houston* from October 1939 to August 1941, when he was promoted to rear admiral and relieved by Capt. Albert Rooks. Oldendorf achieved fame during World War II commanding a fleet at Surigao Strait, the last surface action fought during the war. (USNHHC.)

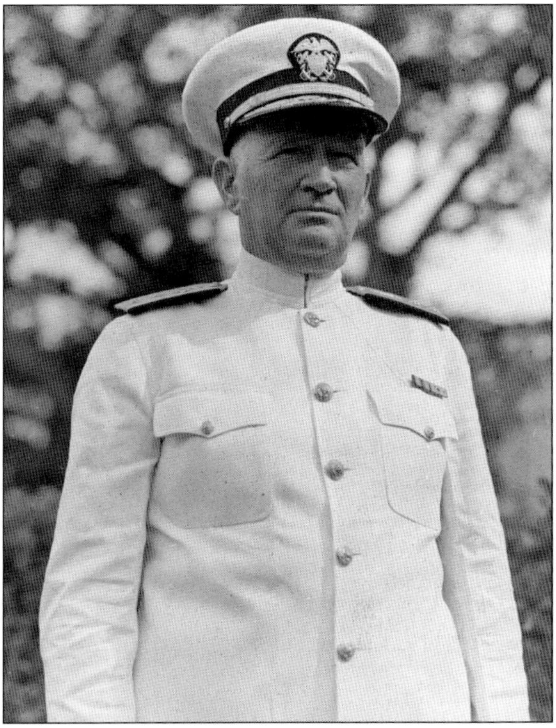

Houston went through a final refit in September 1940, again at Mare Island. This time, significant additions to its antiaircraft defenses were made. Four 5-inch/25-caliber guns were added, doubling the number carried. Two sets of quad 1.1-inch antiaircraft guns and twenty 20mm cannon were installed. (USNHHC.)

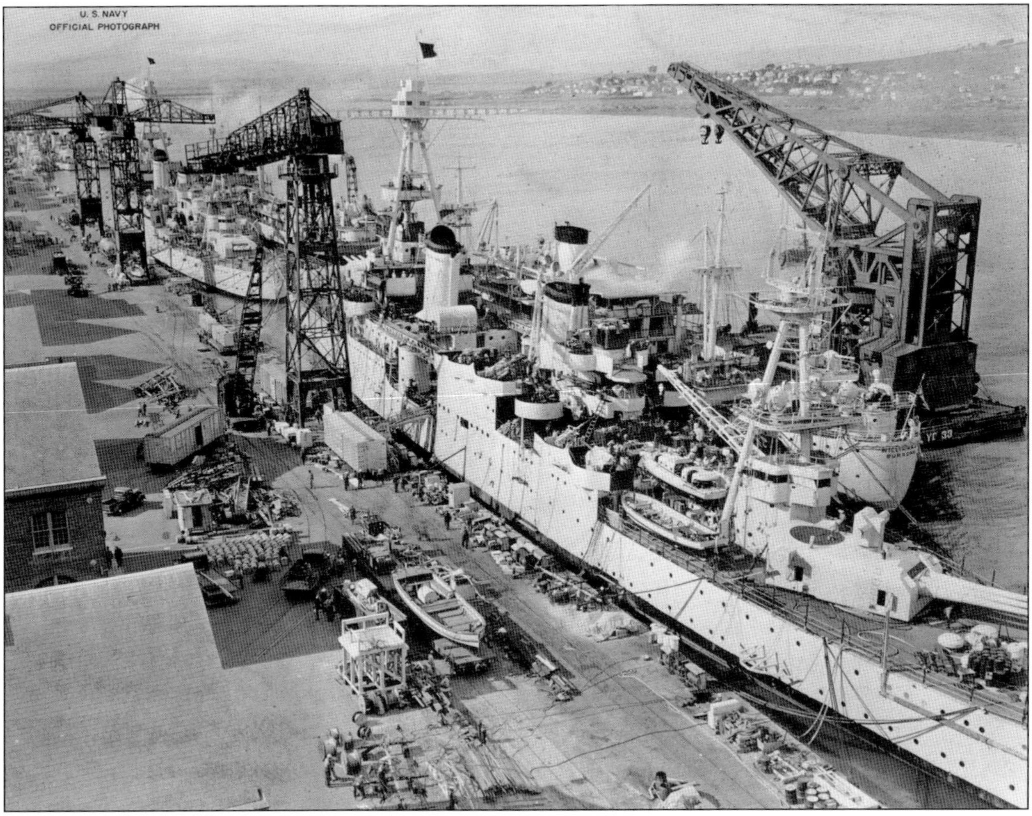

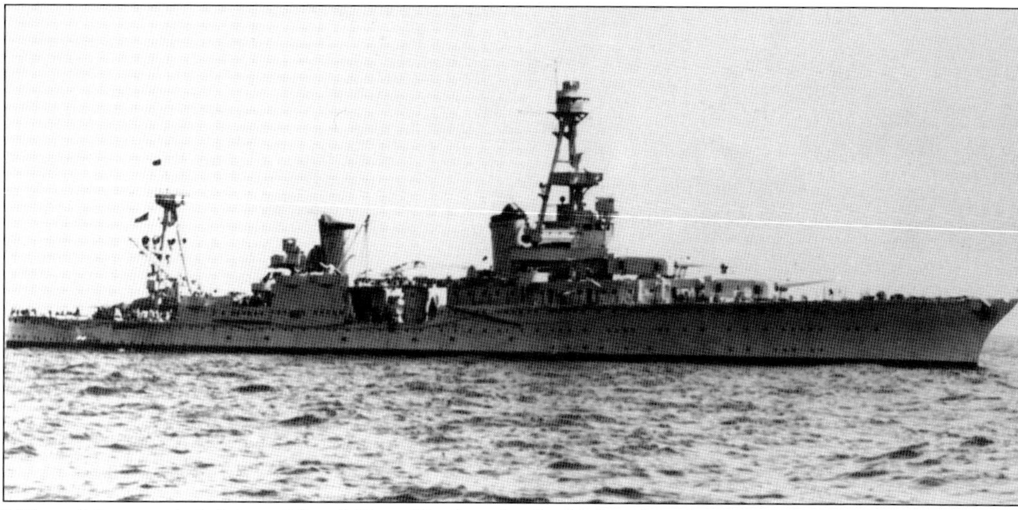

When *Houston* left Mare Island Ship Yard, it looked like this, bristling with antiaircraft guns. From there, it would sail to the Hawaiian islands and then to the Philippines, where it once again became flagship of the Asiatic Fleet. (USN.)

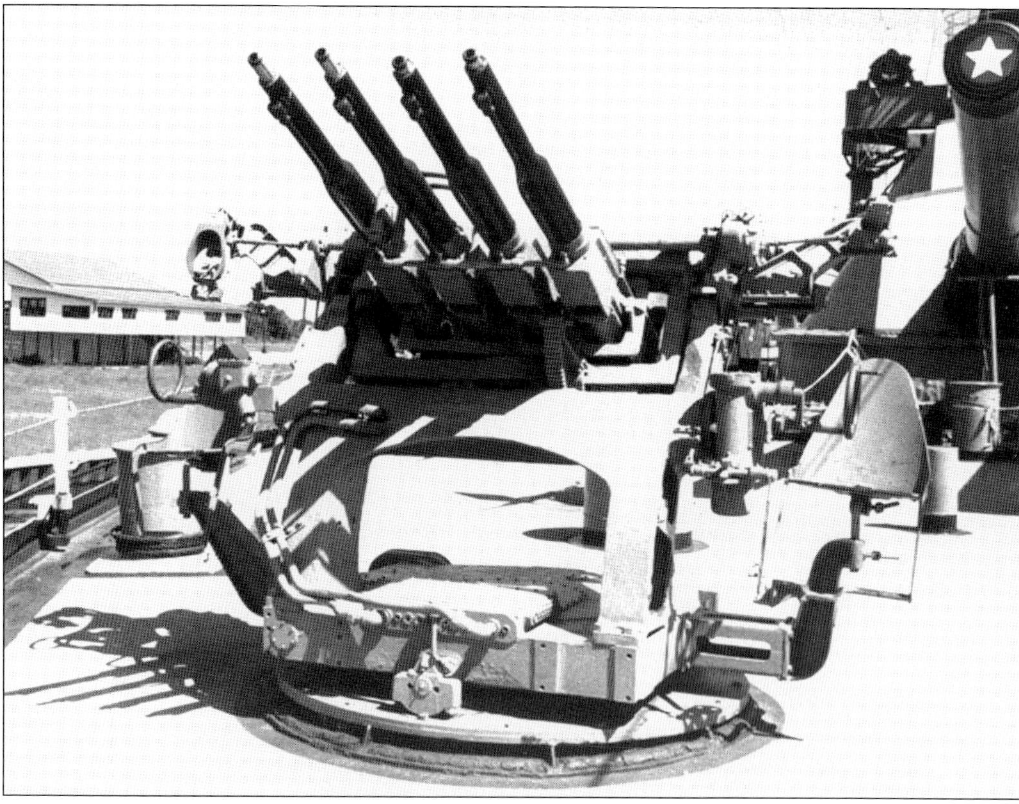

One final alteration was made in the Philippines, just before the war started. Four additional quad 1.1-inch guns were installed, bringing the total to six sets. The 1.1-inch gun pictured was on the Battleship *Texas* prior to its 1989 refit. The 1.1-inch gun was known as the "Chicago Piano." It lacked the punch needed and was phased out in favor of the 40mm Bofors, but not until after *Houston* sank. (TPWD, Battleship *Texas*.)

Two

THE PRESIDENT'S YACHT

No American president more enjoyed the sea than Franklin Delano Roosevelt. His older cousin, Theodore, came close, writing a groundbreaking history of the War of 1812 from the naval perspective. Both served as assistant secretary of the Navy, Theodore at the start of the Spanish-American War and Franklin during World War I. Still, FDR spent a lot more time messing about with boats than any other president. An ardent yachtsman until polio paralyzed him, Roosevelt afterwards continued spending as much time on ships as his schedule permitted.

That included naval vessels. Roosevelt visited more different naval vessels, made more visits to naval vessels, and spent more time aboard naval vessels while president than any other president before or since. And of all the warships in the US Navy during Roosevelt's long presidency, *Houston* was his favorite.

Roosevelt would make four multiweek voyages aboard *Houston* in 1934, 1935, 1938, and 1939. His longest trip, in 1934, lasted over a month. His shortest, in 1939, was two weeks. In all, Roosevelt spent 92 days aboard *Houston* and steamed over 25,400 nautical miles while on the ship—all during his first two terms as president.

The first trip, which traversed 11,783 nautical miles, helped give *Houston* its peacetime nicknames, the "Wanderer" and the "Rambler." The trips were vacations for Roosevelt, and after the first trip, vacations for the crews. By presidential decree, there were no field days (an all-hands cleanup) and no inspections while Roosevelt was aboard.

These voyages did ramble. Three started on one US coast and ended on the other, passing through the Panama Canal. Roosevelt took *Houston* as far west as Hawaii, as far north as Portland, Oregon, as far south as the Galapagos Islands, and as far east as the US Virgin Islands. On one voyage, *Houston* crossed the equator, an opportunity for "shellbacks" (those who had previously crossed the equator) to haze those aboard who had not. The crew discovered that their president was the ship's senior shellback, with 18 crossings—more than anyone else.

Roosevelt loved *Houston*—he kept visiting it—and in turn, its crew loved their president. This chapter presents some reasons why.

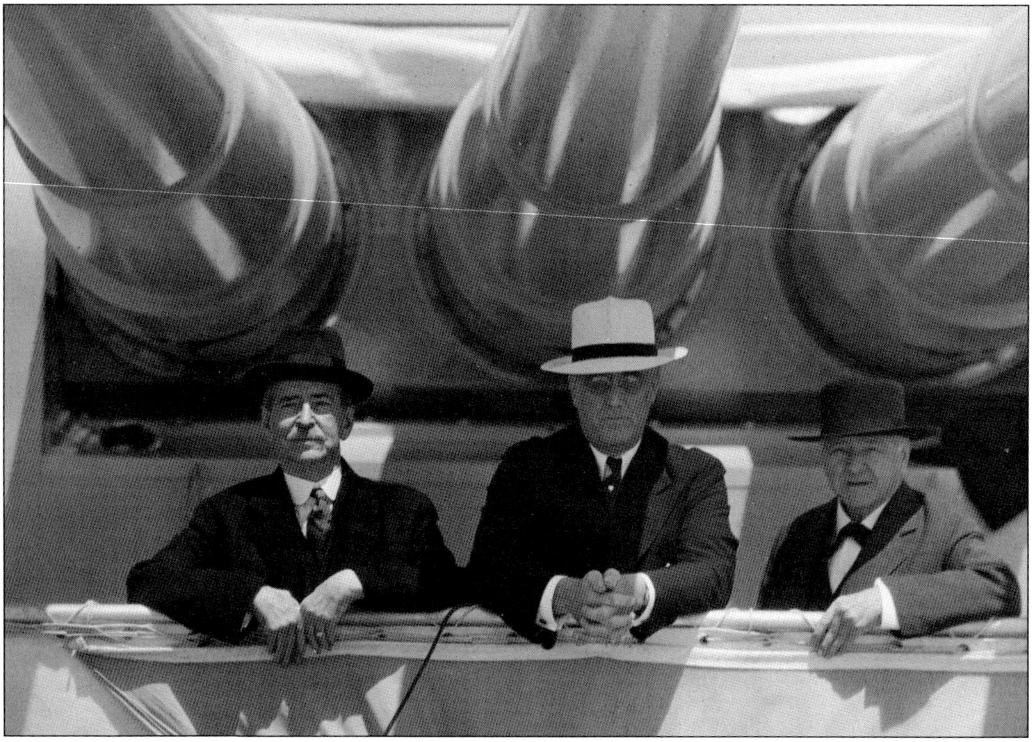

Pres. Franklin Roosevelt's favorite place was aboard a ship. An ardent yachtsman and sailor before being paralyzed by polio, he still loved being at sea afterwards. He is pictured here aboard USS *Indianapolis* with Secretary of the Navy Claude A. Swanson (left) and Ambassador Josephus Daniels during the 1934 Presidential Fleet Review. (USNHHC.)

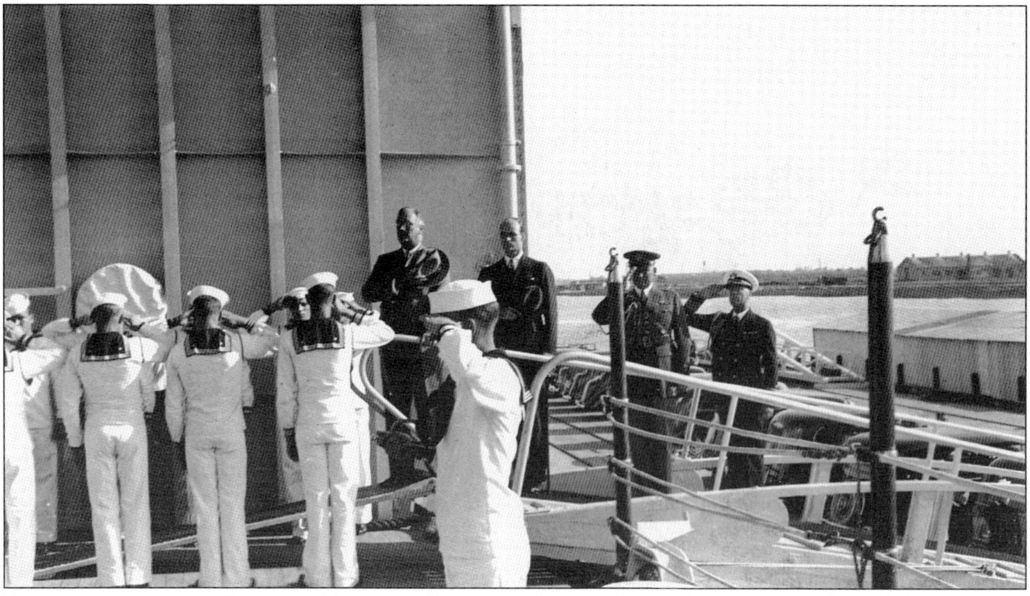

Roosevelt's favorite ship was *Houston*. He spent four multiweek vacations aboard. Here, he is boarding *Houston* during his first stay in 1934. Note that he returns the sailors' salute by removing his hat and placing his hand over his heart, the practice at the time. (HMM.)

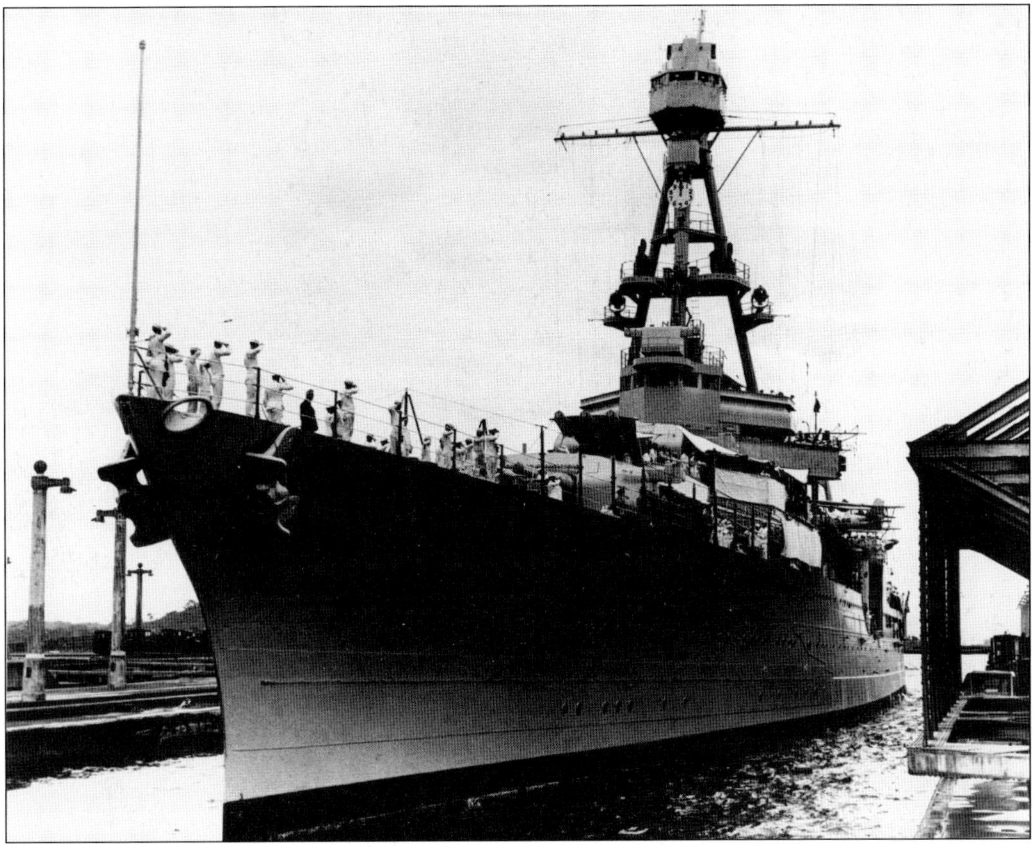

Roosevelt is boarding *Houston* at Annapolis, Maryland. The ship traveled through the Caribbean, making stops at Cap-Haïtien, Haiti; Puerto Rico; the US Virgin Islands; and Cartagena, Colombia, before reaching the Panama Canal. It is shown entering the Gatun Lock. (USNHHC.)

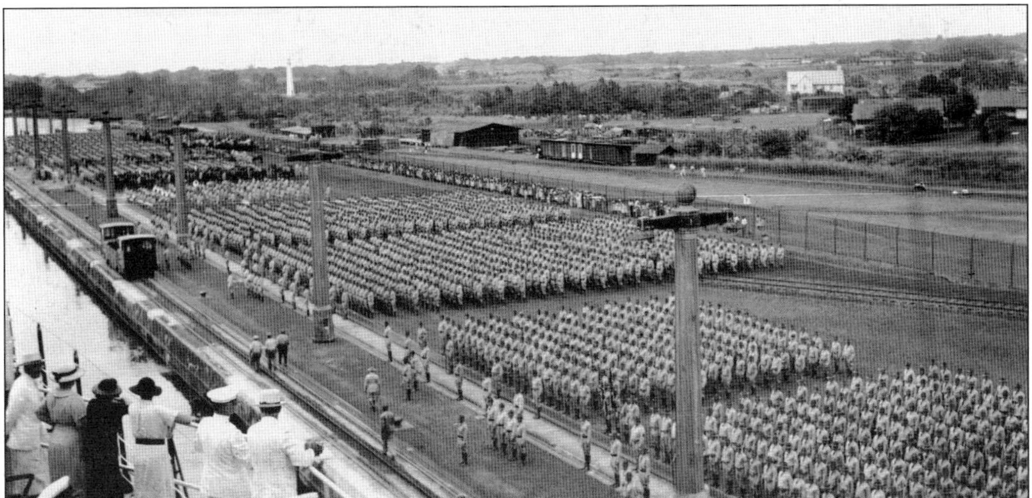

Roosevelt reviewed US Army troops stationed in Panama at each end of the Panama Canal. Here, Army forces render passing honors to the president and presidential party while *Houston* is in the Gatun Lock. (HMM.)

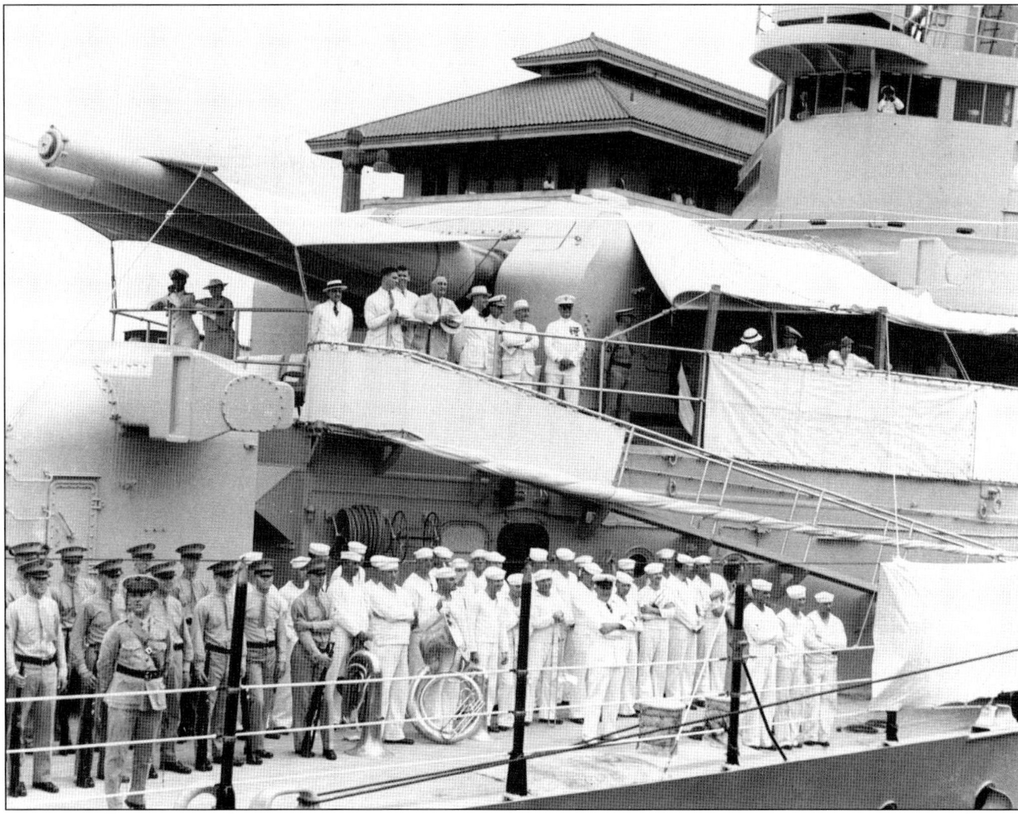

Houston's crew turned out for these reviews, lining the rails in their whites, as President Roosevelt and his party observe from an upper deck, forward of the No. 2 turret. Note the temporary ramp installed for the president. (USNHHC.)

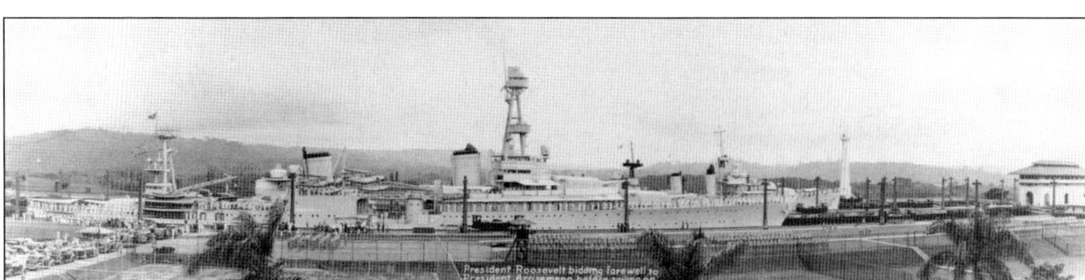

The whole scene—ships, troops, and canal—is captured in this panoramic photograph. Roosevelt left *Houston* to meet Panamanian president F.H. Arosemena. Roosevelt is shown about to board after saying goodbye. He is in the automobile just to the left of the catapult. (USNHHC.)

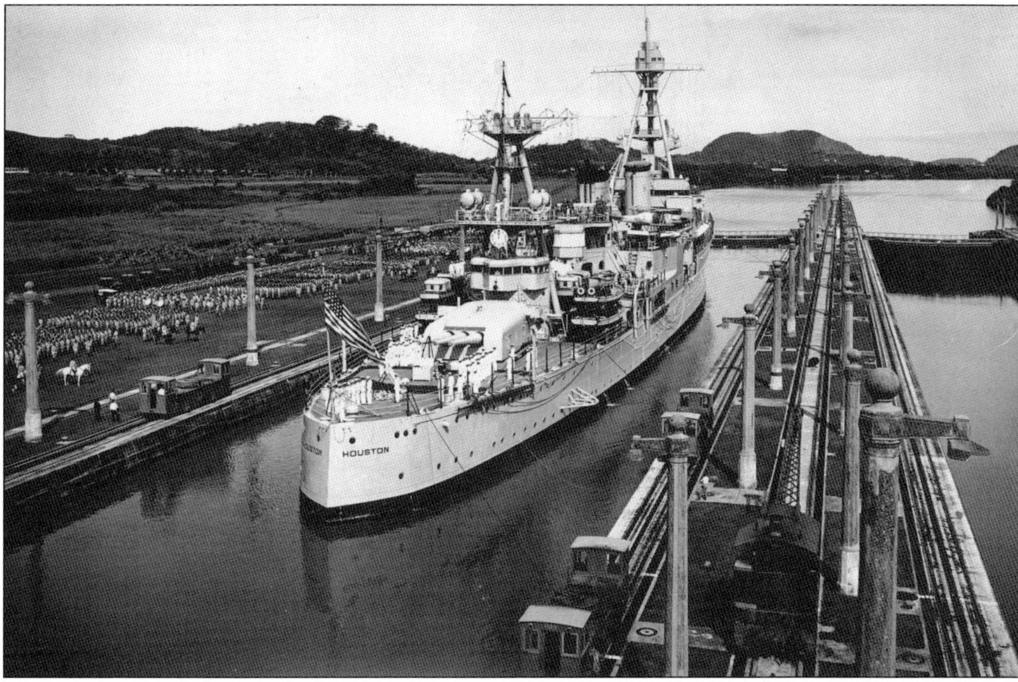

In this view, *Houston*, with Roosevelt aboard, readies to leave the Gatun Lock and enter the Pacific. Ships are pulled through the lock by electric locomotives, known as mules, seen here on both sides of the lock. (USN.)

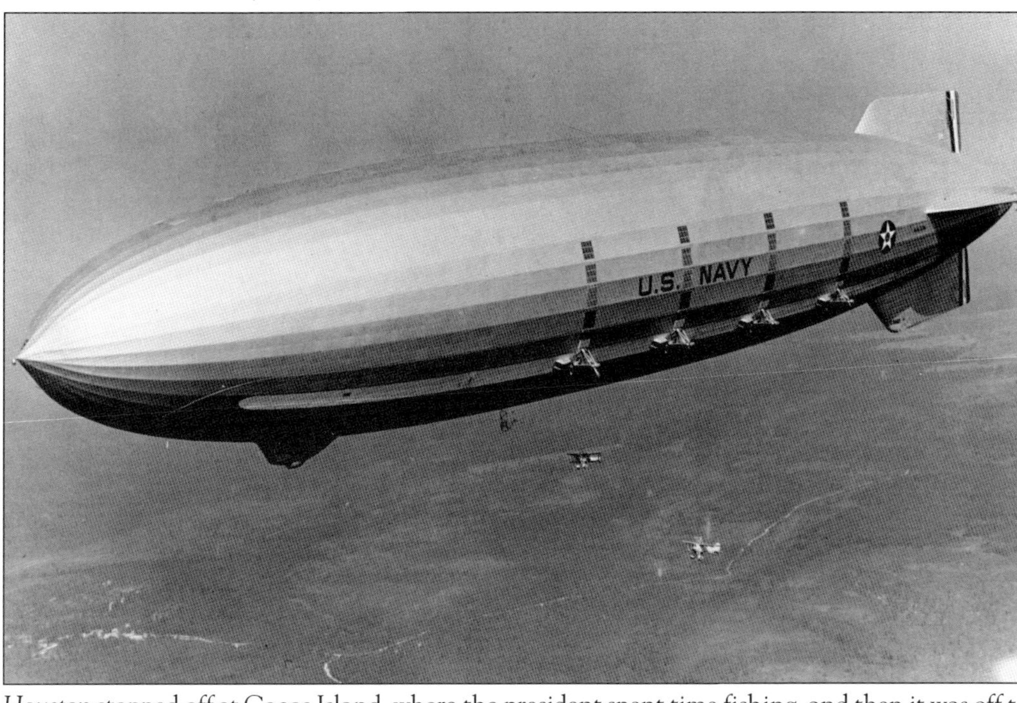

Houston stopped off at Cocos Island, where the president spent time fishing, and then it was off to Hawaii. En route to Hawaii, the airship *Macon* rendezvoused with *Houston* in mid-ocean. *Macon* carried Sparrowhawk aircraft, which flew over *Houston* to drop papers for Roosevelt. (NARA.)

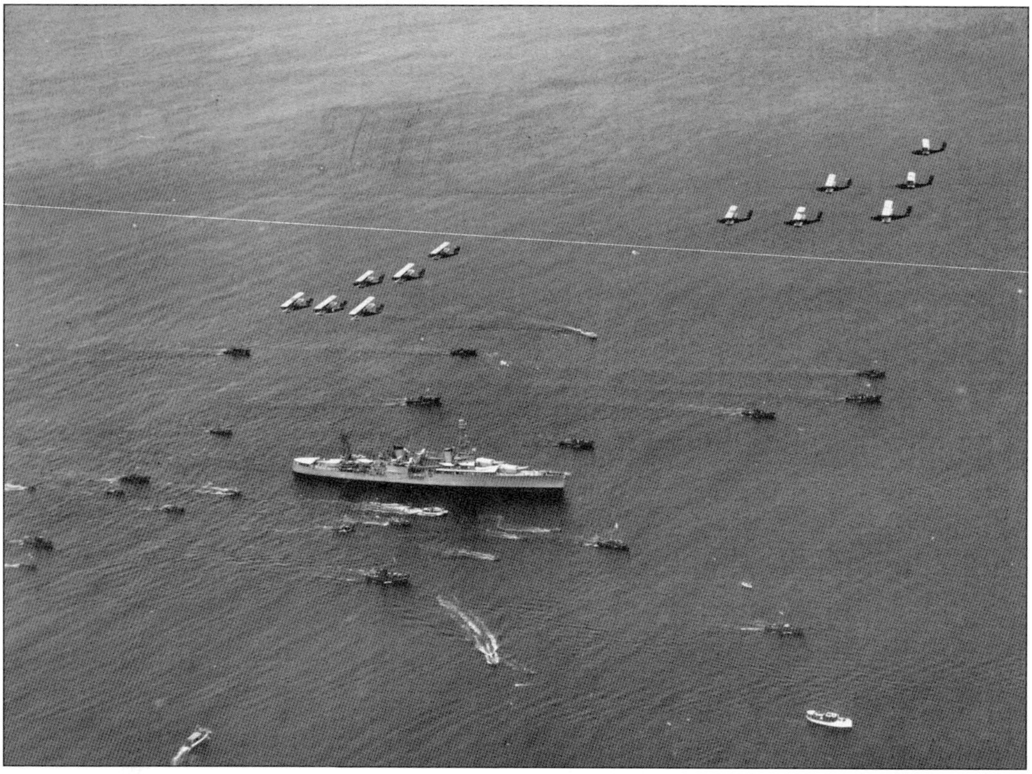

At Hawaii, *Houston* was escorted into Pearl Harbor by naval ships of all kinds as formations of aircraft flew overhead. (NARA.)

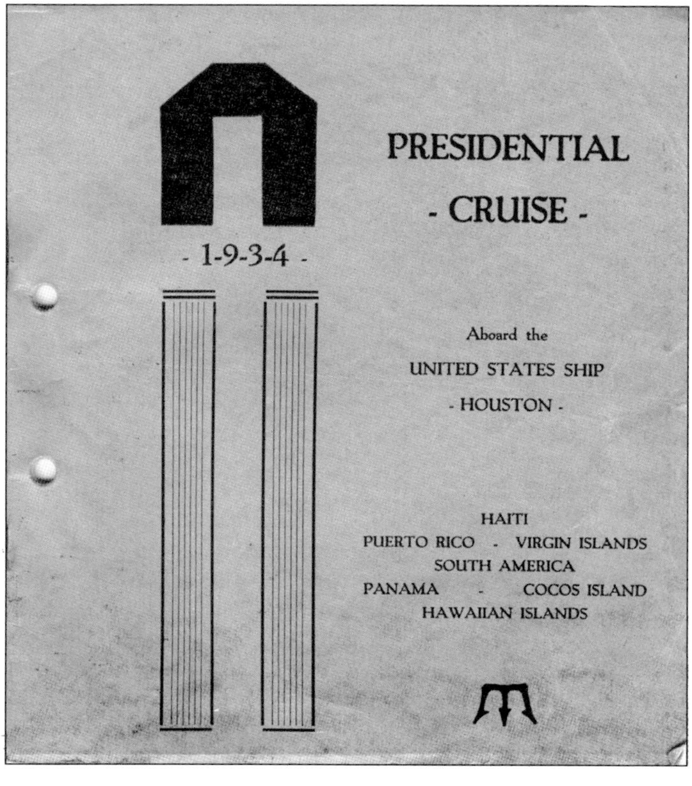

PRESIDENTIAL
- CRUISE -

- 1-9-3-4 -

Aboard the
UNITED STATES SHIP
- HOUSTON -

HAITI
PUERTO RICO - VIRGIN ISLANDS
SOUTH AMERICA
PANAMA - COCOS ISLAND
HAWAIIAN ISLANDS

After the cruise ended, *Houston's* crew put together a pamphlet describing the cruise and distributed them to those aboard. (HMM.)

THE BLUE BONNET

★ U.S.S. HOUSTON ★

Volume II. San Diego, California., Sept. 30, 1935. Number XXXVIII

Second Presidential Cruise

During the coming week the HOUSTON will proceed to sea on her second cruise with our Commander in Chief, President F. D. Roosevelt on board. Two notable personages in our Government sailing in the C in C's party are: Secretary of the Interior, Harold B. Ickes and Works Progress Administrator, Harry Hopkins.

As we go to press our tenative schedule is not definitely known, but we, the crew of the United States Ship HOUSTON feel proud to have our distinguished shipmates on board. We all look forward with happy anticipation to the coming cruise, as memories of the pleasant cruise last year are still fresh in our minds.

It was with pardonable pride we received news of the forthcoming cruise, forthwith proceedings with preparations, intent on making this a far greater and more successful cruise than the last whether it be shorter or longer in duration.

This cruise is a fine opportunity for us, the entire crew, to demonstrate clearly to you, our cooperative ability in carrying out each evolution as a smoothly functioning and thoroughly schooled unit of our great Naval Forces.

President Roosevelt, we members of the HOUSTON crew welcome you and your party aboard, both as Commander in Chief of our Navy and as a former, distinguished shipmate.

We hope this cruise is as enjoyable and pleasant to you and your party as it will be to us in having such distinguished shipmates.

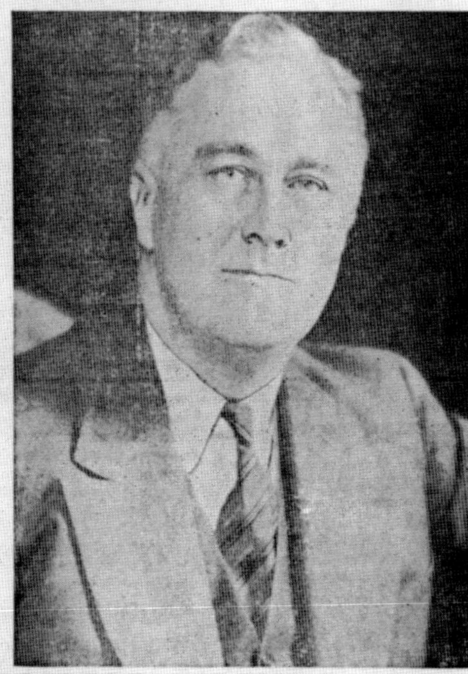

Franklin D. Roosevelt

Houston's newspaper, *The Blue Bonnet*, did not exist when Roosevelt made his first cruise. It had been in business for nearly a year when Roosevelt decided to take a second trip aboard *Houston*. The paper announced the event on its front page, complete with photograph. (UHDL.)

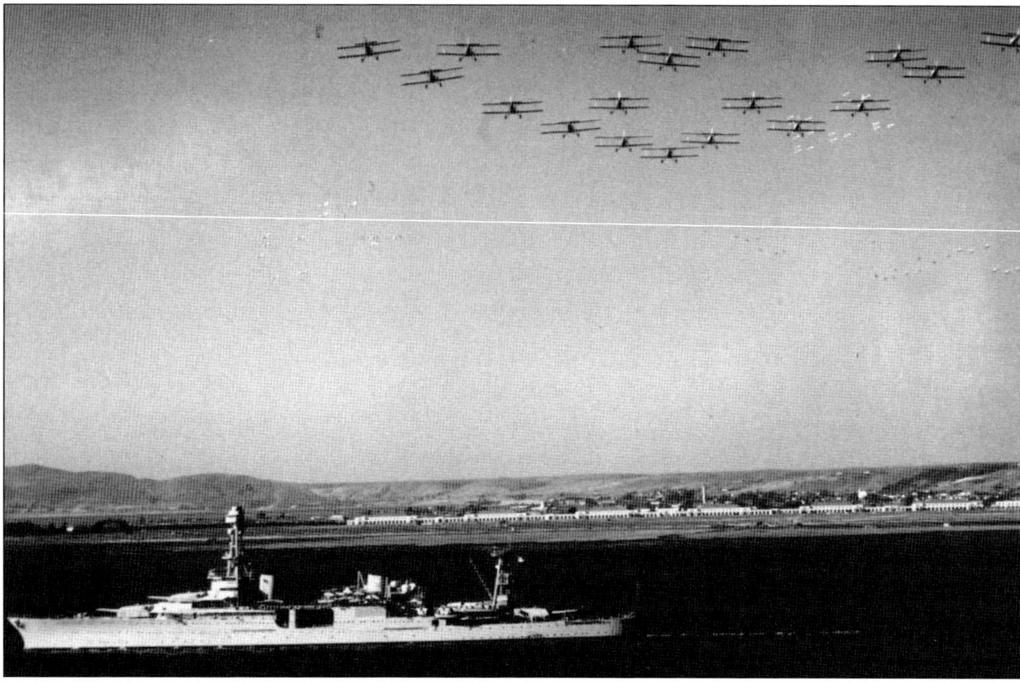

Houston left San Diego on October 2, 1935, with Roosevelt aboard. There was as much fanfare for the departure as there was for *Houston's* arrival at Hawaii the year before, with Army aircraft making formation flights overhead. (NARA.)

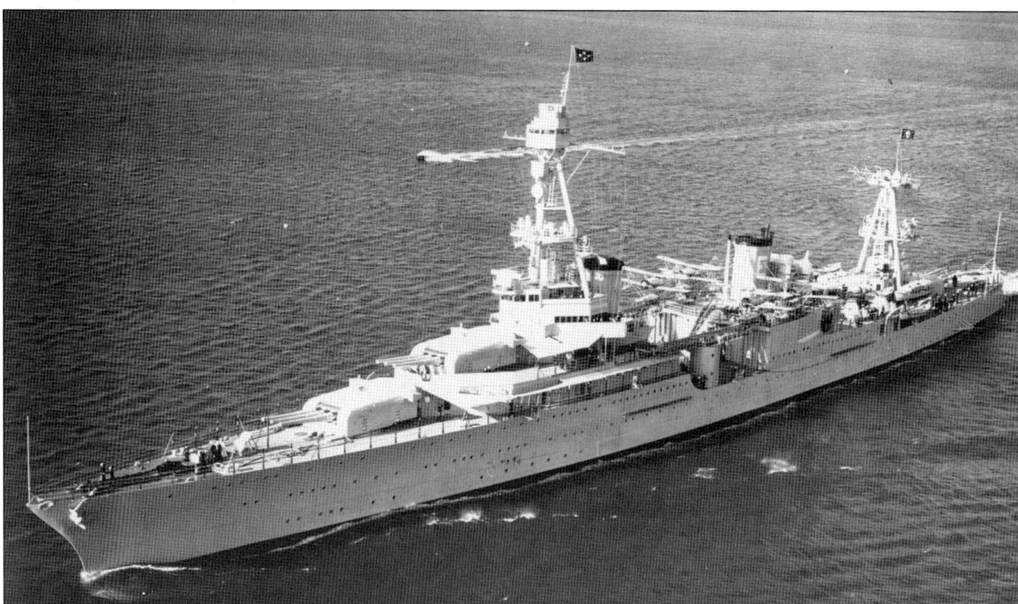

Houston is seen steaming off San Diego. It flies the flag of a full (four-star) admiral at the foremast, and the presidential flag at the peak of the mainmast. By this time, *Houston* had an elevator installed, allowing Roosevelt to travel from the forecastle deck, where his cabin was, to the bridge four levels up. (USNHHC.)

Pictured is the *Houston's* boat deck when the president was aboard. The highly polished and elaborately decorated presidential launch (with the presidential seal at its bow) is at left. The presidential flag is flying atop the mainmast. (USNHHC.)

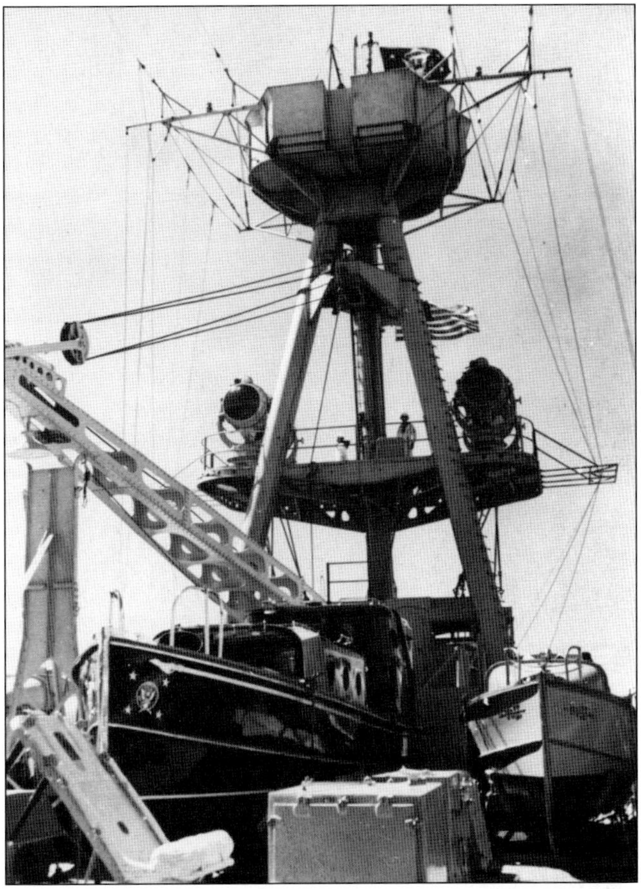

This voyage also saw a stop at Cocos Island, where the fishing was good. While Roosevelt fished, the crew of *Houston*, pictured at anchor at the island, enjoyed liberty. (USNHHC.)

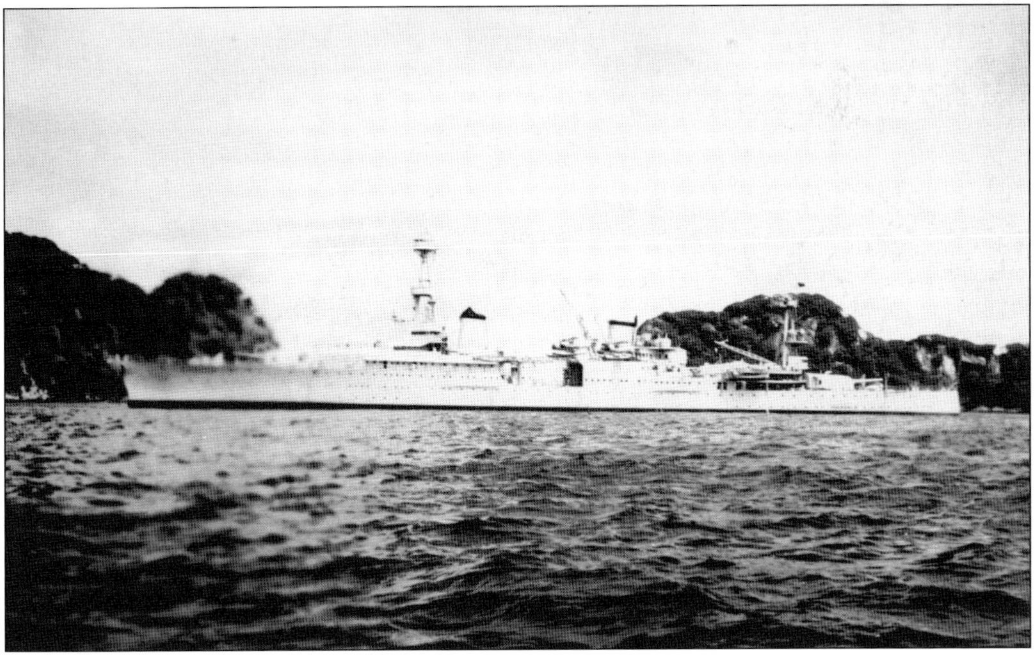

THE BLUE BONNET
★U.S.S. HOUSTON★

Volume VII, Number 3. Off Socorro Island 20 July, 1938.

PRESIDENT ROOSEVELT BOARDS HOUSTON

Ship Honored by Distinguished Guest

President Roosevelt boarded our ship while we were moored to the dock in Oakland, California. Shortly afterward, the ship got underway for the fleet review in San Francisco Bay. Amid the booming of saluting guns and the rendering of the National Anthem by each large ship passed by the HOUSTON our Chief Executive reviewed the fleet units concentrated there. That same night he took his departure for a tour of Yosemite and points south towards San Diego. At San Diego he came aboard again to remain for a cruise in Southern waters, to fishing grounds off the beaten track of commerce.

So it is our privilege and honor to be the ship chosen. The Captain, officers, and men of the U.S.S Houston take this opportunity of expressing to the President a welcome deep from their hearts. We appreciate the fact that you have given us an opportunity to serve you.

Our ship is only one unit of a highly efficient fighting force. It is our duty as a unit to carry you on this cruise—a duty tinged with gladness which we eagerly except.

On the other former cruises which you made on this vessel many of us were not aboard, but we who are now attached, sincerely hope to make this the most enjoyable and pleasant you have ever had.

Welcome aboard shipmate.

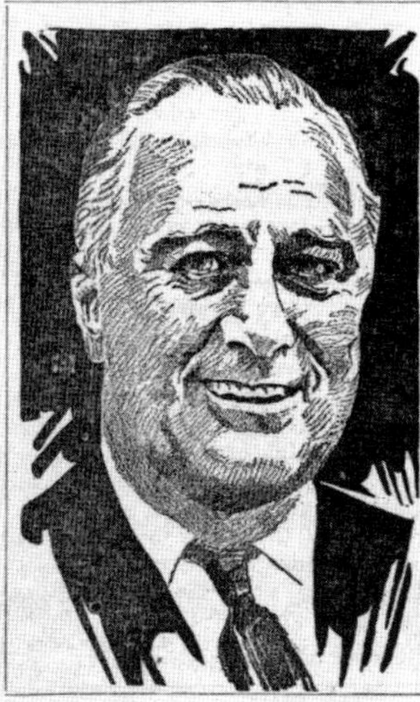

President Franklin D. Roosevelt

Domain of Neptunus Rex
The Royal Palace

Latitude-000
Longitude-1 to 360 degrees

Greetings, Thrice Greetings, True Sons of The Seas, I Send From My Most Equatorial Chambers.

It is with anxious and most pleasurable anticipation that I, Neptunus Rex, Ruler of the Raging Main, await the moment when, once again, I will be privileged to WELCOME YOU TO MY DOMAIN.

The Queen is all aflutter. Thrice she has "beaned" my Royal Dome when I dared interrupt whilst she was engaged in "Planning" just what or what not she would or would not wear for the Auspicious Occasion. Aye, True Sons of the Seas, the Queen is more Queenly than ever.

The Princess, Beauteous and Spritely Maiden as ever graced the Lilting Waves of my Domain, is all athrill to welcome you too.

Long John Silver, My Most Secret Emissary, has long since been aboard with you. Hour after hour, day after day, night after night, his reports have come to me. There is a Royal Commendation for My Trusted Sons of the Seas, But, Dire, Fearful, and Painful will be the Exquisite Tortures to be inflicted upon unregenerate Pollywogs who have dared to decry my Royal Person and power. Their cries and prayers for mercy will fall upon the ears of my Torturer Buccaneers as falls the softest, musical dew drop on the lightly opening buds on a Spring Morn.

(Continued on Pg. 3)

Roosevelt made his third trip on *Houston* in July 1938, spending three weeks aboard. His arrival made the front page of *The Blue Bonnet* again, although this time the president had to share it with another sovereign, King Neptune. (UHDL.)

As on the earlier voyages, Roosevelt spent time fishing. He did not fish from the cruiser, but would board one of the ship's motor launches, fish from that, and transfer the catch aboard at the end of the session. In 1938, Roosevelt insisted on using a 20-year-old coxswain as his fishing guide. (HMM.)

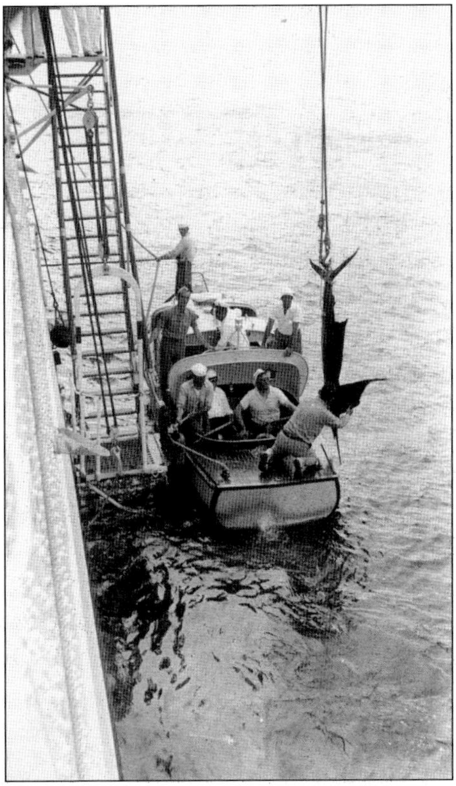

Like fishermen everywhere, Roosevelt enjoyed posing with his catch. With a shark he caught behind him, he is seated in the well deck just forward of *Houston's* aircraft hangar. The president may be delighted, but the officer at far left has the expression of a man concerned about getting the deck spotless again. (USNHHC.)

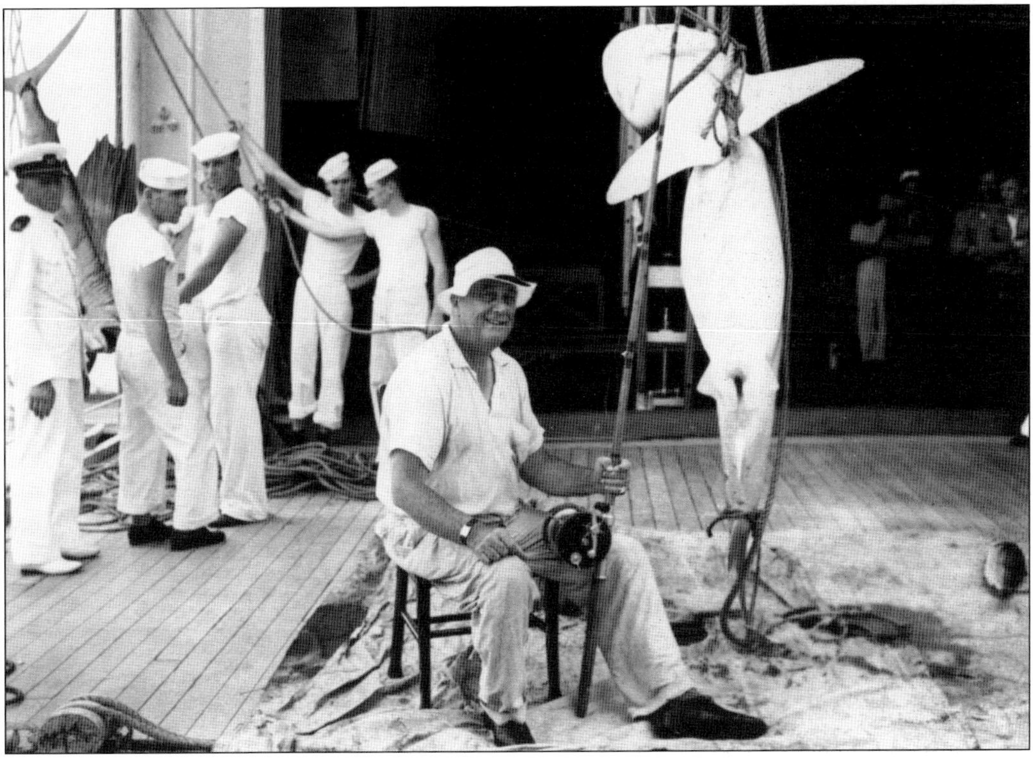

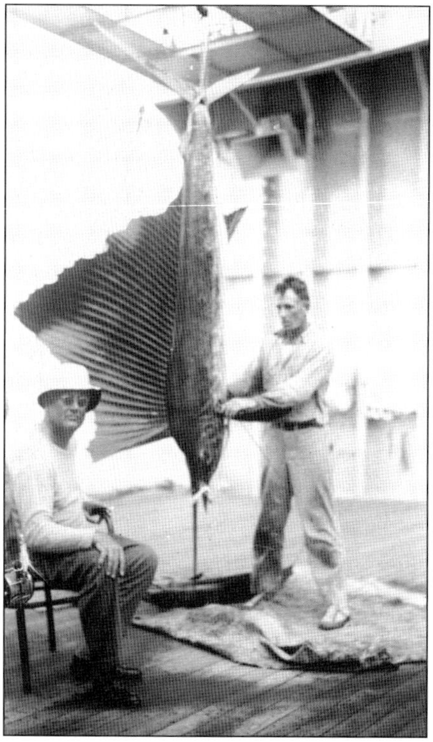

Here, Roosevelt is seated in front of a sailfish, which is being steadied by one of *Houston's* crewmen. (HMM.)

Roosevelt also found time to pose with members of the ship's crew. In this photograph, he is shown with the ship's Marine contingent, in their dress blues. (USNHHC.)

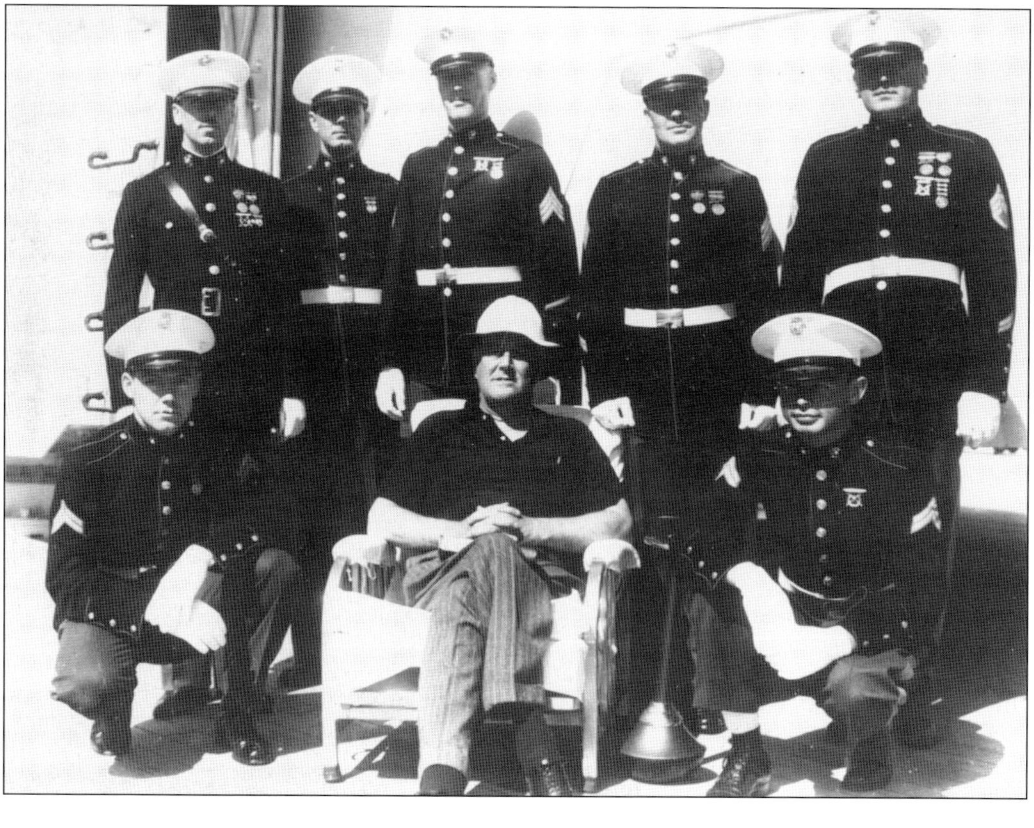

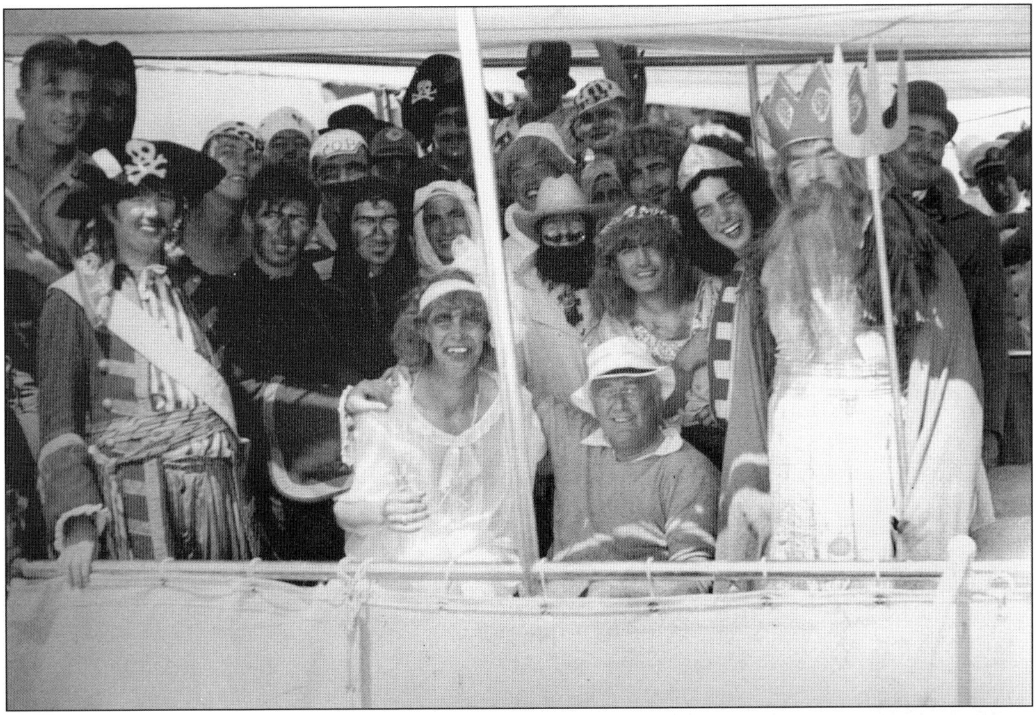

Roosevelt took time out for foreign affairs on this voyage, meeting with King Neptune and his court when they boarded for the line-crossing ceremony. Since Roosevelt had crossed the equator before, he was already a shellback. (HMM.)

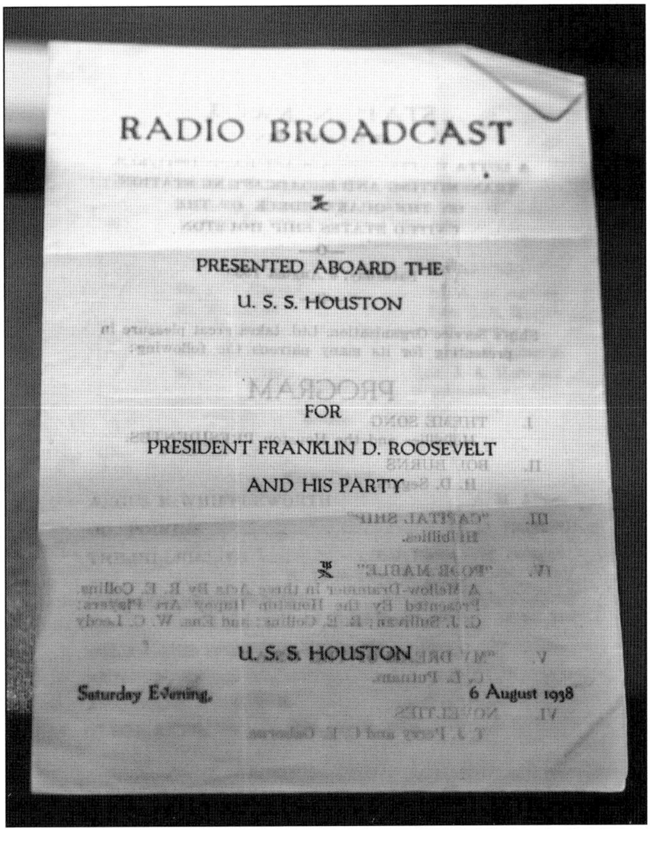

RADIO BROADCAST

PRESENTED ABOARD THE

U. S. S. HOUSTON

FOR

PRESIDENT FRANKLIN D. ROOSEVELT

AND HIS PARTY

U. S. S. HOUSTON

Saturday Evening, 6 August 1938

Roosevelt's fondness for *Houston* was reciprocated. Its crew did what they could to make his stays special. During the 1938 voyage, they put together a radio program for Roosevelt, broadcasting it from *Houston's* radio room. (WL.)

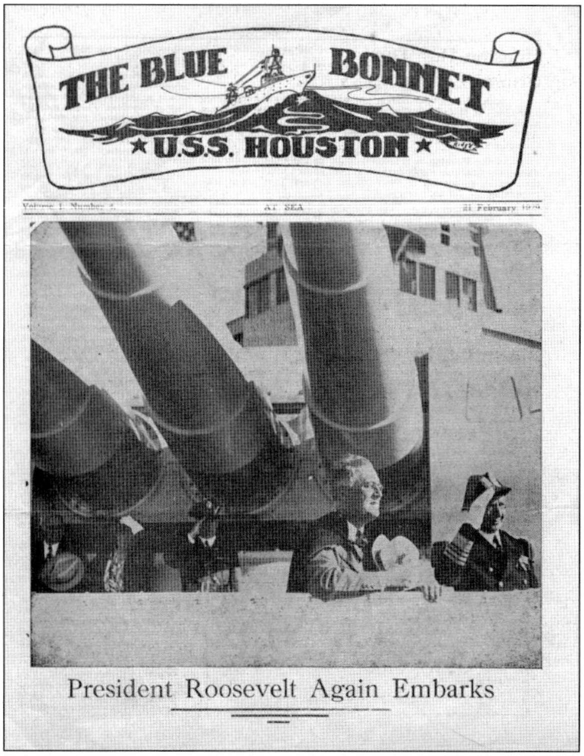

THE BLUE BONNET

★U.S.S. HOUSTON★

AT SEA

President Roosevelt Again Embarks

Roosevelt's fourth and final voyage aboard *Houston* took place in February 1939. World War II would not start for another six months, but war seemed inevitable by then. Again, *The Blue Bonnet* gave the event front-page treatment. (UHDL.)

Because war clouds were gathering, the 1939 voyage was less a vacation and more a planning session than previous trips. Roosevelt is shown here seated with Adm. William D. Leahy, then the Navy's chief of naval operations. (USNHHC.)

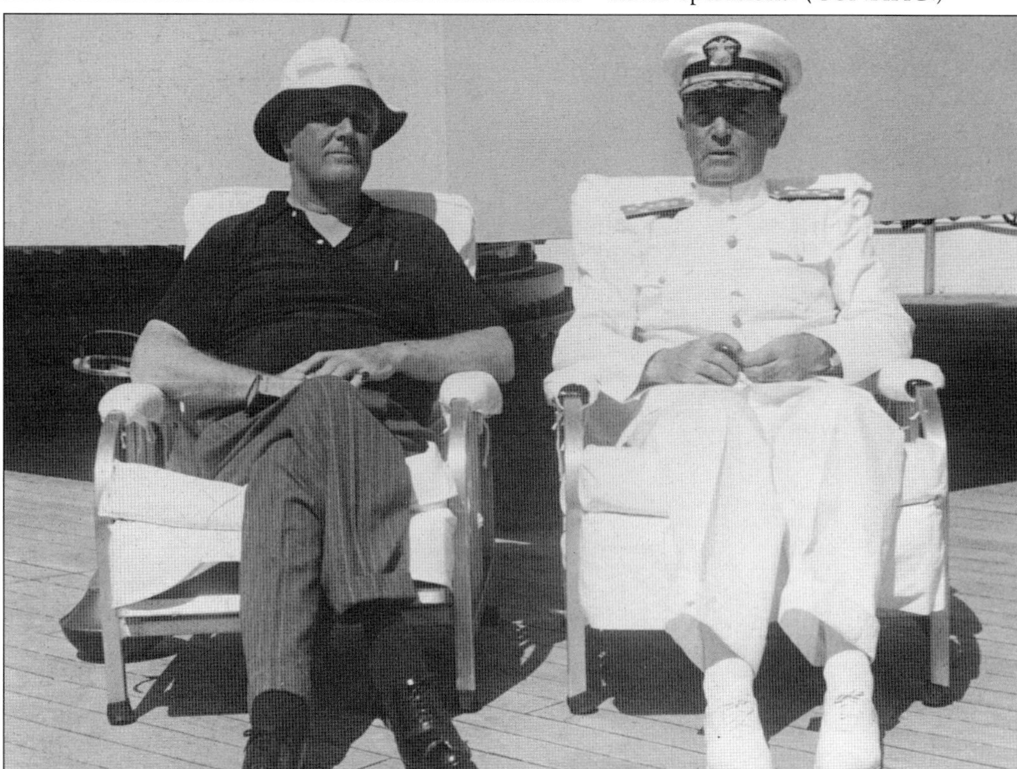

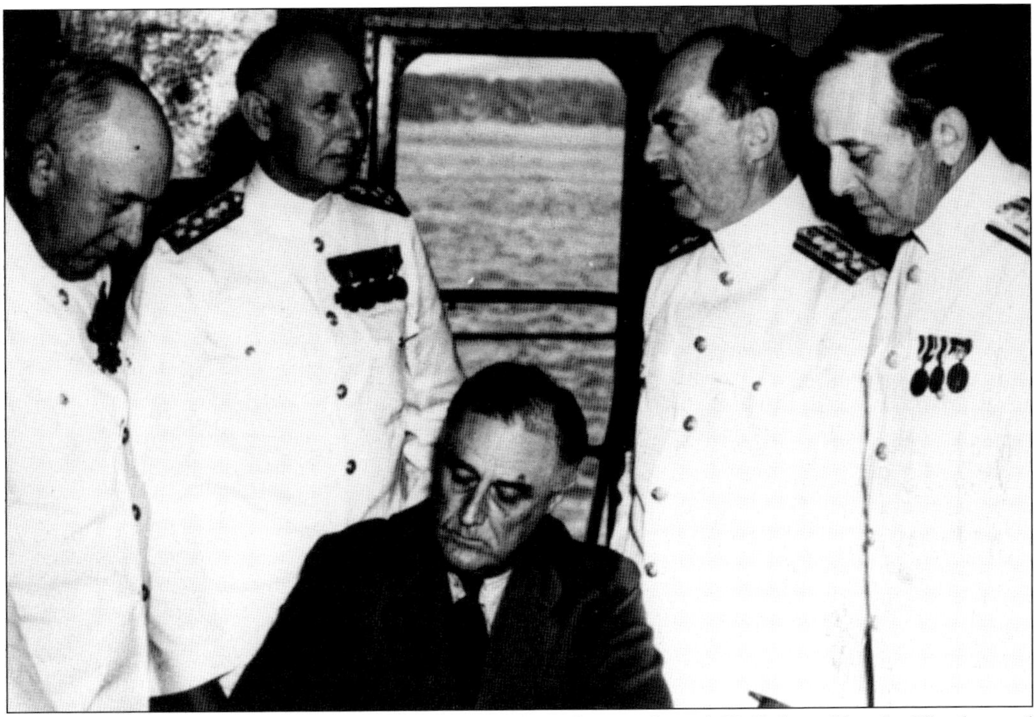

Roosevelt is shown in a planning session with Adms. Edward Kalbfus, Claude Bloch, and William Leahy and Vice Adm. Adolphus Andrews in a room aboard *Houston* in February 1939. Kalbfus was commander Battle Force, US Fleet (COMBATFOR); Bloch was commander in chief, US Fleet (CINCUS); and Andrews was commander Scouting Force, US Fleet (COMSCOFOR). (USNHHC.)

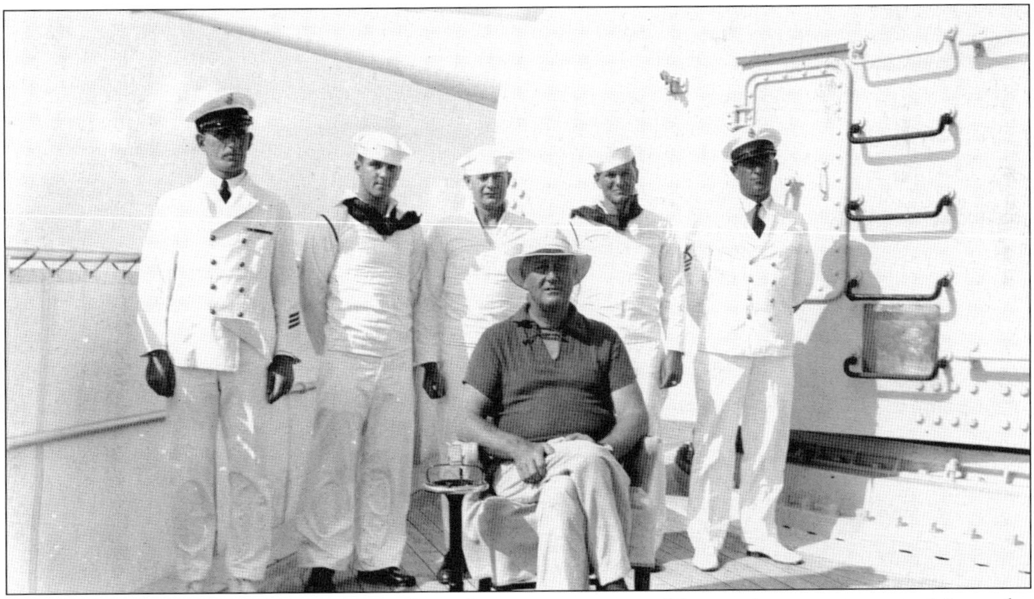

It was not all work, however. Roosevelt took time out to give *Houston's* crew opportunities to be photographed with him. Here, he is posing with a bosun's mate and his team. (HMM.)

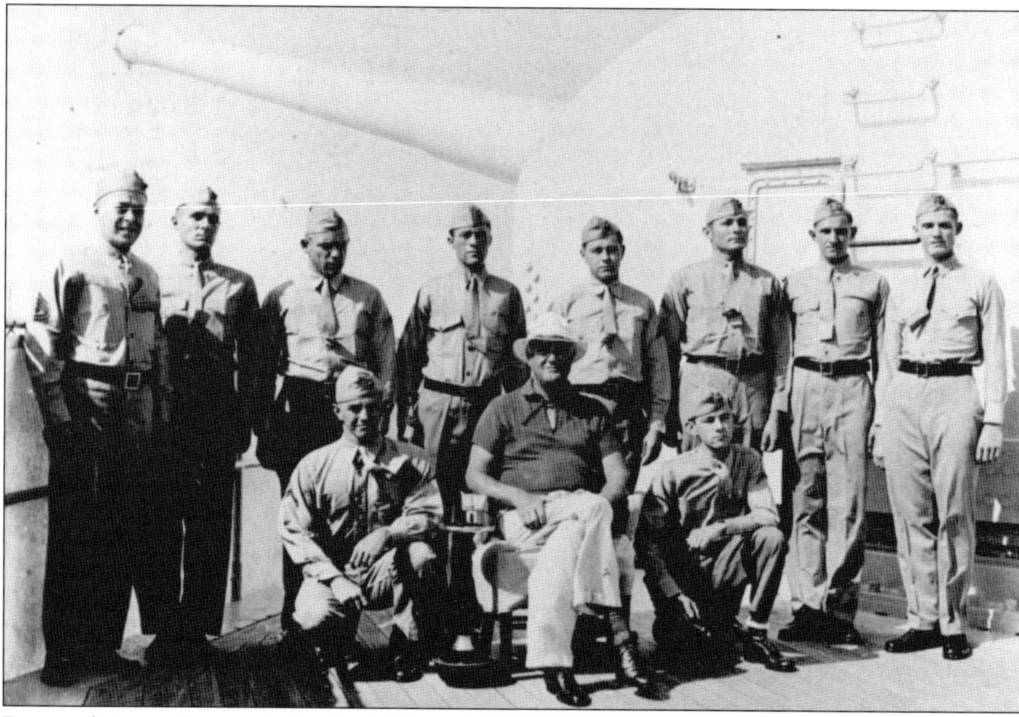

Roosevelt is seen here with the ship's Marine contingent once again. This time, they are in khakis. Both this and the photograph on page 42 were taken in front of the No. 2 turret. (HMM.)

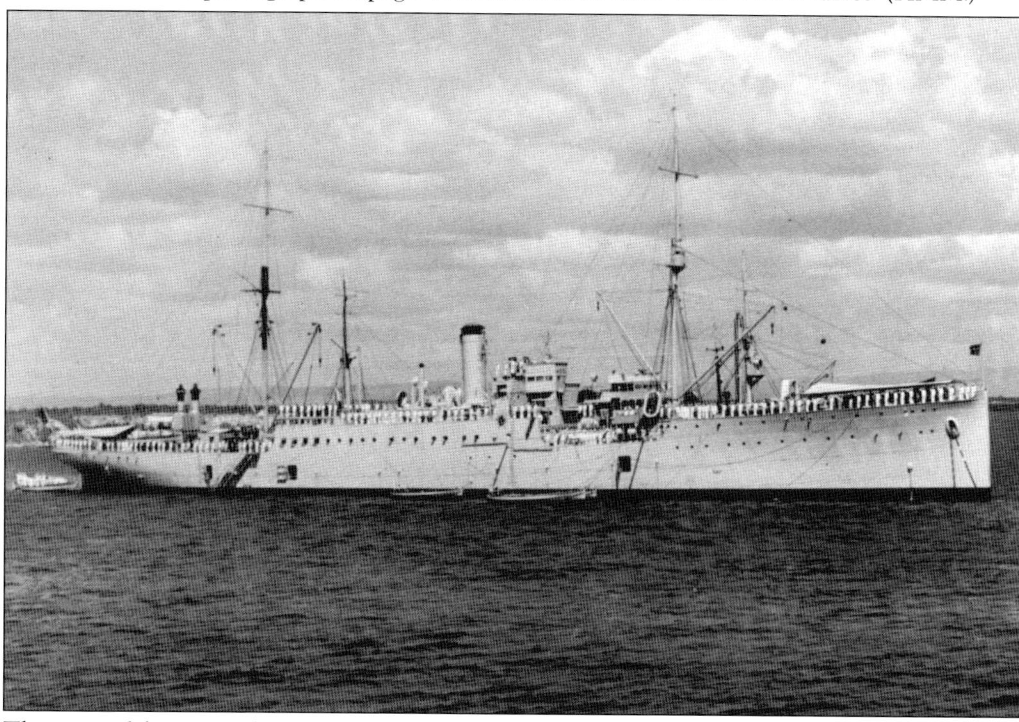

The crew of the repair ship *Vestal* mans the rails to honor President Roosevelt as *Houston* steams past *Vestal* at Guantanamo Bay, Cuba, on February 20, 1939. (USNHHC.)

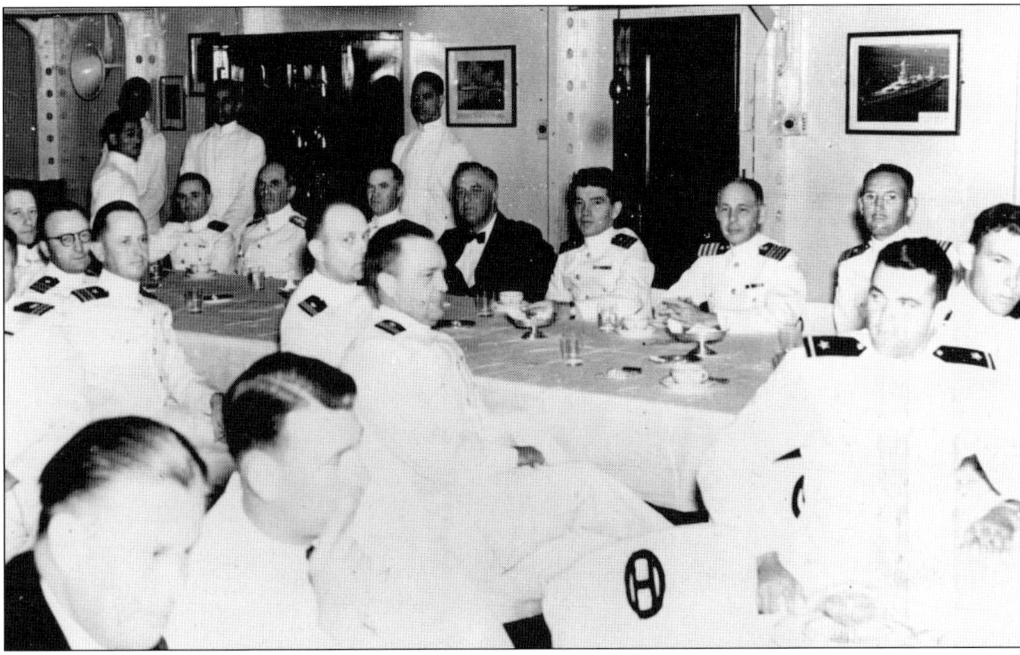

Of course, there was always at least one formal dinner in *Houston's* wardroom during Roosevelt's visits. Guest of honor Roosevelt, a civilian, is in dinner dress, and the officers wear dress whites. *Houston's* captain, George N. Barker, is second from Roosevelt's left. (USNHHC.)

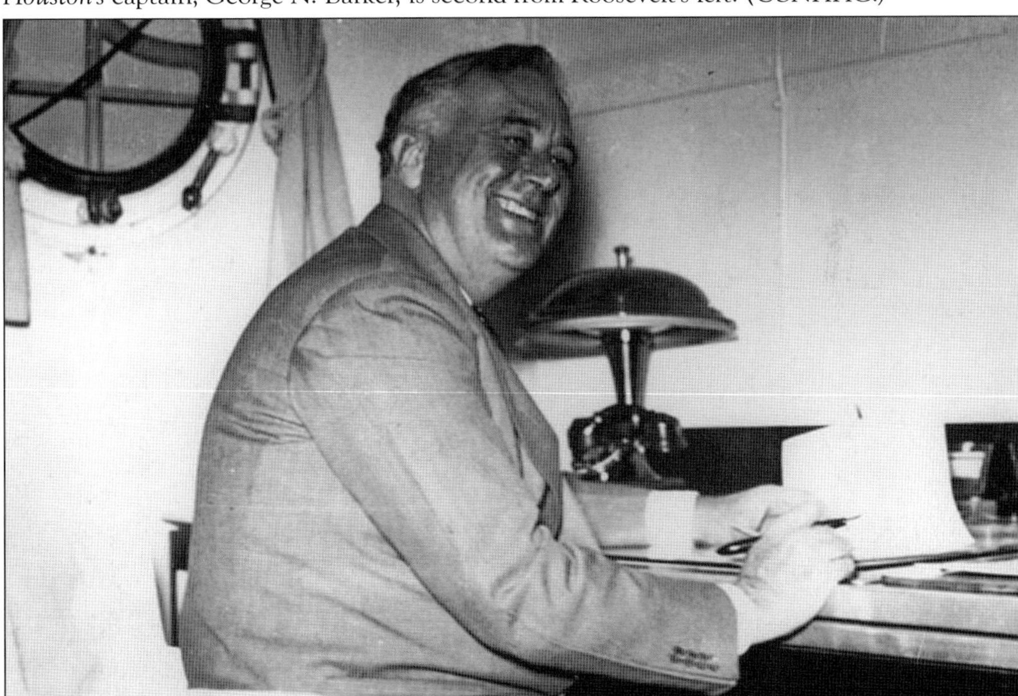

When Roosevelt traveled on *Houston*, he took the admiral's cabin, which was included in *Houston's* design to help it fill its role as a flagship. This is Roosevelt in his *Houston* home during his 1939 voyage. (NARA.)

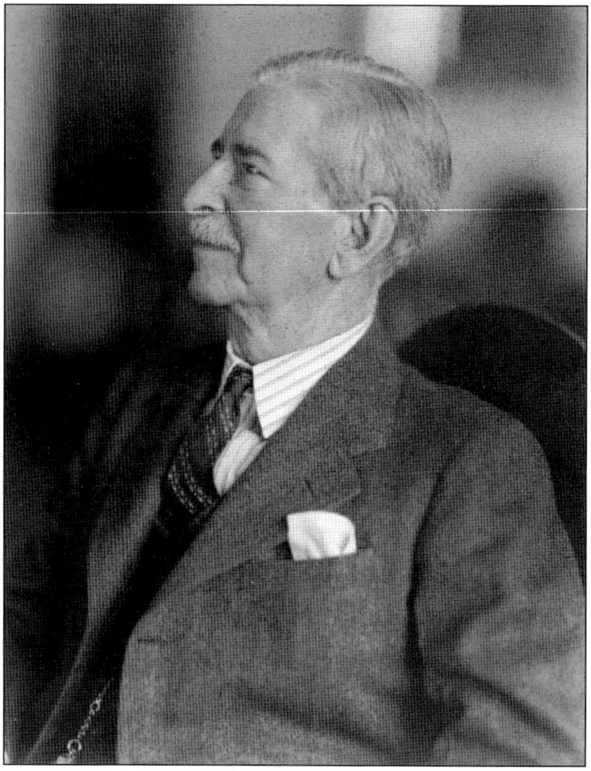

President Roosevelt was not the only dignitary to spend a week or two in the admiral's suite aboard *Houston*. Secretary of the Navy Claude Swanson was aboard from March 11 through March 23, 1939, one week after the president left the ship. (USNHHC.)

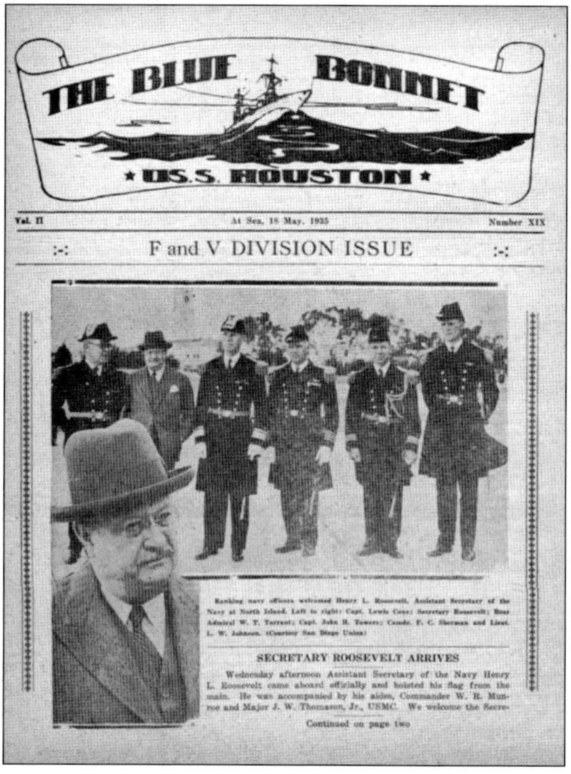

THE BLUE BONNET

U.S.S. HOUSTON

Vol. II | At Sea, 18 May, 1935 | Number XIX

F and V DIVISION ISSUE

Ranking navy officers welcomed Henry L. Roosevelt, Assistant Secretary of the Navy at North Island. Left to right: Capt. Lewis Coxe; Secretary Roosevelt; Rear Admiral W. T. Tarrant; Capt. John H. Towers; Comdr. F. C. Sherman and Lieut. L. W. Johnson. (Courtesy San Diego Union)

SECRETARY ROOSEVELT ARRIVES

Wednesday afternoon Assistant Secretary of the Navy Henry L. Roosevelt came aboard officially and hoisted his flag from the main. He was accompanied by his aides, Commander W. R. Munroe and Major J. W. Thomason, Jr., USMC. We welcome the Secre-

Continued on page two

Assistant Secretary of the Navy Henry L. Roosevelt used *Houston* to get to Hawaii when he did an inspection of Pearl Harbor and the Hawaiian area in 1935. He stayed on *Houston* from May 15 through May 31, and even made the front page of *The Blue Bonnet*. (UHDL.)

Three

China Station

Houston spent five years—over 40 percent of its 12 years as a commissioned warship—as the flagship of the Asiatic Fleet. The Asiatic Fleet was the Navy's smallest. It usually had one heavy cruiser to serve as flagship, one or two light cruisers, a dozen destroyers, and a collection of auxiliary support ships, motley ocean-going gunships, and river gunboats. The ocean-going gunships showed the American flag in the various European colonies then dotting the Asian mainland and scattered islands between Asia and Australia.

The river gunboats patrolled Chinese rivers—as far inland as 1,300 miles—to protect American and European interests within China. In the 1800s, after losing the Opium Wars, China had opened its rivers to foreign warships and opened several ports, known as treaty ports, to foreign nations. The most important treaty port was Shanghai, although the British Crown Colony of Hong Kong might have disputed that.

In many ways, *Houston's* job while in the Asiatic Fleet was to look good. It was the most powerful US warship in the fleet at China station, as the posting in one of the Chinese treaty ports was called. This was where the world's navies visited to show their flags. A smart appearance was required lest one's nation lose prestige, and *Houston* was always a smart ship.

Houston's two tours in the Asiatic Fleet came during critical periods in Pacific history. Its first tour was from 1931 through 1933. Those three years saw the opening round of hostilities that led to the Second Sino-Japanese War, which started in 1937. Its second tour, from 1940 through 1942, saw the start of the Pacific phase of World War II. *Houston* was present when the Shanghai Incident began in January 1932, and during the run-up to the Japanese attacks at Pearl Harbor and the Philippines.

For *Houston's* sailors, the Far East offered adventure of a sort they had never dreamed of while growing up in the Great Plains, Midwest, or Deep South. It was as different from home as it got. This chapter captures that adventure in pictures.

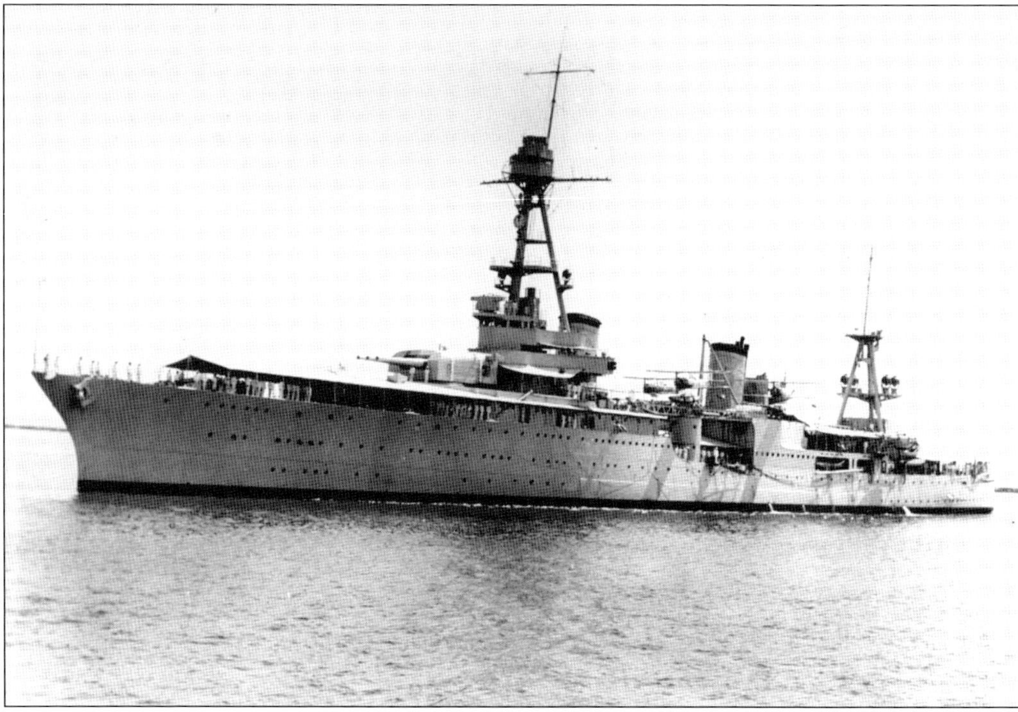

Houston was twice the flagship of the Asiatic Fleet, once from 1931 to 1933 and again from 1940 to 1942. This 1931 photograph shows *Houston* in Manila Bay shortly after arriving. It looks every inch a peacetime flagship with everything squared away. Note the torpedo tubes on the left side aft of the second funnel. These were removed after *Houston's* 1933 return to the states. (USNHHC.)

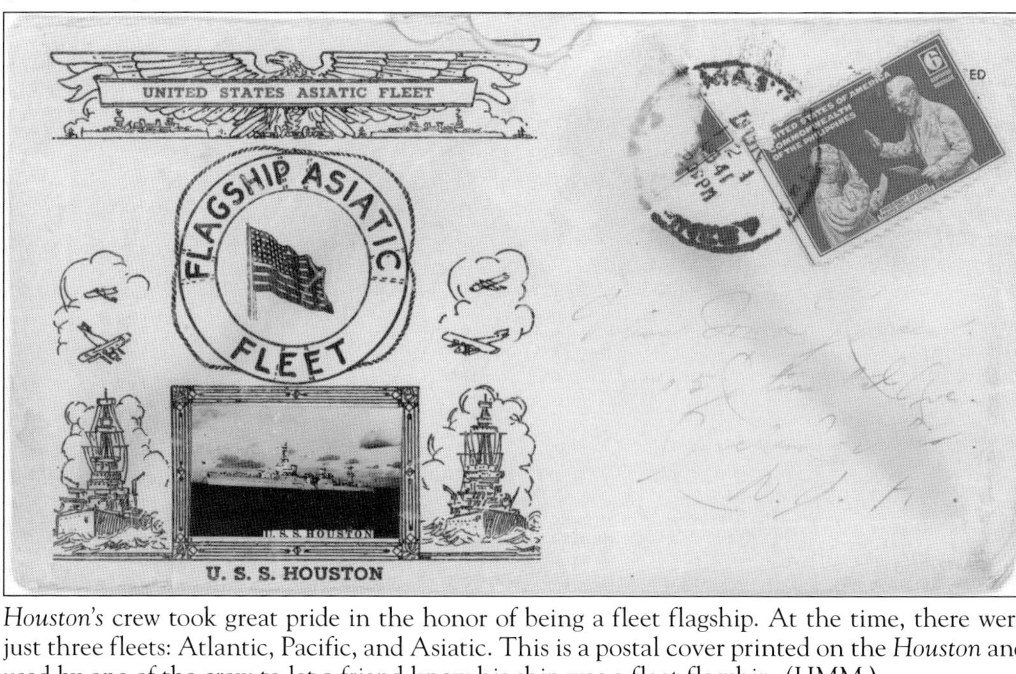

Houston's crew took great pride in the honor of being a fleet flagship. At the time, there were just three fleets: Atlantic, Pacific, and Asiatic. This is a postal cover printed on the *Houston* and used by one of the crew to let a friend know his ship was a fleet flagship. (HMM.)

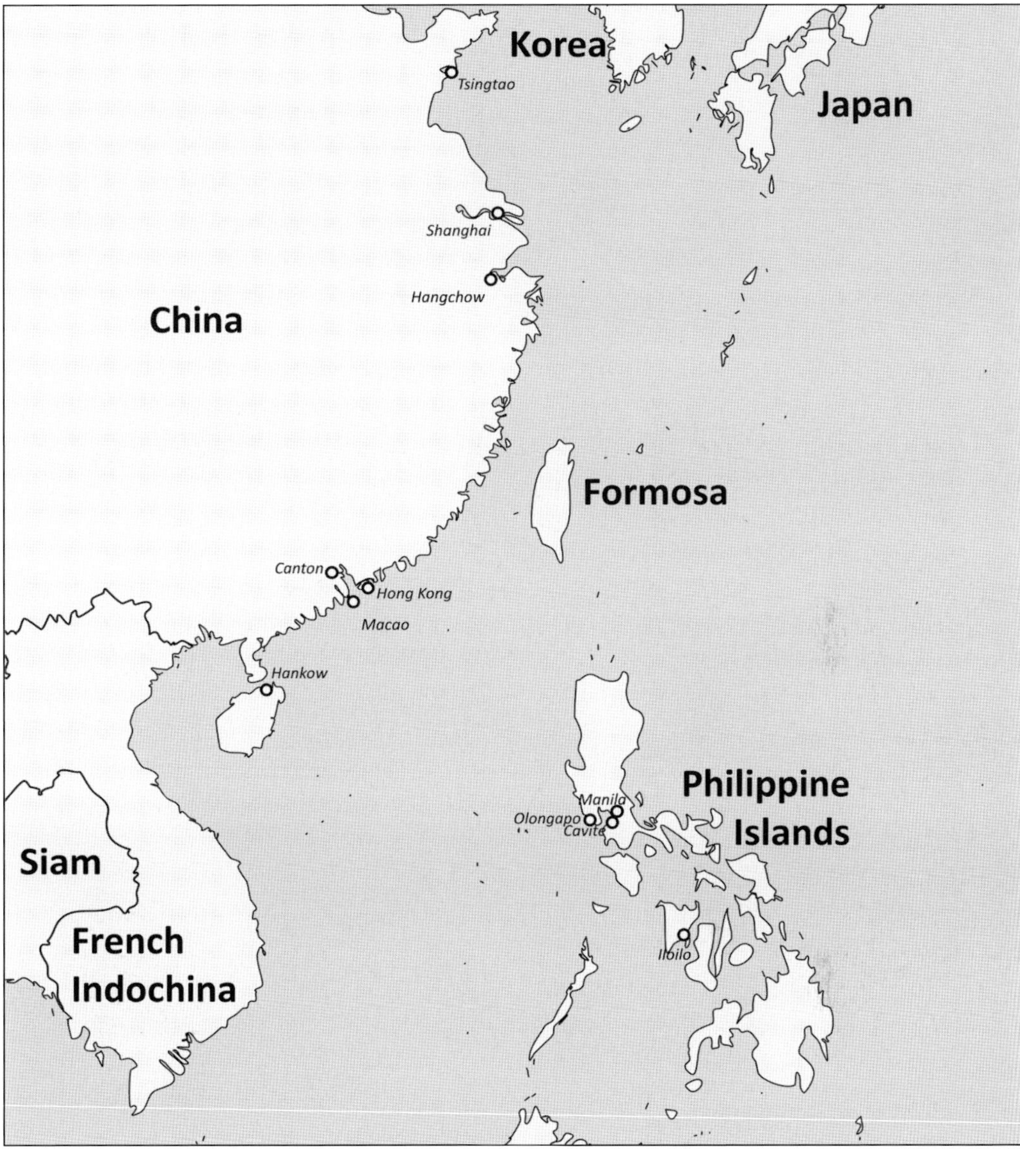

The geographical area covered by the Asiatic Fleet was big, technically including the seas as far west as India and as far south as Australia. The Asiatic Fleet's core area of responsibility—mainly Philippine waters and China's coast, with occasional diplomatic stops at Japan—is shown on this map. (AC.)

Pride in being the flagship of the Asiatic Fleet was manifested in many ways. The Chinese character for bird was adopted as the insignia for *Houston's* air group the first time the ship served in the Asiatic Fleet. (USNHHC.)

The insignia was maintained with pride by *Houston's* air group. Here, a sailor paints the insignia on one of the cruiser's Curtiss SOC Seagull floatplanes in the late 1930s or early 1940s. (HMM.)

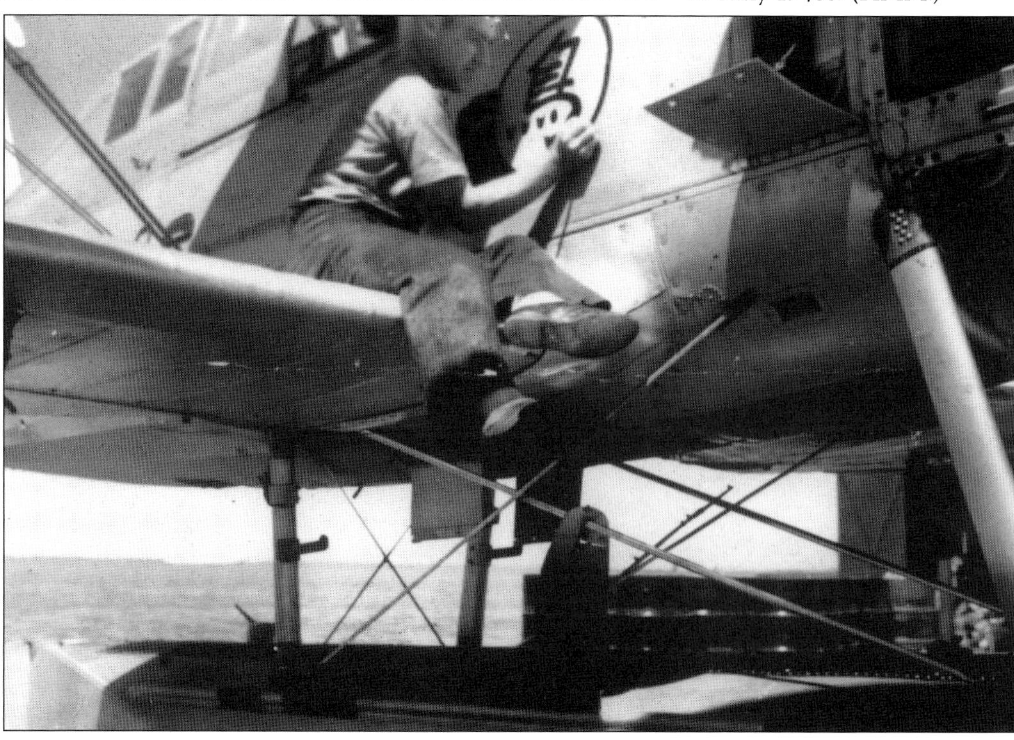

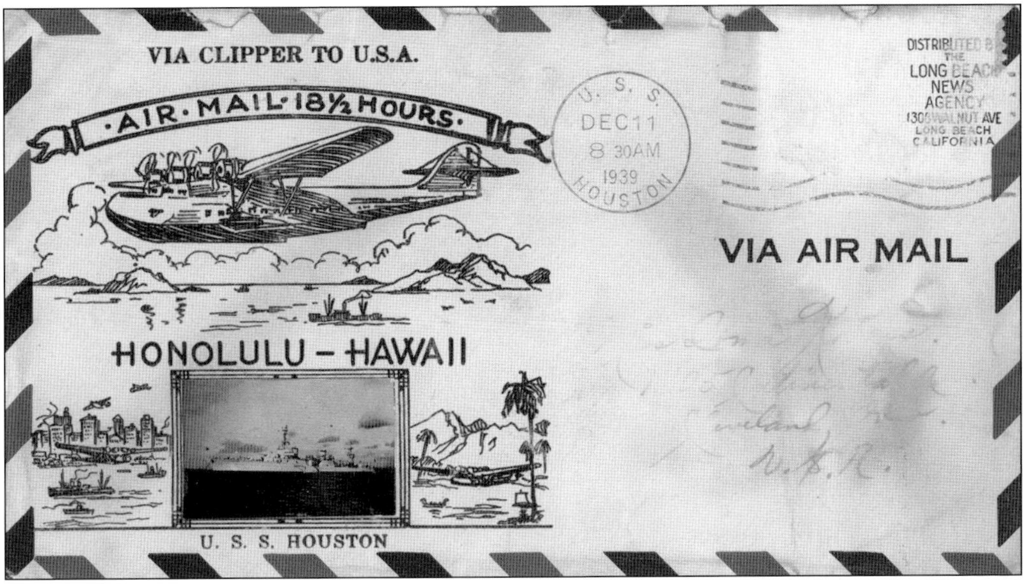

Asiatic Fleet sailors were seen as a breed apart. Between the world wars, most US Navy sailors rarely ventured west of Hawaii. It was sufficiently distant that visiting Hawaii merited special notice, like mailing, via Pan Am Clipper, a letter proclaiming one's post in Honolulu to someone in the states. (HMM.)

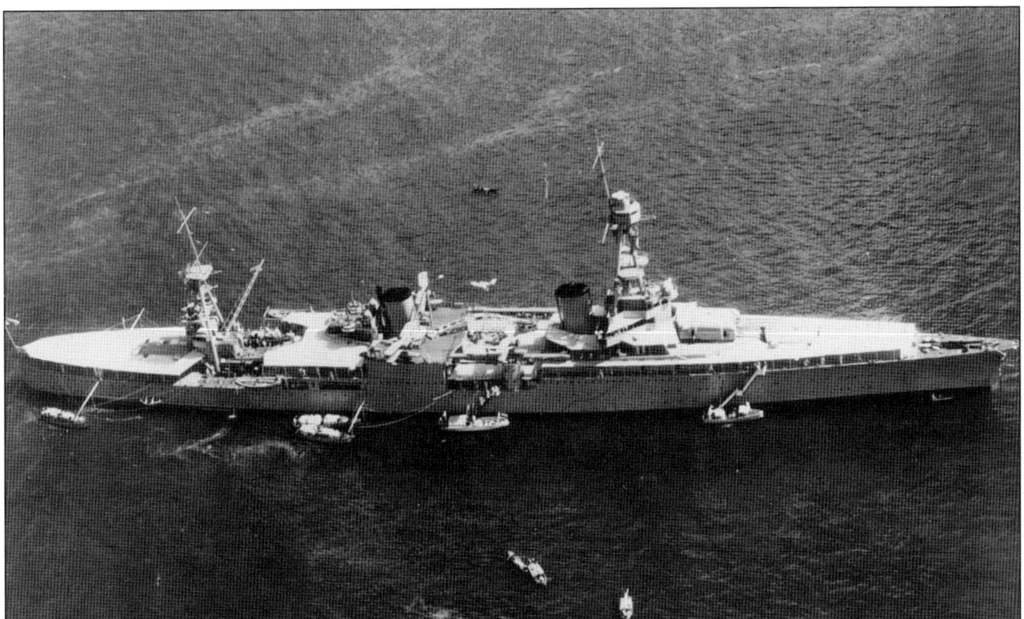
The home port for the Asiatic Fleet was Manila in the Philippines. This photograph shows *Houston*, newly arrived to assume its responsibilities as flagship of the Asiatic Fleet, in Manila Bay in February 1931. It has awnings set to provide shade on the deck and a suite of ship's boats tied up alongside. (USNHHC.)

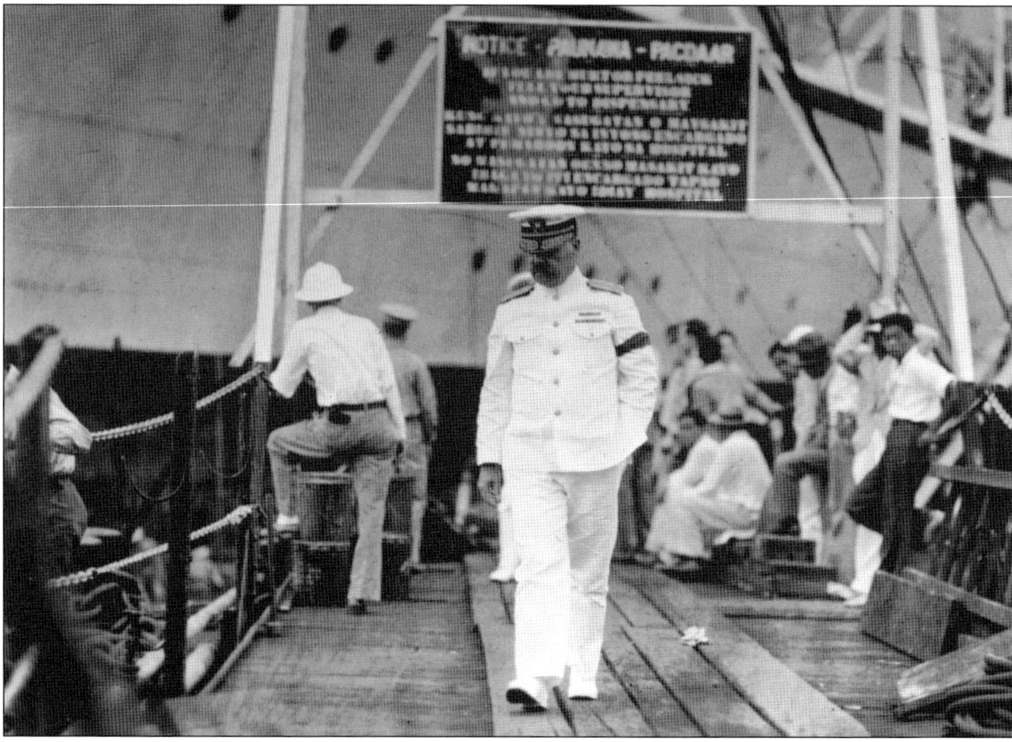

Adm. Montgomery M. Taylor was commander of Asiatic Fleet between September 1931 and August 1933. He was no stranger to these waters. As a lieutenant, he fought at the Battle of Manila Bay. He was battery commander for Commodore George Dewey's flagship *Olympia*. Taylor is shown here going ashore at Olongapo Naval Station. *Houston*, Taylor's flagship, is in the background. (USNHHC.)

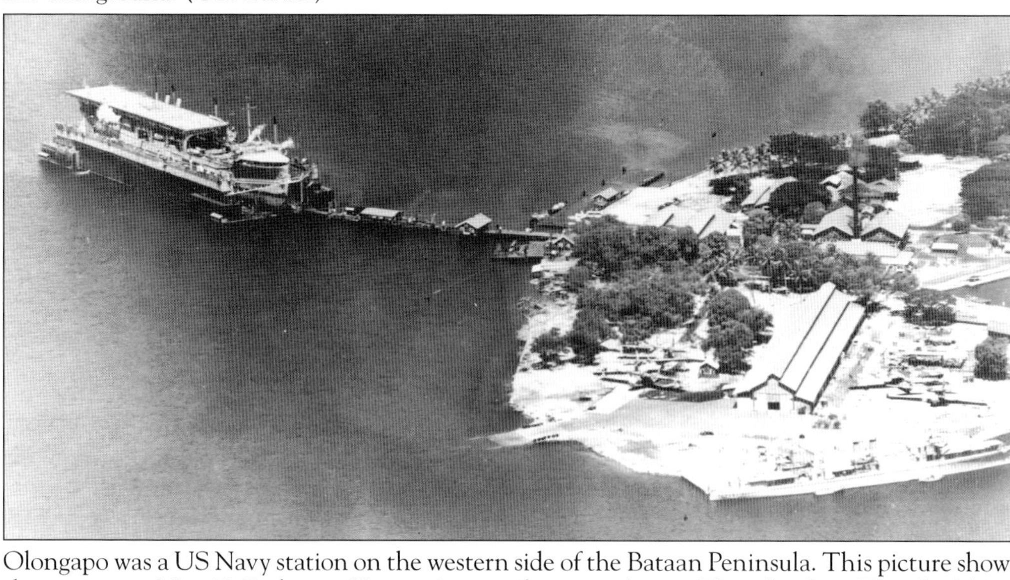

Olongapo was a US Navy station on the western side of the Bataan Peninsula. This picture shows the station in May 1941, during *Houston's* second tour as Asiatic Fleet flagship. The "building" on the left is actually the seaplane tender (former aircraft carrier) *Langley* in the Dewey floating dry dock. (USNHHC.)

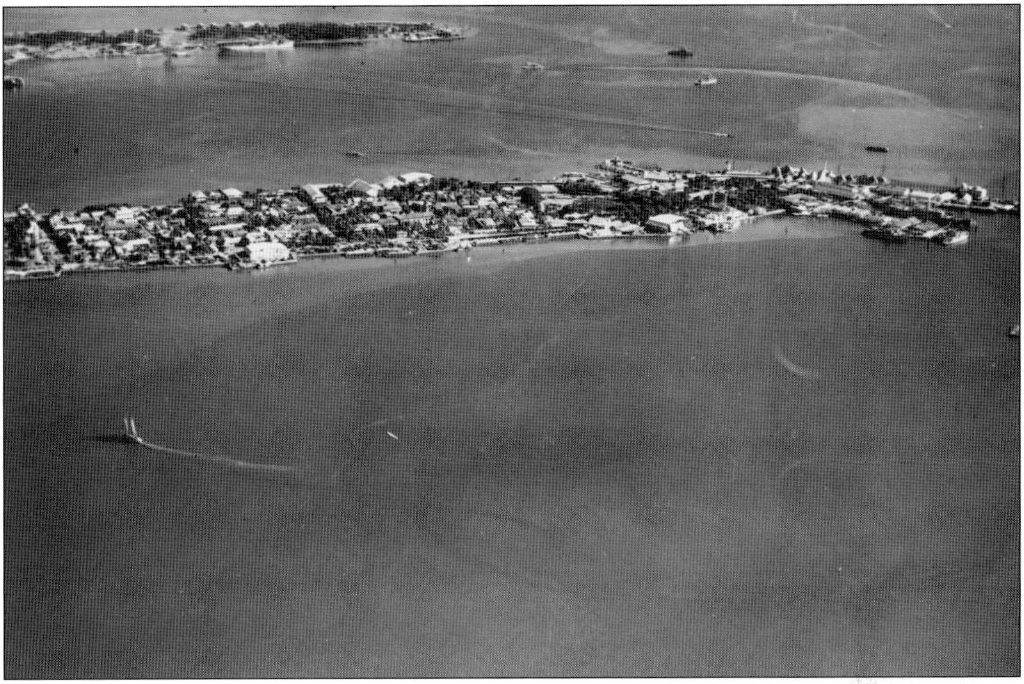

Cavite Navy Yard, on the south side of Manila Bay, was the Asiatic Fleet's main base, filling the same role in the Far East that Pearl Harbor did in the Central Pacific. *Houston* was normally based out of here. Cavite is seen here in October 1941. (USNHHC.)

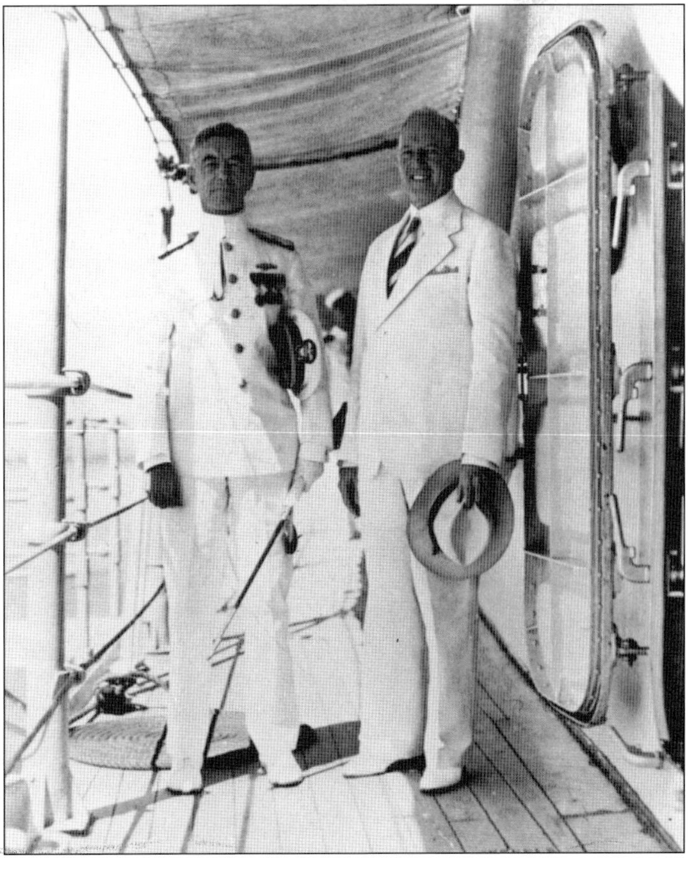

Adm. Thomas Hart led the Asiatic Fleet during *Houston's* second tour, when the cruiser served as his flagship. He is pictured aboard *Houston* meeting with Francis Sayre, the US high commissioner to the Commonwealth of the Philippines. Hart is turned out in immaculate dress whites with full medals. (USNHHC.)

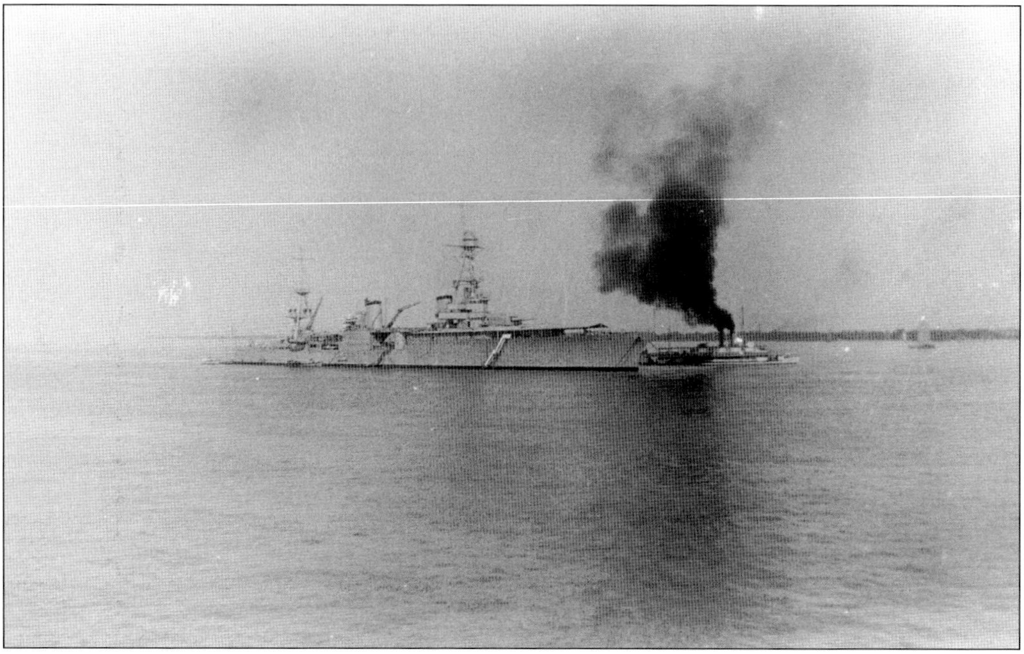

Houston spent most of its time with the Asiatic Fleet outside the Philippines. The 1930s were an age of gunboat diplomacy, in which the United States and European nations had the right to patrol China's coast and rivers to protect citizens. *Houston* is pictured off Hankow, a port on the north side of Hainan Island. Behind it can be seen smoke from the coal-burning USS *Palos*. Designed as a Yangtze River gunboat, *Palos* was on temporary duty at Hainan at the time. (USNHHC.)

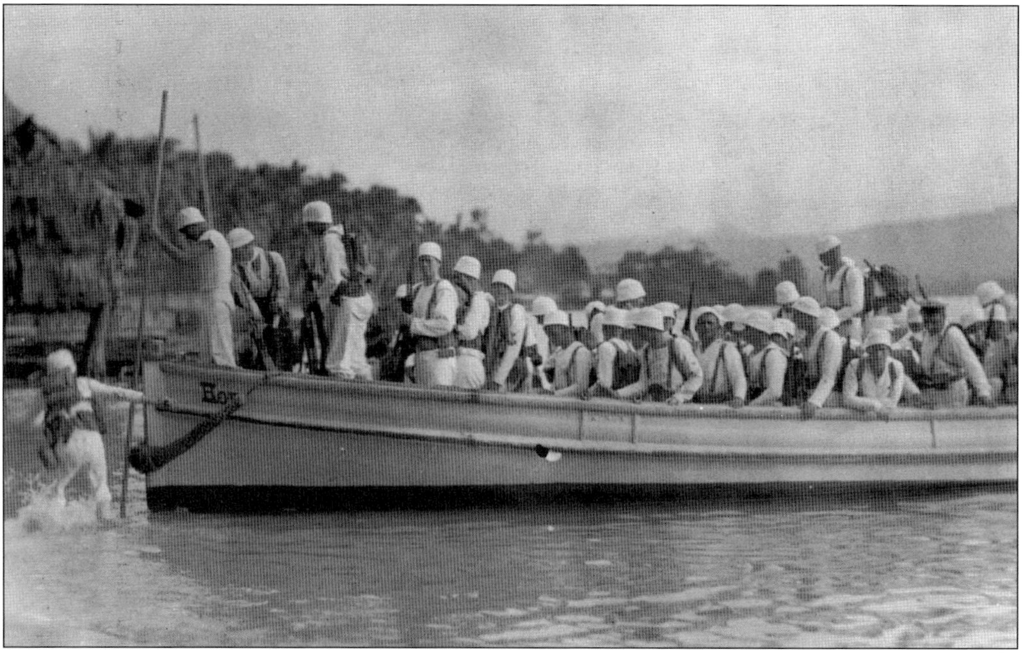

Because the Navy was expected to aid US citizens abroad in a muscular manner during the early 1930s, Navy ships practiced landing armed shore parties. In this photograph, armed sailors from *Houston* are coming ashore on the ship's motor launch. (USNHHC.)

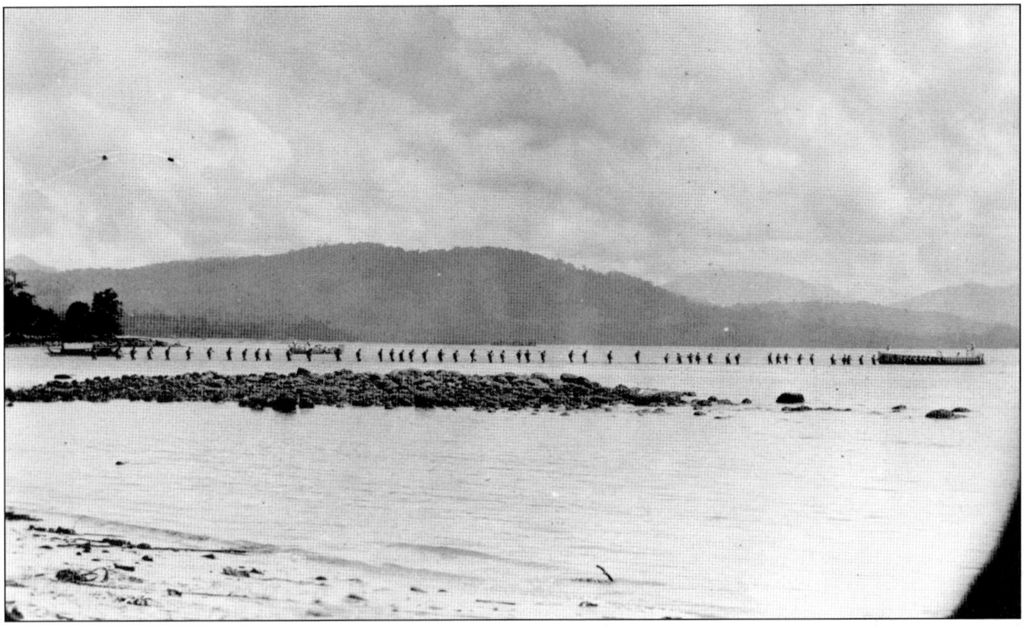
This exercise was carried out in Dumanquilas Bay, Mindanao, in the Philippines. Having reached shallow water, the sailors form a skirmish line and wade ashore. (USNHHC.)

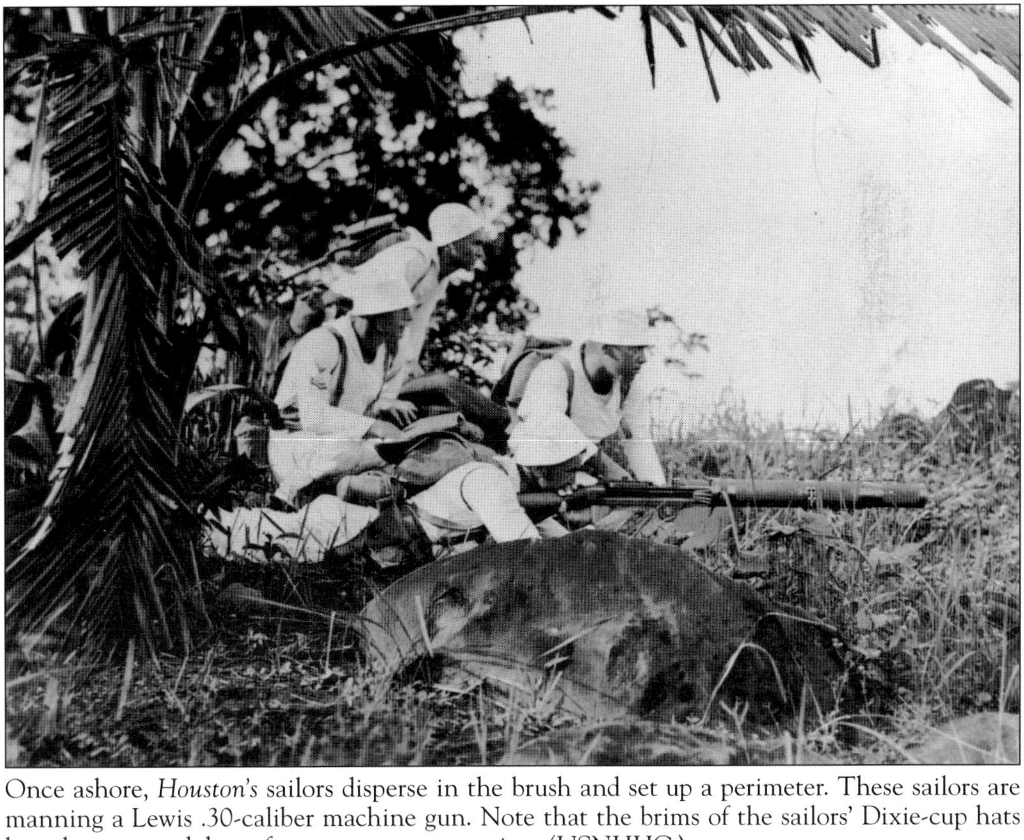
Once ashore, *Houston's* sailors disperse in the brush and set up a perimeter. These sailors are manning a Lewis .30-caliber machine gun. Note that the brims of the sailors' Dixie-cup hats have been turned down for greater sun protection. (USNHHC.)

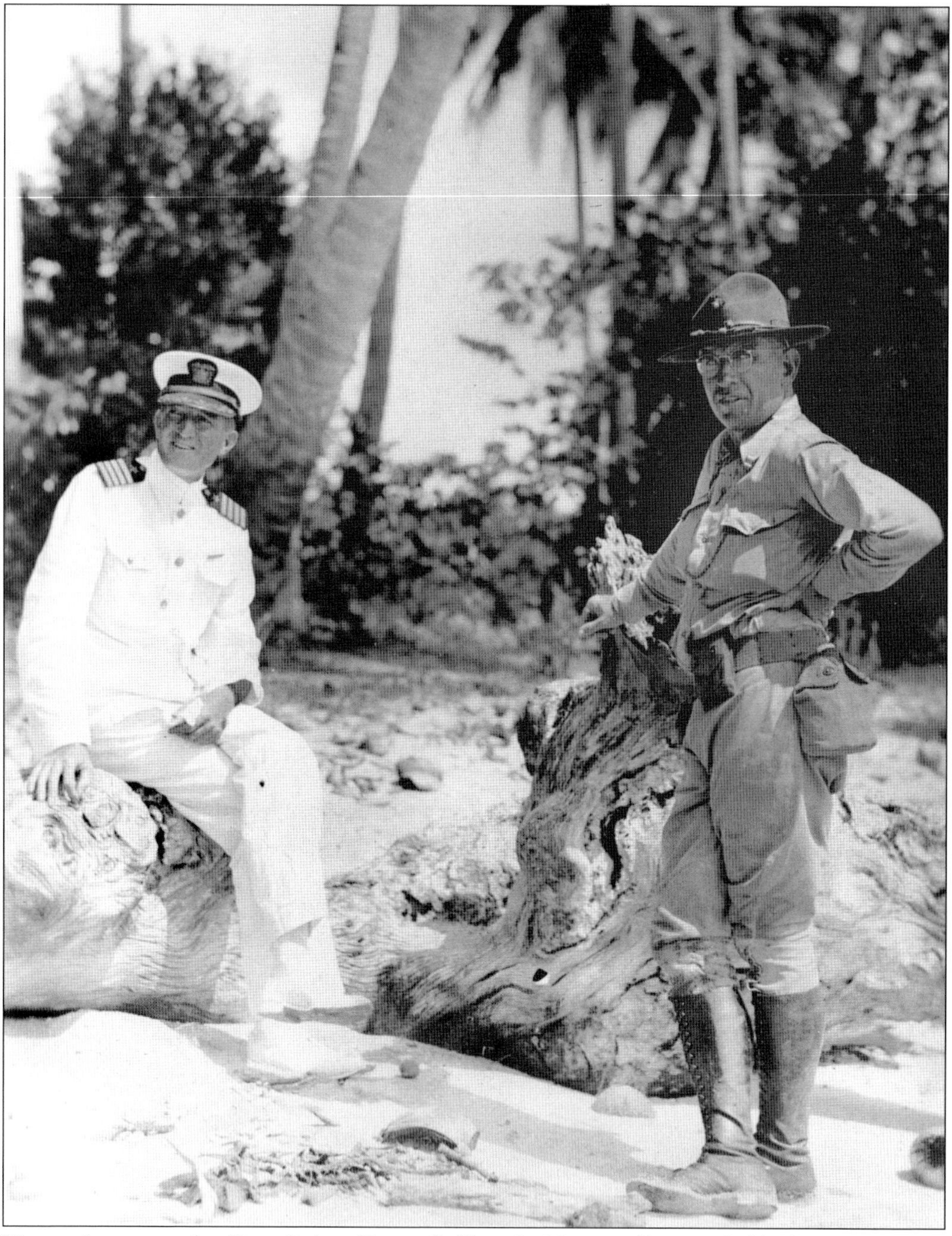

Houston's commander, Capt. Robert Dawes (left), and a Marine officer, probably Capt. D. Curtiss, observe the progress of the exercise from shore. It looks as if Captain Dawes is enjoying the break in routine. Dawes was *Houston's* second captain. (USNHHC.)

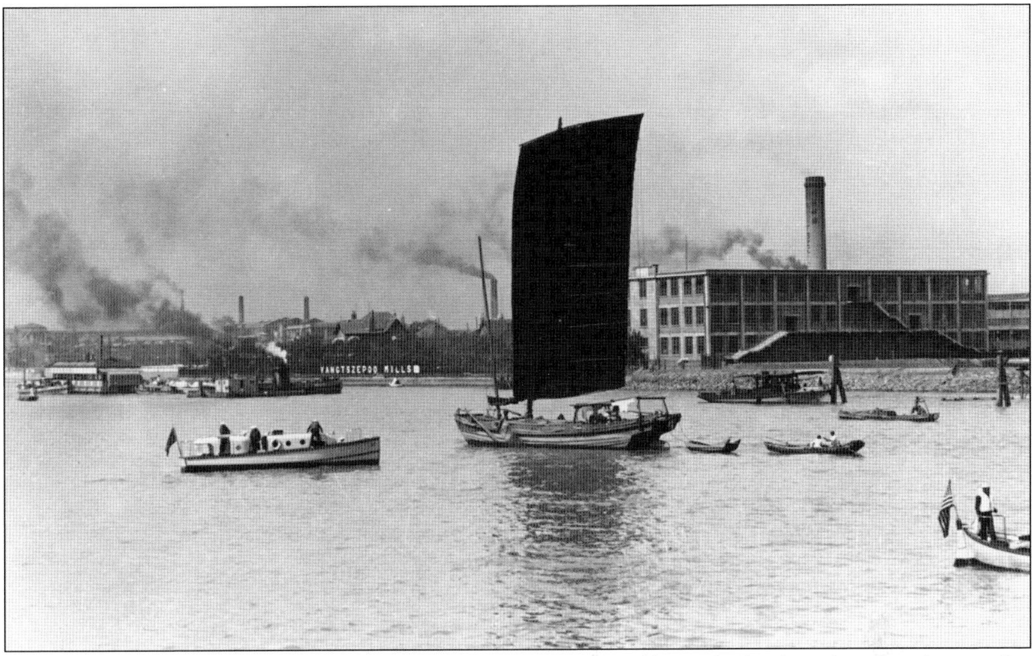

Even for *Houston* sailors who grew up on the coast, regardless of whether they lived near the Atlantic, Pacific, Gulf, or Great Lakes, the Far East offered a far different waterfront than they were familiar with. The rigs on the sailing vessels were unfamiliar, and instead of dories and dinghies, the Asian waterfront was filled with sampans and junks. (USNHHC.)

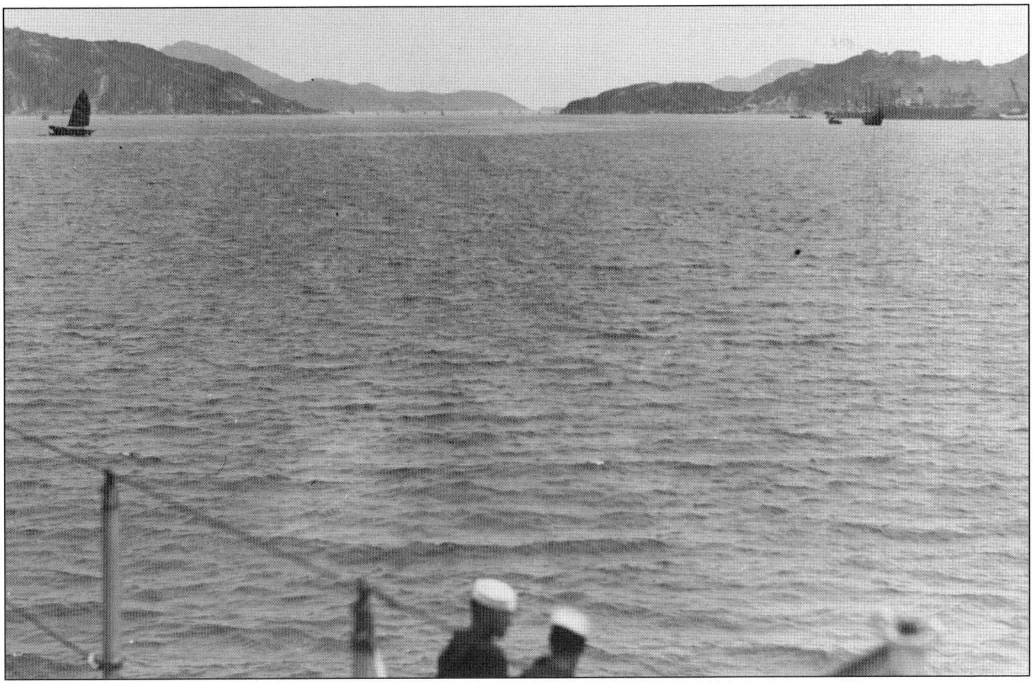

Hong Kong was Great Britain's most important naval outpost in China. As such, it was a frequent destination for *Houston*. This picture, taken aboard the cruiser in 1932, shows the entrance to Hong Kong's harbor as *Houston* steams in. (USNHHC.)

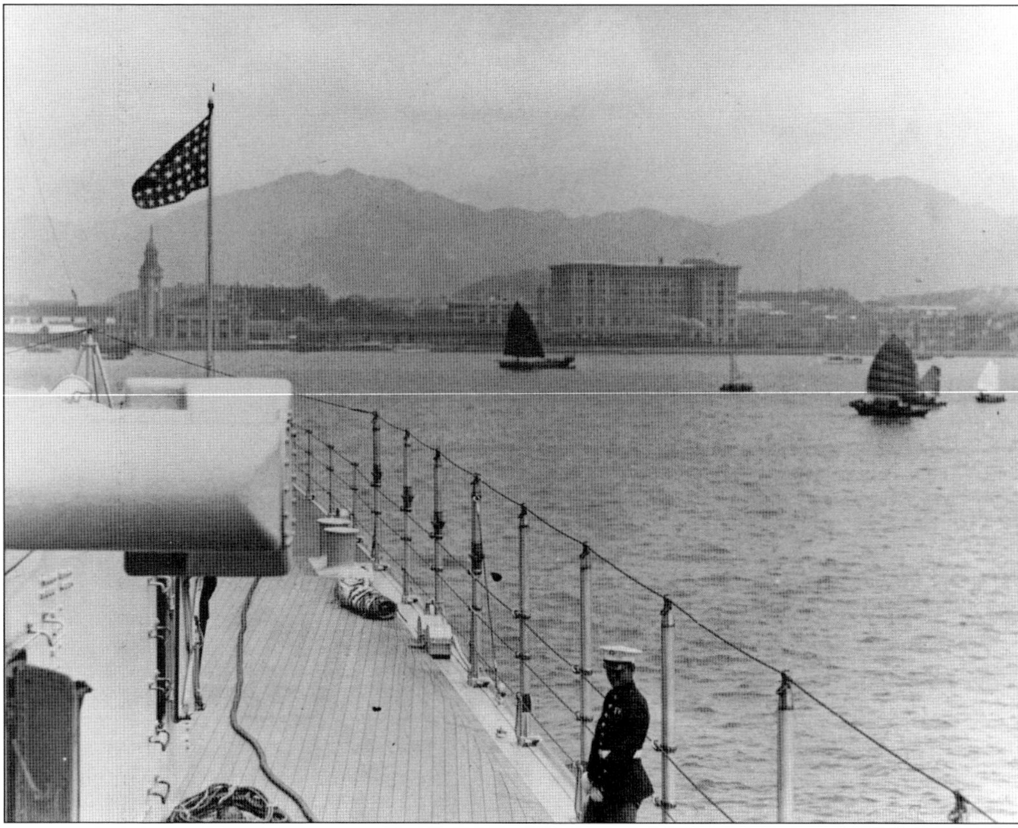

This photograph of Kowloon, the mainland "new city" of Hong Kong, was taken from *Houston's* bridge, looking forward. The object on the left in the foreground is the second turret rangefinder. While Hong Kong has changed dramatically since this picture was taken in 1932, the Canton Railway Clock Tower (on the left, between the rangefinder and the flag) still stands. (USNHHC.)

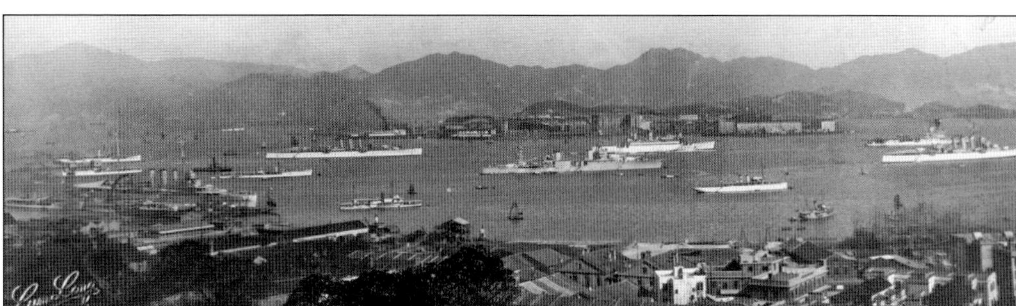

Here is a panoramic view of Hong Kong Harbor taken from Hong Kong Island in the early 1930s, when *Houston* was visiting and the British fleet was in. *Houston* is at center. Behind it is the Royal Navy submarine tender *Medway.* Three of the five *Kent*-class heavy cruisers that served in the Royal Navy's 5th Cruiser Squadron are present (the large three-funnel ships), the British aircraft carrier *Hermes* (behind the cruiser, right); the US patrol boat *Isabel,* in front and ahead of *Houston*; and a French river gunboat aft of Houston. (USNHHC.)

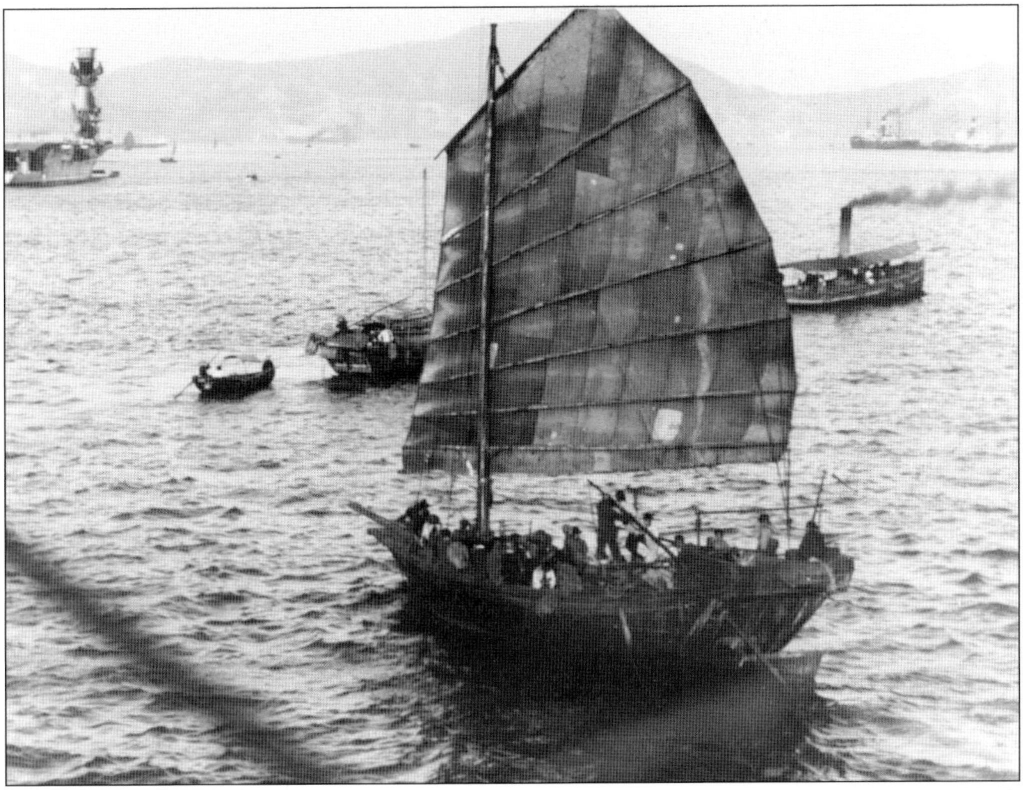

Here is the Hong Kong harbor in 1932, as captured in a photograph taken from *Houston*. A junk is sailing past in the foreground. In the background on the left is HMS *Hermes*, a British aircraft carrier. (USNHHC.)

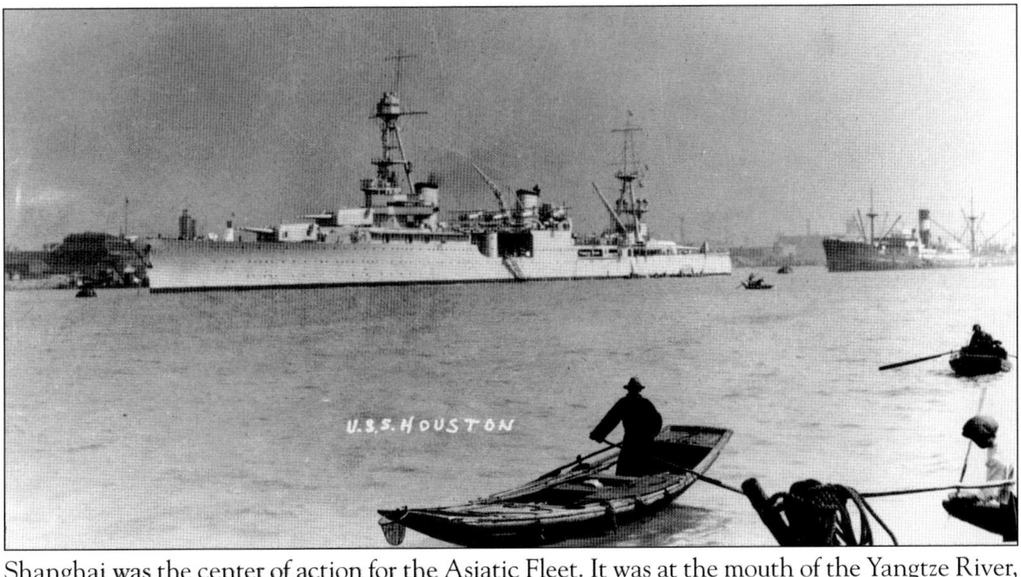

Shanghai was the center of action for the Asiatic Fleet. It was at the mouth of the Yangtze River, one of China's most important waterways. It was also a treaty port, with foreign nations granted extraterritorial rights. This shows *Houston* anchored at Shanghai, with the Bund, the heart of the Shanghai International Settlement, in the background. (USNHHC.)

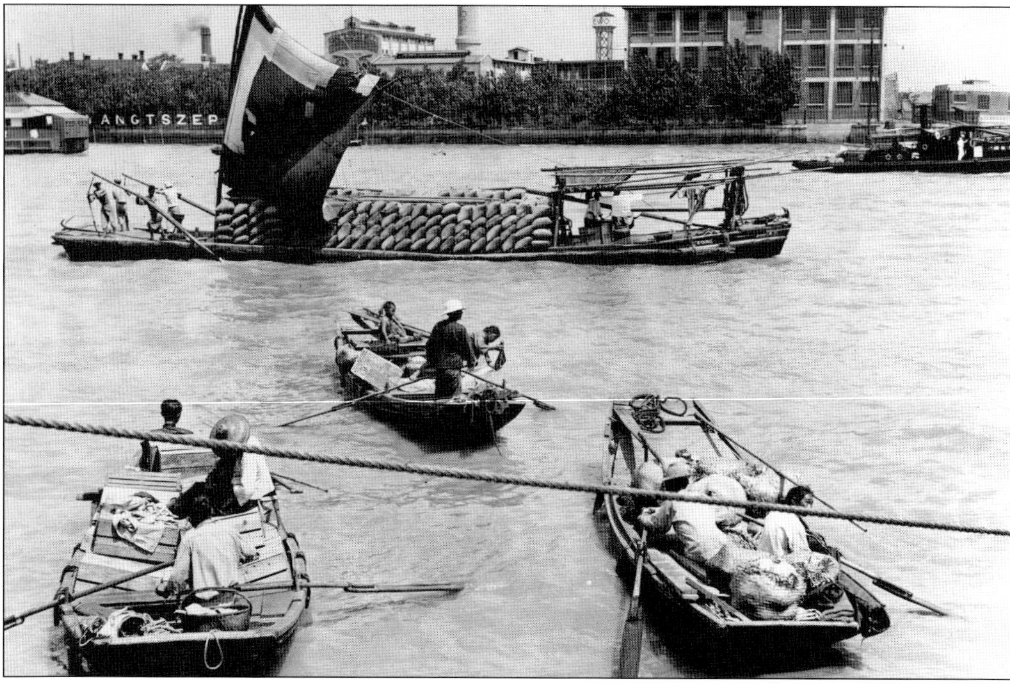

Here is Shanghai harbor in 1932, as captured in a photograph taken from *Houston*. Water taxies carry passengers and cargo, while a rice-filled barge sails past. The powered boat at upper right is a river police vessel. On shore, the Yangtszepoo Cotton Mill (left) and the Ewo Brewery (right) can be seen. (USNHHC.)

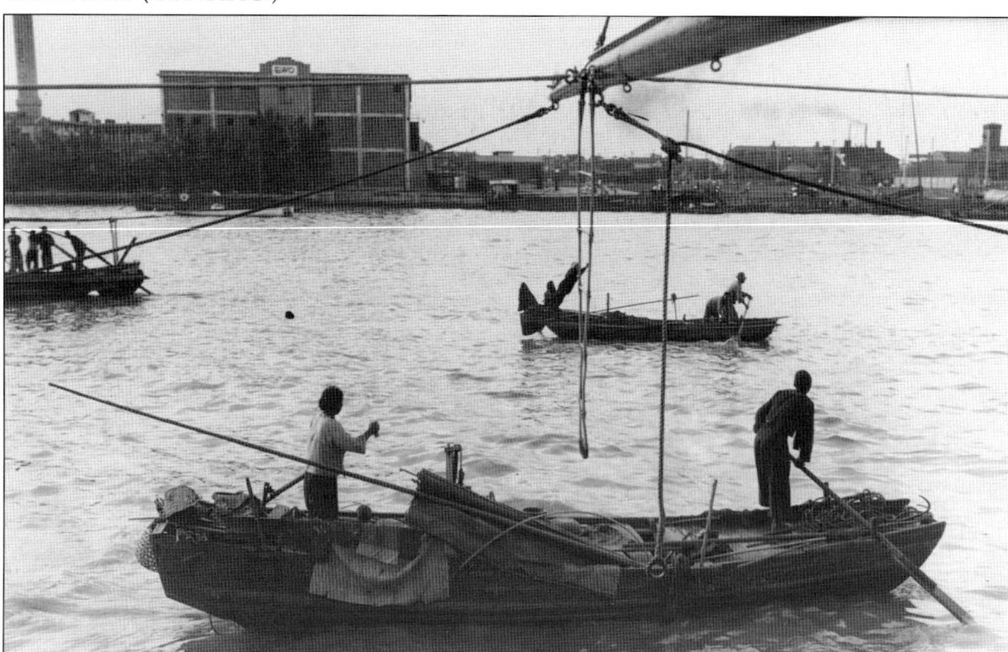

This is another view of the Ewo Brewery. More harbor boats are in the water. The boom at top is one of *Houston's* boats' booms. Its boats, and those of visitors, tie up to these booms. (USNHHC.)

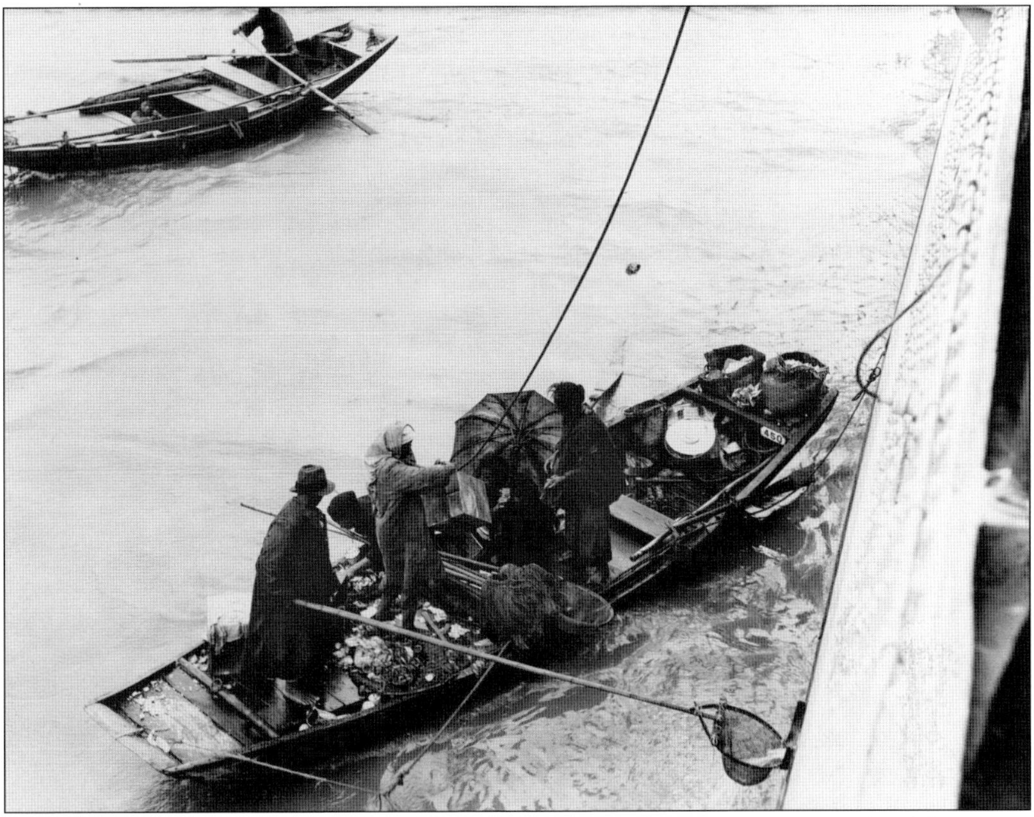

Houston used the harbor boats for its own needs. Here, a garbage scow ties up next to *Houston* to carry off trash. One reason sailors loved serving in the Asiatic Fleet was the types of services they could get from local entrepreneurs. Carry-out garbage service sounded good. (USNHHC.)

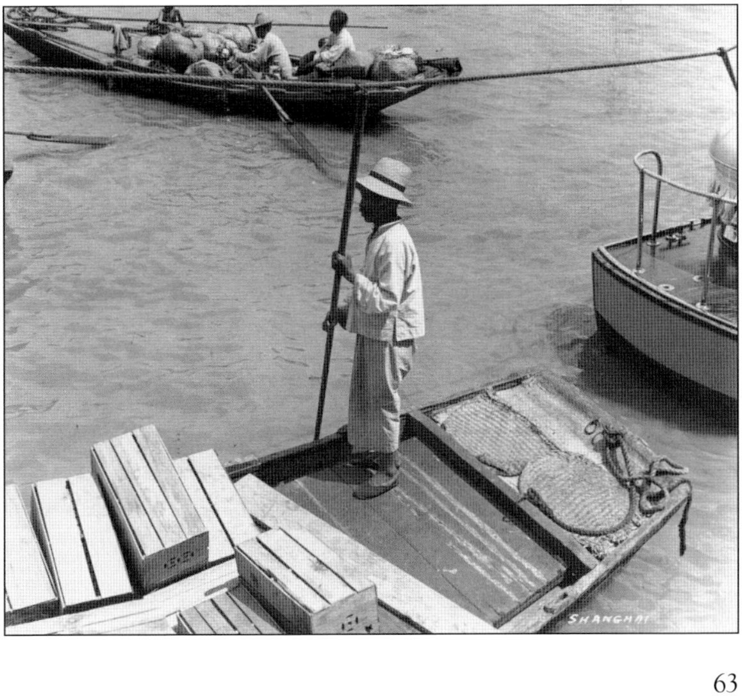

Not only did harbor boats carry trash away from *Houston* in Chinese ports, they brought goods to the ship. This sampan is hooking up to a boat line alongside *Houston* during a Shanghai visit. The crates contain goods this man plans to sell to *Houston's* crew. It could be anything from food to souvenirs. (USNHHC.)

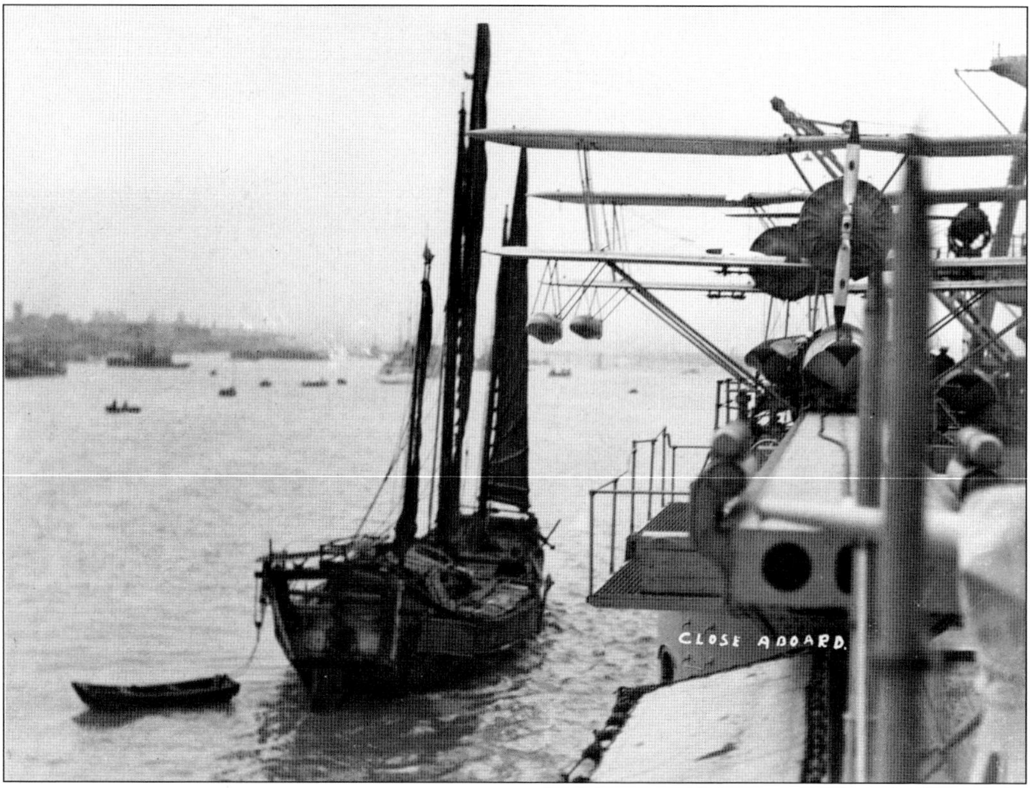

A large junk is seen close aboard *Houston*. As it appears stopped, this Shanghai bumboat was probably taking care of business aboard *Houston*. Note the two Corsair seaplanes on the *Houston*. (USNHHC.)

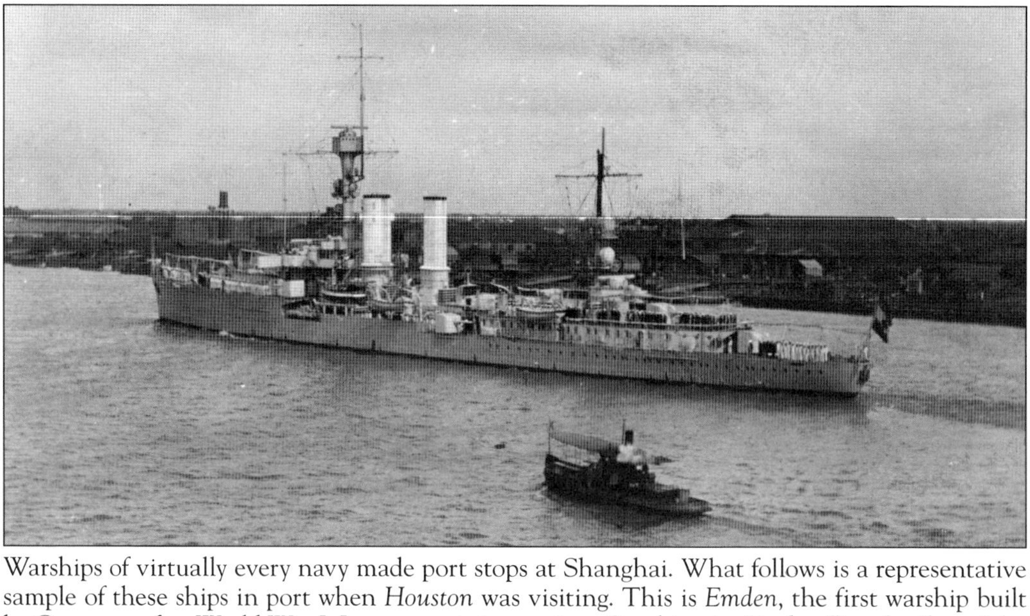

Warships of virtually every navy made port stops at Shanghai. What follows is a representative sample of these ships in port when *Houston* was visiting. This is *Emden*, the first warship built by Germany after World War I. It was a training cruiser. On this trip, *Emden* flies the flag of the Weimar Republic. Hitler took over two years after this 1931 visit. (USNHHC.)

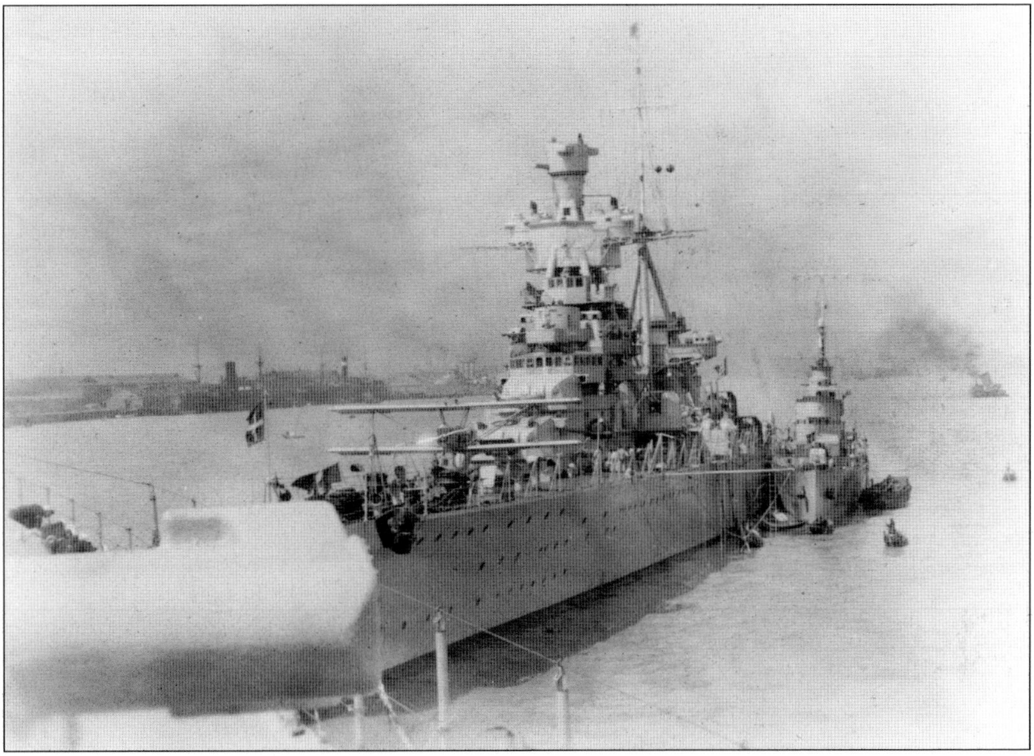

Italy, a World War I ally and World War II foe, also sent warships on show-the-flag cruises. Heavy cruiser *Trento* visited Shanghai in 1932, accompanied by the destroyer *Espero*. *Trento* was an Italian counterpart to *Houston*, a treaty cruiser with eight 8-inch guns, built in 1927. (USNHHC.)

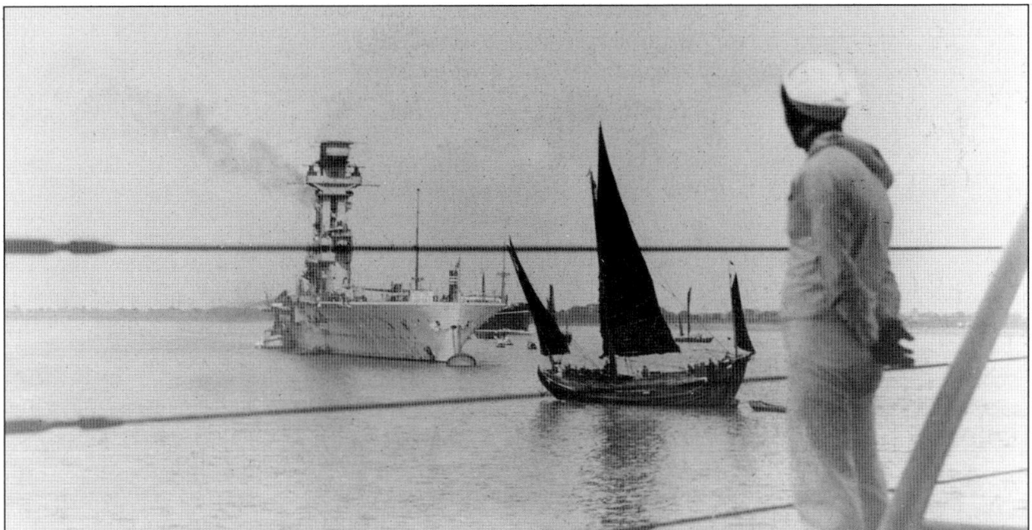

Britain was another frequent visitor to Shanghai. HMS *Eagle* was one of two aircraft carriers the Royal Navy stationed in the Far East during *Houston's* first tour there. It started out as a battleship for the Chilean navy, but World War I began while it was under construction in Britain. When finally launched, it had become an aircraft carrier and Chile did not want it back, so the Royal Navy kept it. (USNHHC.)

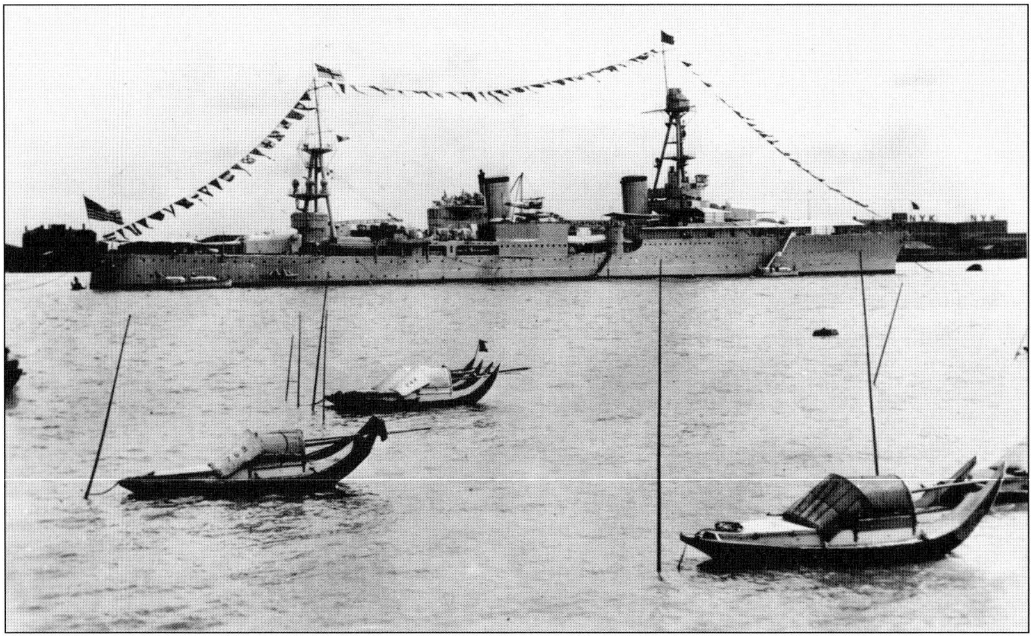

The special relationship between the United States and Great Britain dates to 1859 in the Far East, when a US Navy squadron went to the aid of the Royal Navy. That relationship is highlighted in this photograph. *Houston* is dressed with flags celebrating a holiday. Since it is flying the British white ensign at the mainmast, it is most likely a British holiday. (USNHHC.)

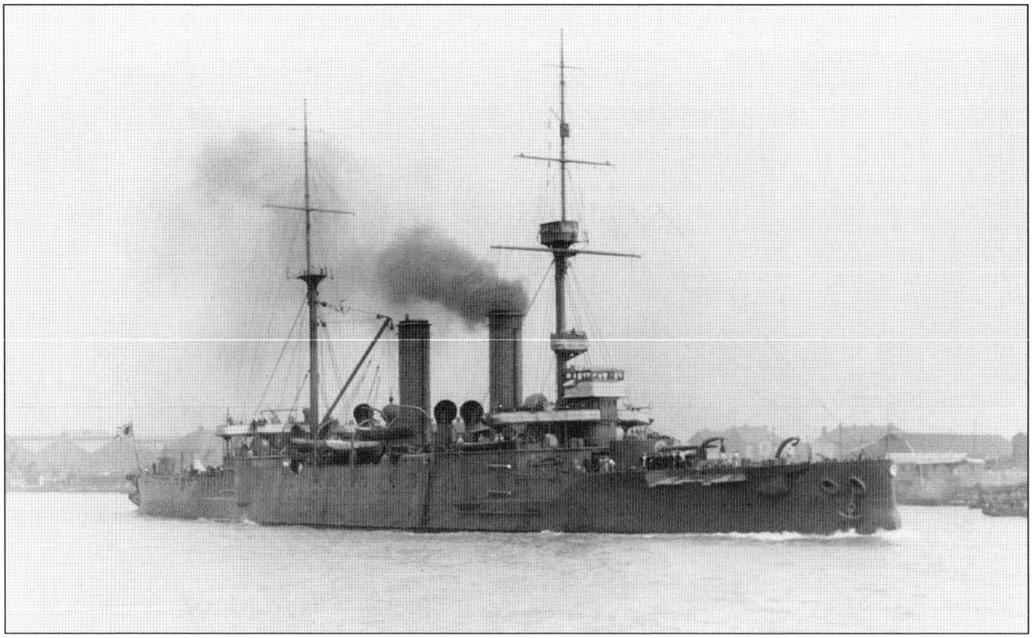

Another major naval presence in Shanghai in addition to the Royal Navy and the US Navy was the Imperial Japanese Navy. Its ships were regular visitors to Shanghai. This is the *Tokiwa*. An armored cruiser launched in 1898, it was a veteran of the Japanese victory at Tsushima. Not only was it still a warship in 1931 when this picture was taken, it also survived World War II. (USNHHC.)

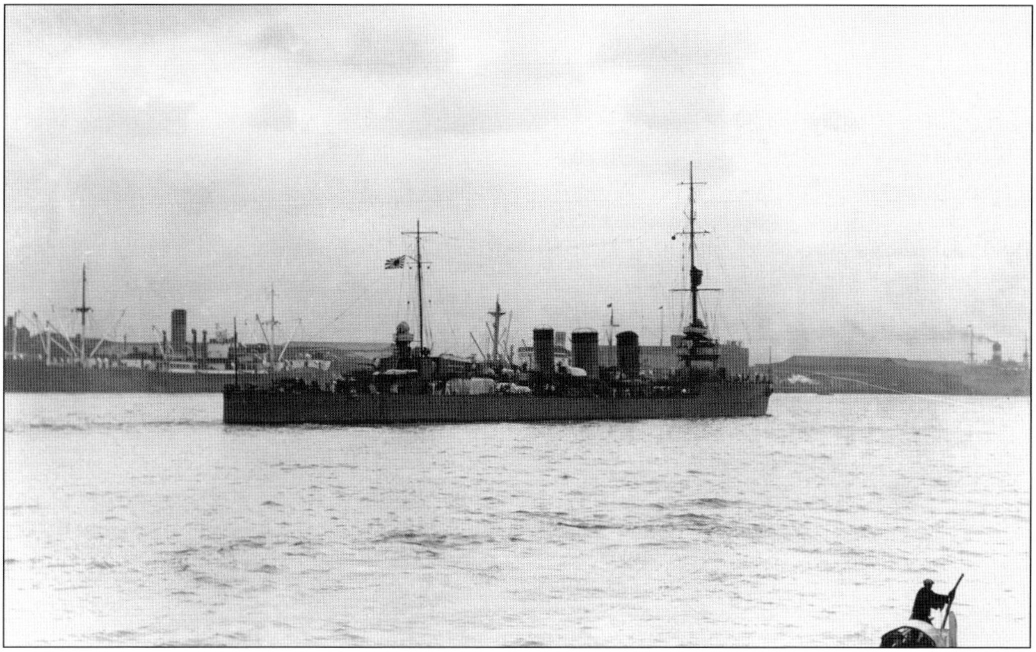

A more modern warship, from the perspective of 1931, was the Japanese light cruiser *Tenryu*. Launched in 1918, it was an old-style light cruiser, intended for scouting and leading destroyer flotillas. It was in Shanghai in February 1932, when this picture was taken, as part of a Japanese show of force against the Chinese Nationalist government. (USNHHC.)

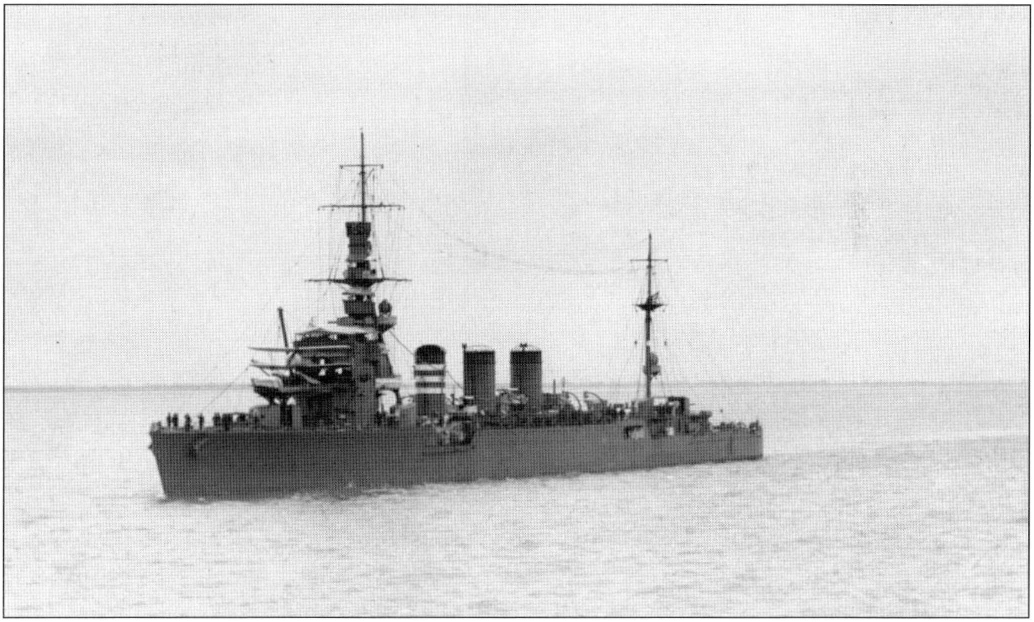

The Japanese cruiser *Yura* is captured by a photographer on *Houston* as it steams up the Whangpoo River at Shanghai. *Yura* is minutes away from beginning a bombardment of the Woosung Forts guarding Shanghai. The bombardment, which took place on February 20, was part of the January 28 Incident, a six-week battle marking the beginning of Japanese aggressions leading to World War II. (USNHHC.)

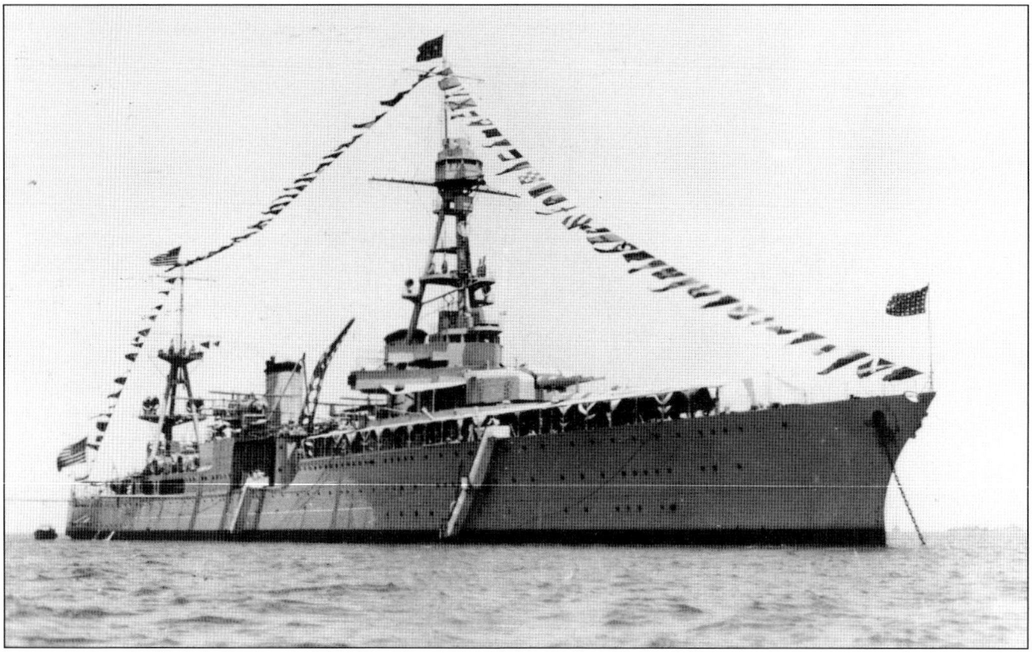

Houston is pictured in Tsingtao, China, on July 4, 1933. The ship is dressed with flags to celebrate Independence Day and is flying Admiral Montgomery's flag at the mainmast. Tsingtao played a major role during World War I when the Japanese took it from Germany, but it was controlled by China in 1933. (USNHHC.)

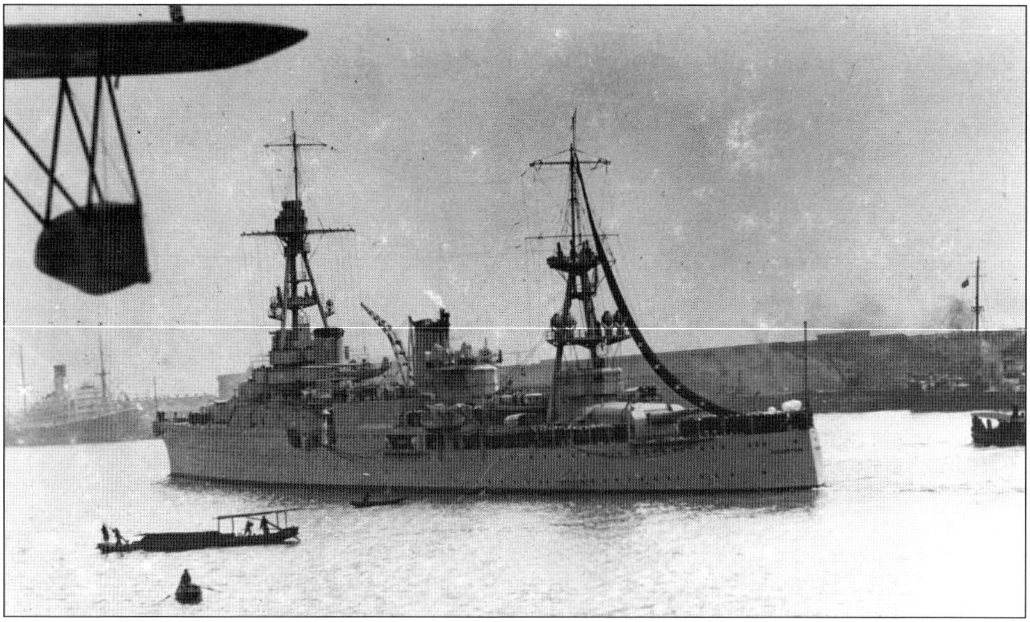

Houston is seen back in Shanghai at the end of its first tour in the Asiatic Fleet. It has been relieved by sister ship *Augusta.* The long pennant spilling down from the mainmast to the deck is the "homeward bound pennant." It is unofficial but traditional. It is supposed to be one foot long for every sailor overseas for the commission, up to the length of the ship. Houston had a peacetime crew of 785. This pennant was 600 feet long, due to the length of *Houston.* (USNHHC.)

Four

A Home

In his novel *The Sand Pebbles*, Richard McKenna described life in the Asiatic Fleet during the period when *Houston* was assigned to it. McKenna stated that sailors labeled ships two ways: They could be a madhouse or a home. A madhouse was a ship where everything went wrong. A home was a ship that was homelike—a ship where life was enjoyable. The food was good, the living quarters were clean, discipline predictable, and off-duty hours comfortable.

By all accounts, *Houston* was a home. As a flagship, it was run by the book. To many sailors, that was a plus. Having a dependable routine was appreciated in Depression-era America. The Navy provided a place to sleep, three meals a day, and worthwhile work. In a world where millions were unemployed, men joined the Navy for just those things.

Living aboard *Houston* was like living in a small company town (population 1,071) with one employer. *Houston* had its own laundry, post office, newspaper, and shops. Community celebrations and festivities took place. Thanksgiving and Christmas were big events. The Navy's version of carnival occurred when a ship crossed the equator.

Houston even carried its own sports teams. Team sports were big in the 1930s Navy, and the crew participated with enthusiasm. Being part of a winning team, which brought trophies to *Houston*, made a sailor a hero to his shipmates.

More than that, the Navy offered opportunity for travel. Recruiting posters promised "Join the Navy and see the world." In the 1930s, Great Plains farm boys and sons of city factory workers joined up for just that. For many, the trip to boot camp took them farther from home than they had ever previously traveled. *Houston* took them still farther—to exotic locations seen by many only in movies: China, Central America, Hawaii, and the Philippines. This chapter explores life aboard *Houston*.

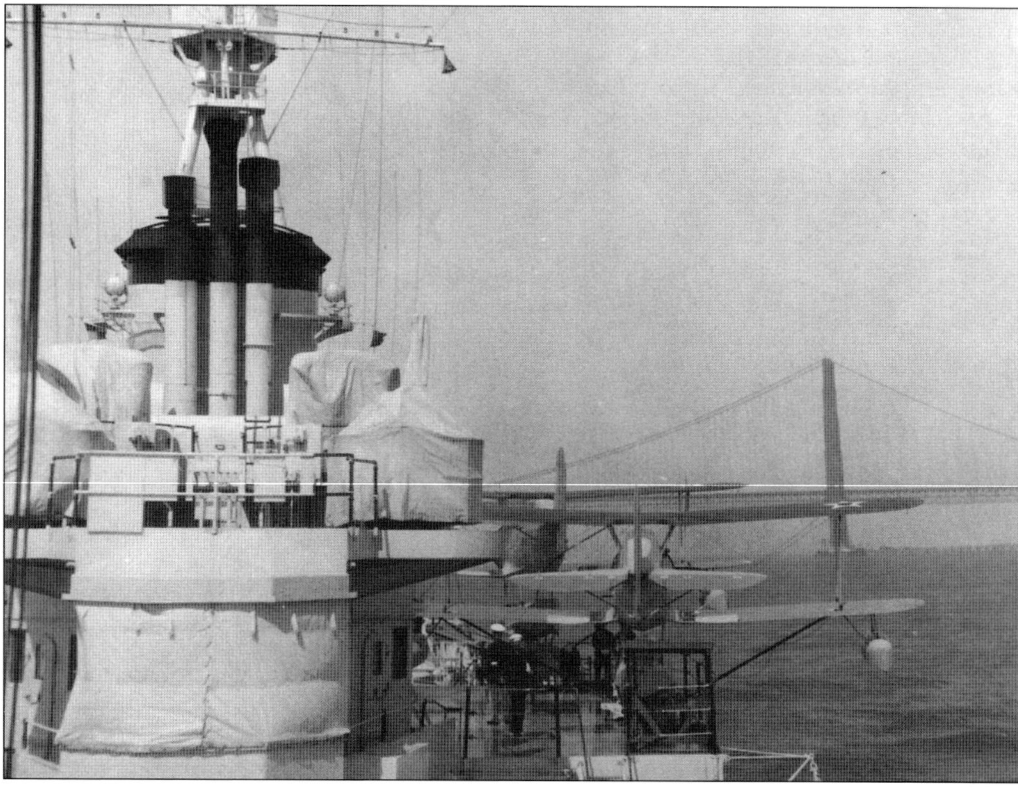

During *Houston's* dozen years in the Navy, it traveled many places and did many things. Here, it steams out of San Francisco Bay with the Golden Gate dead ahead. Yet wherever it went and whatever it did, it was also a home for the 1,071 officers and men aboard. (NARA.)

In many ways, a warship was like a small town. It had its own post office. Letters mailed from the cruiser were postmarked "USS Houston." They were also sent in envelopes, printed aboard *Houston* proclaiming their origin and the ship's status. (HMM.)

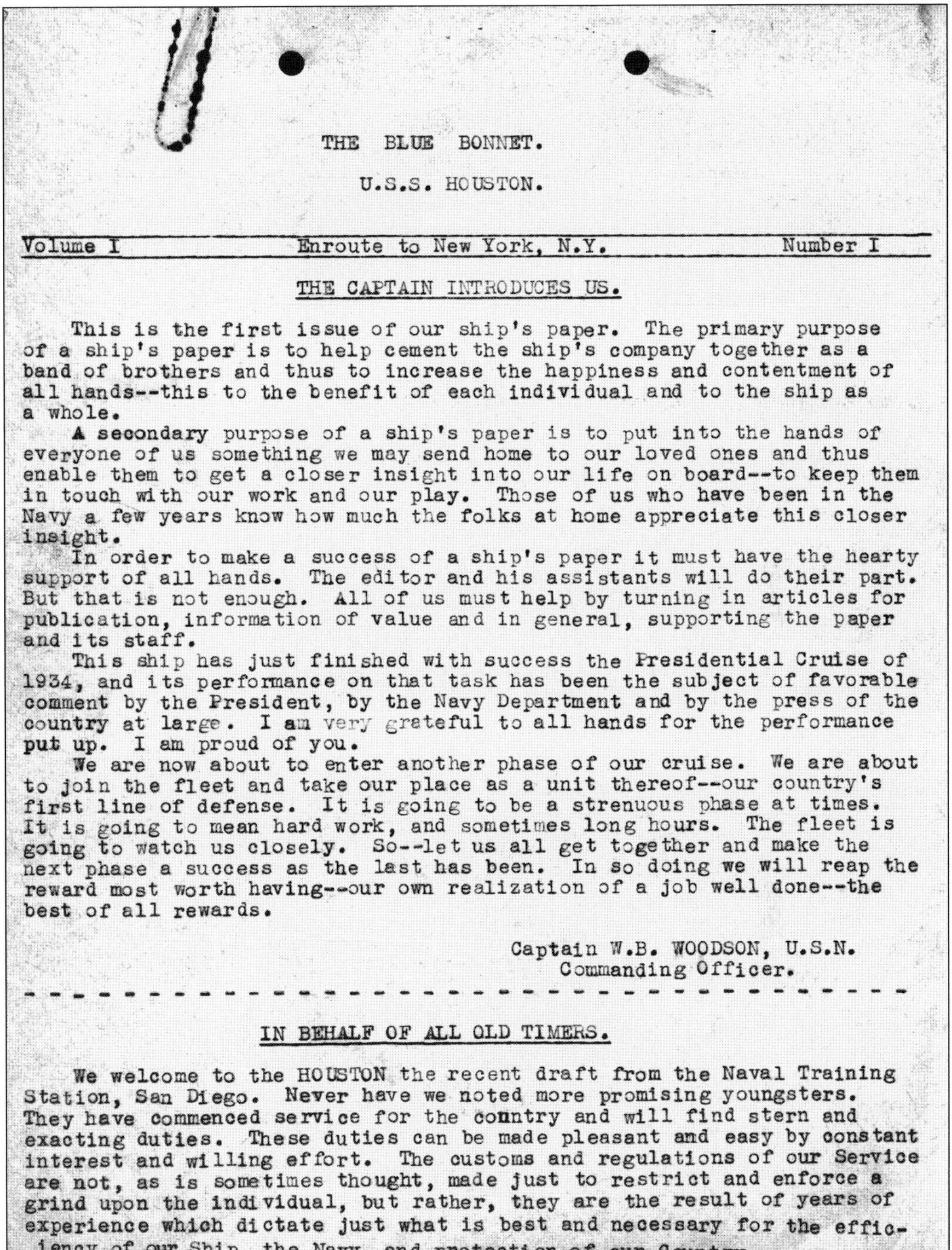

THE BLUE BONNET.

U.S.S. HOUSTON.

Volume I	Enroute to New York, N.Y.	Number I

THE CAPTAIN INTRODUCES US.

This is the first issue of our ship's paper. The primary purpose of a ship's paper is to help cement the ship's company together as a band of brothers and thus to increase the happiness and contentment of all hands--this to the benefit of each individual and to the ship as a whole.

A secondary purpose of a ship's paper is to put into the hands of everyone of us something we may send home to our loved ones and thus enable them to get a closer insight into our life on board--to keep them in touch with our work and our play. Those of us who have been in the Navy a few years know how much the folks at home appreciate this closer insight.

In order to make a success of a ship's paper it must have the hearty support of all hands. The editor and his assistants will do their part. But that is not enough. All of us must help by turning in articles for publication, information of value and in general, supporting the paper and its staff.

This ship has just finished with success the Presidential Cruise of 1934, and its performance on that task has been the subject of favorable comment by the President, by the Navy Department and by the press of the country at large. I am very grateful to all hands for the performance put up. I am proud of you.

We are now about to enter another phase of our cruise. We are about to join the fleet and take our place as a unit thereof--our country's first line of defense. It is going to be a strenuous phase at times. It is going to mean hard work, and sometimes long hours. The fleet is going to watch us closely. So--let us all get together and make the next phase a success as the last has been. In so doing we will reap the reward most worth having--our own realization of a job well done--the best of all rewards.

Captain W.B. WOODSON, U.S.N.
Commanding Officer.

- -

IN BEHALF OF ALL OLD TIMERS.

We welcome to the HOUSTON the recent draft from the Naval Training Station, San Diego. Never have we noted more promising youngsters. They have commenced service for the country and will find stern and exacting duties. These duties can be made pleasant and easy by constant interest and willing effort. The customs and regulations of our Service are not, as is sometimes thought, made just to restrict and enforce a grind upon the individual, but rather, they are the result of years of experience which dictate just what is best and necessary for the efficiency of our Ship, the Navy, and protection of our Country.

Like many small towns in mid-20th-century America, *Houston* even had its own newspaper, *The Blue Bonnet*, named for Texas's state flower. The first issue, printed in 1934, was typewritten, and probably reproduced on a mimeograph machine. (UHDL.)

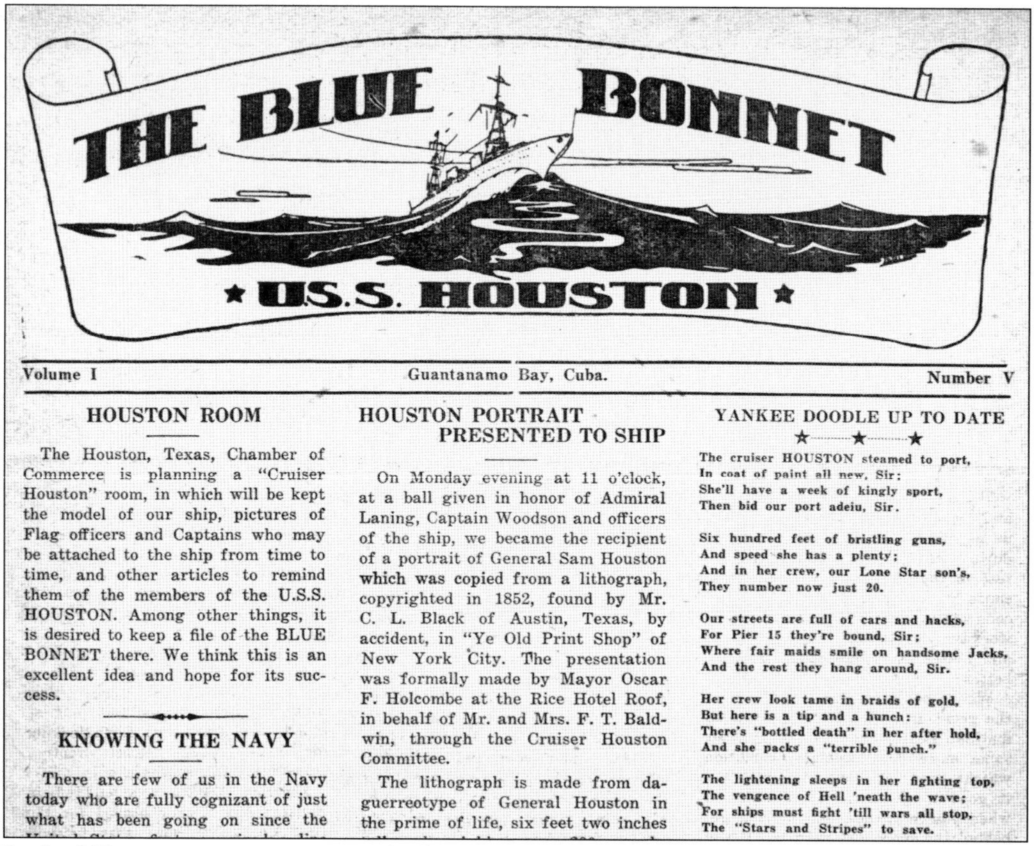

THE BLUE BONNET

★ U.S.S. HOUSTON ★

Volume I | Guantanamo Bay, Cuba. | Number V

HOUSTON ROOM

The Houston, Texas, Chamber of Commerce is planning a "Cruiser Houston" room, in which will be kept the model of our ship, pictures of Flag officers and Captains who may be attached to the ship from time to time, and other articles to remind them of the members of the U.S.S. HOUSTON. Among other things, it is desired to keep a file of the BLUE BONNET there. We think this is an excellent idea and hope for its success.

KNOWING THE NAVY

There are few of us in the Navy today who are fully cognizant of just what has been going on since the

HOUSTON PORTRAIT PRESENTED TO SHIP

On Monday evening at 11 o'clock, at a ball given in honor of Admiral Laning, Captain Woodson and officers of the ship, we became the recipient of a portrait of General Sam Houston which was copied from a lithograph, copyrighted in 1852, found by Mr. C. L. Black of Austin, Texas, by accident, in "Ye Old Print Shop" of New York City. The presentation was formally made by Mayor Oscar F. Holcombe at the Rice Hotel Roof, in behalf of Mr. and Mrs. F. T. Baldwin, through the Cruiser Houston Committee.

The lithograph is made from daguerreotype of General Houston in the prime of life, six feet two inches

YANKEE DOODLE UP TO DATE

★ ★ ★

The cruiser HOUSTON steamed to port,
In coat of paint all new, Sir:
She'll have a week of kingly sport,
Then bid our port adeiu, Sir.

Six hundred feet of bristling guns,
And speed she has a plenty;
And in her crew, our Lone Star son's,
They number now just 20.

Our streets are full of cars and hacks,
For Pier 15 they're bound, Sir;
Where fair maids smile on handsome Jacks,
And the rest they hang around, Sir.

Her crew look tame in braids of gold,
But here is a tip and a hunch:
There's "bottled death" in her after hold,
And she packs a "terrible punch."

The lightening sleeps in her fighting top,
The vengence of Hell 'neath the wave;
For ships must fight 'till wars all stop,
The "Stars and Stripes" to save.

By the fifth issue, it was typeset instead of being banged out on a typewriter, and gained the masthead it would carry for most of its existence: a drawing showing the cruiser steaming toward the reader on billowing waves, set on a scroll. Its four pages appeared once every two weeks. (UHDL.)

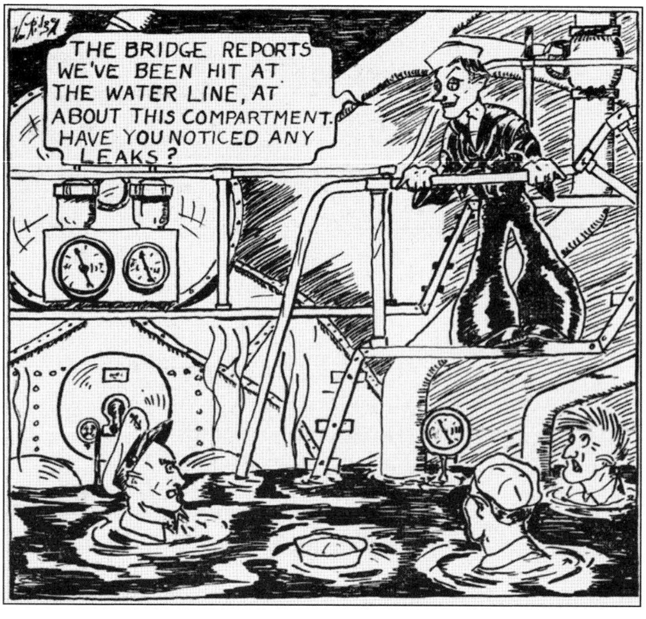

It even had features found in small-town newspapers, including poetry, photographs, and even cartoons. These, like this one, poked gentle fun at life aboard a warship. The cartoonist might not have been as talented as Bill Mauldin, but he knew his audience. (UHDL.)

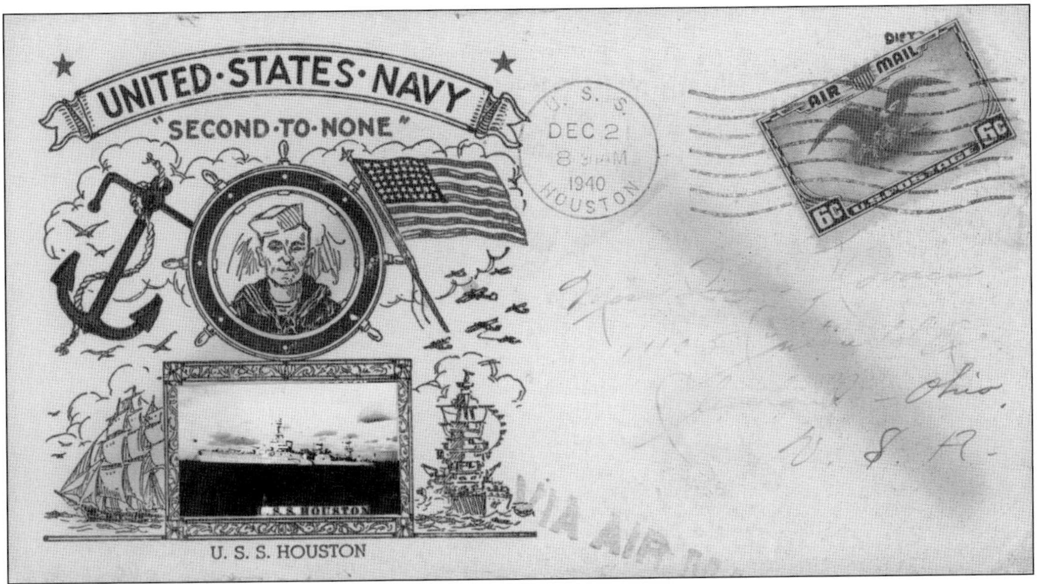

He also appears to be the artist who created *Houston's* postal covers. Compare the sailor in the ship's wheel to the bluejacket in the previous cartoon. (HMM.)

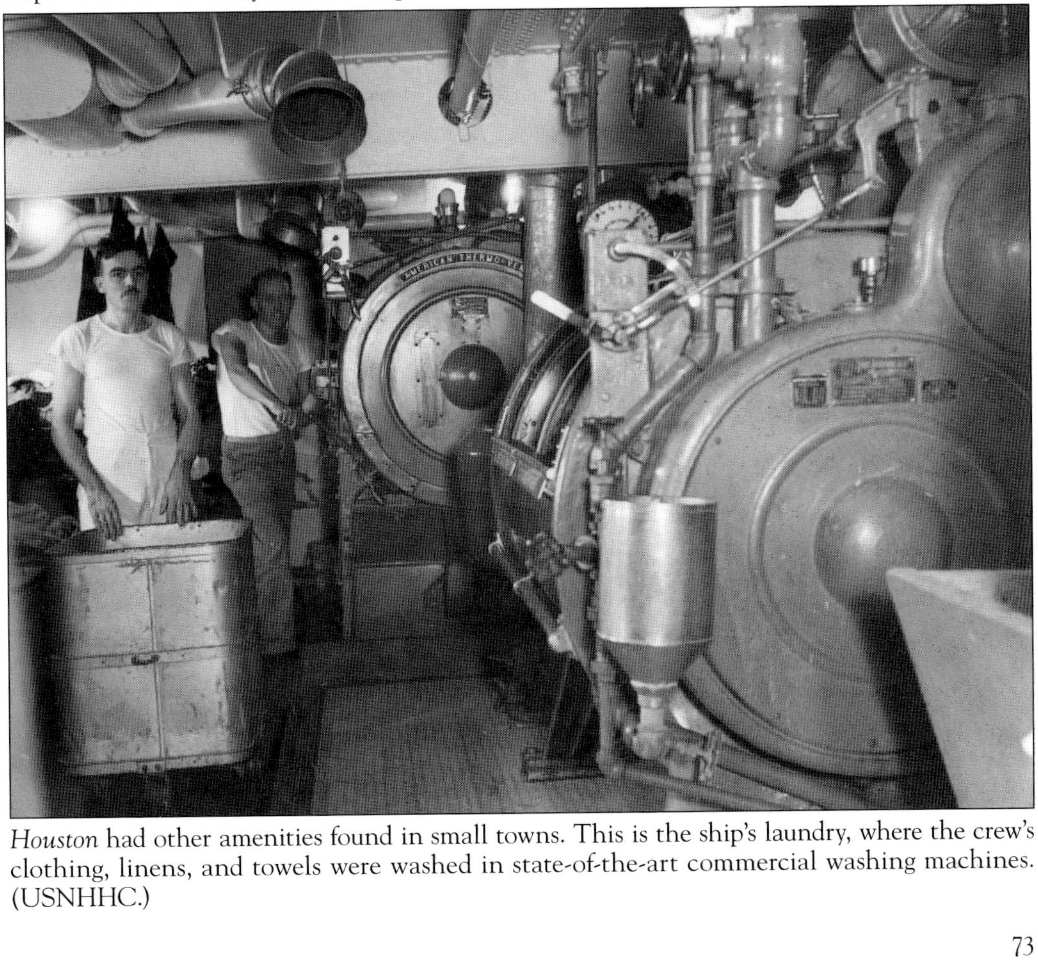
Houston had other amenities found in small towns. This is the ship's laundry, where the crew's clothing, linens, and towels were washed in state-of-the-art commercial washing machines. (USNHHC.)

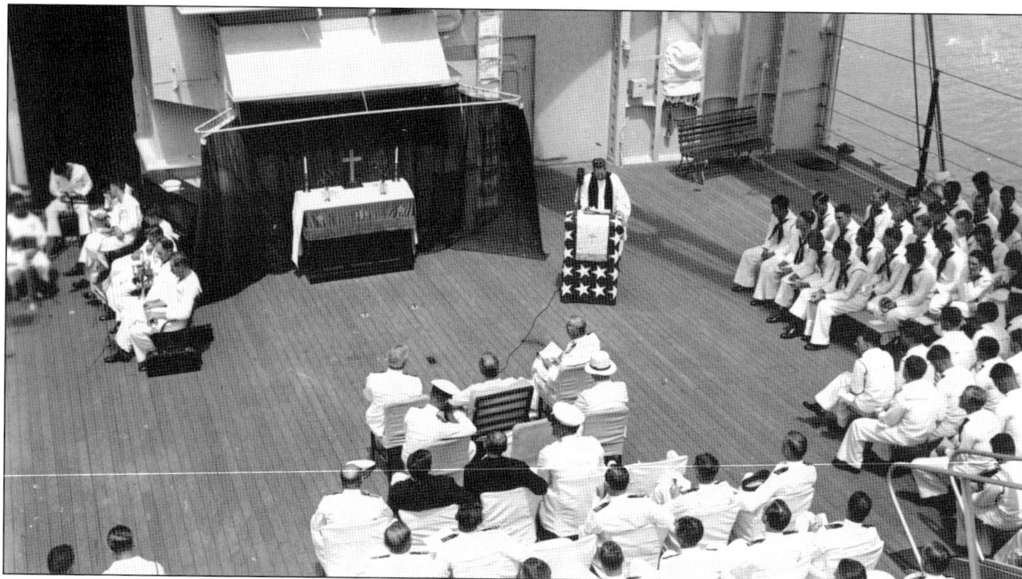

While *Houston* lacked a church with a steeple, church services were held every Sunday, in good weather, as shown here in the well deck amidships. At the time, the captain officiated at the service, but *Houston* carried a chaplain. He presides at this service. (HMM.)

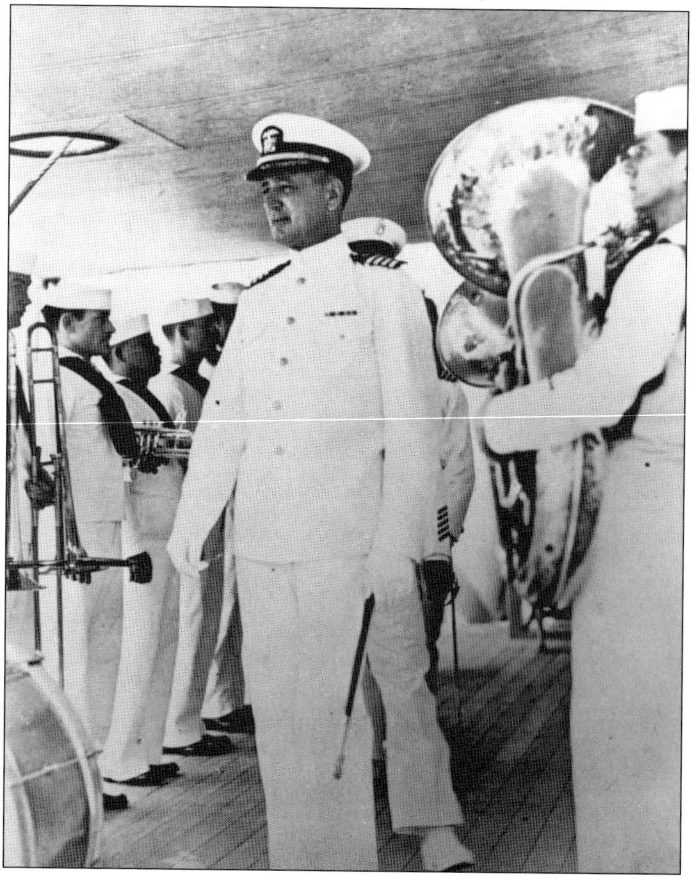

Sunday was the day the captain inspected the ship to ensure everything was ship-shape. Capt. Albert Rooks was *Houston*'s final captain. In this photograph, he is inspecting the ship's band. This is a full-dress inspection, as evidenced by Rooks's dress whites and the sword he is wearing. (USNHHC.)

The inspection continues with Captain Rooks examining the appearance of *Houston's* sailors. The expression "toe the line" comes in part from this exercise, with sailors lining up so the tips of their toes are aligned with a line formed by one of the deck planks. (USNHHC.)

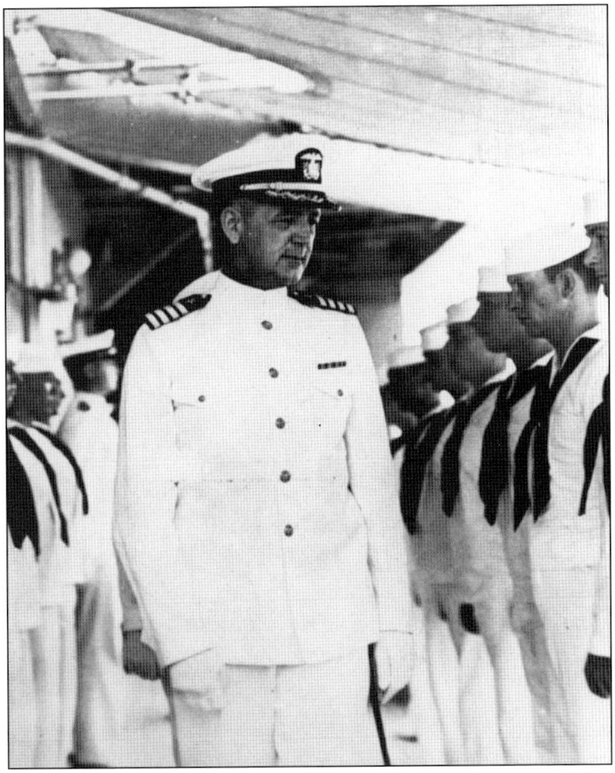

This group photograph was taken during *Houston's* first stint in the Asiatic Fleet. The ship's band is seated in the front, the Marine contingent along the sides, officers in the row behind the band, chiefs and petty officers behind the officers, and the crew behind them. To get everyone in the picture, some men are standing atop the bridge and in the foremast platforms. (USNHHC.)

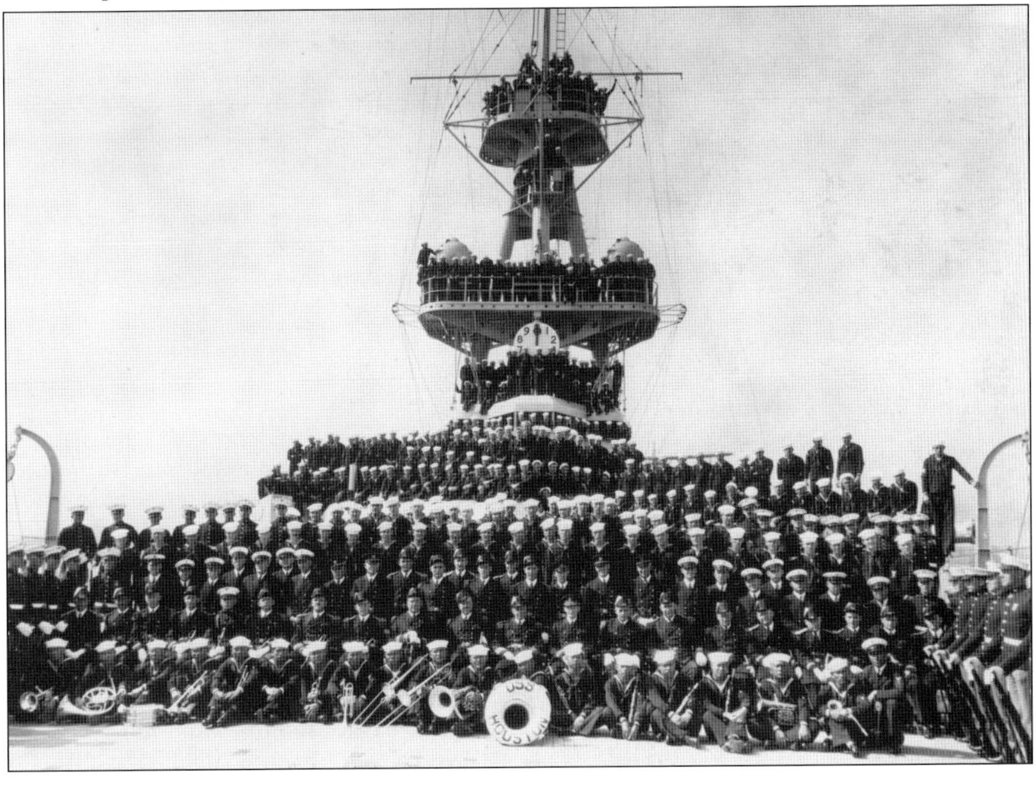

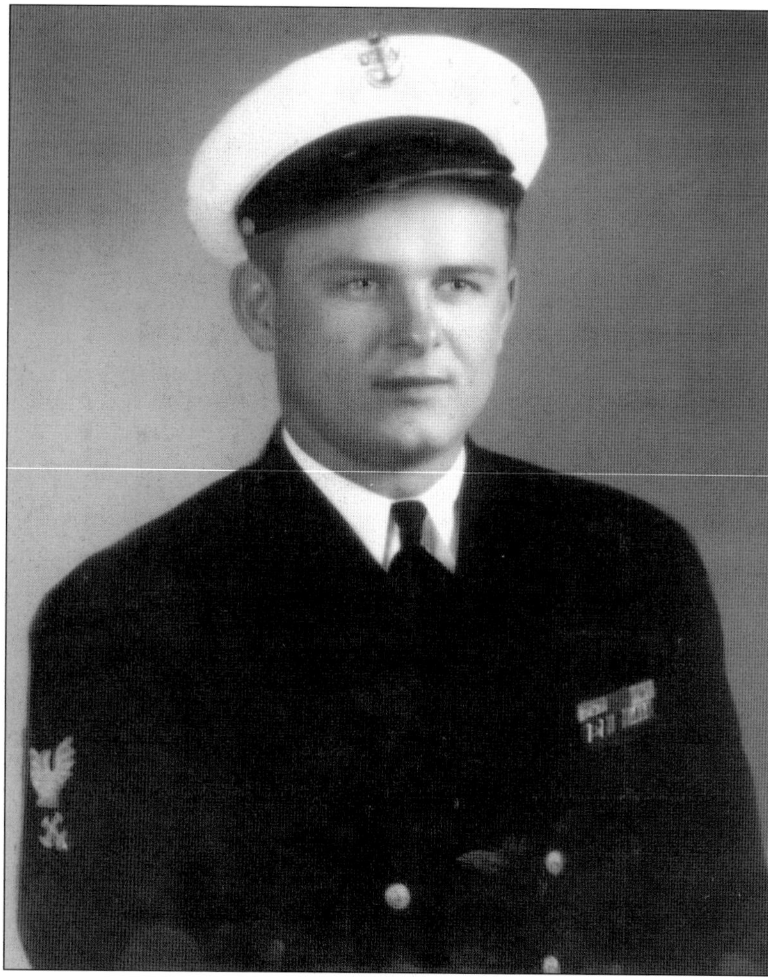

John B. Stefanak was typical of the men volunteering to serve in the pre–World War II Navy. The fourth of nine children of a Cleveland, Ohio, family, Stefanak enlisted for the adventure. A natural athlete, he was on the *Houston's* baseball team and held the rank of coxswain when *Houston* sank. He survived World War II, retiring from the Navy in 1946 as a chief bosun's mate. (HMM.)

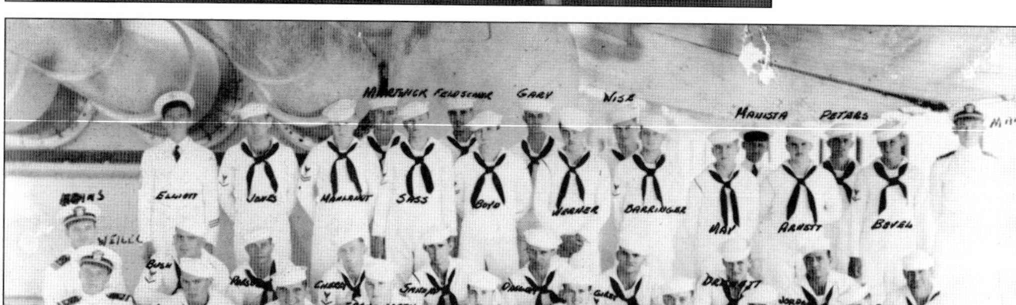

Sailors also liked getting group shots of their particular work team. This is a photograph of the Fire Control Division in 1941. The men in this group were responsible for aiming *Houston's* guns. These men fought at Java Sea and Sunda Strait. (USNHHC.)

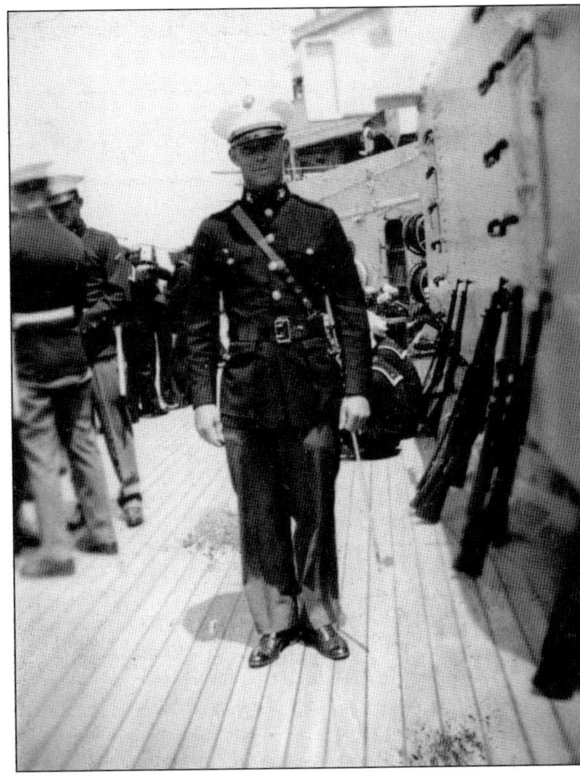

Houston also had a Marine detachment aboard. They served as guards, performed ceremonial duties, and served as the nucleus of landing parties when called upon. This is one of *Houston's* Marine officers, posing for the camera as his men prepare for some ceremonial occasion. (USNHHC.)

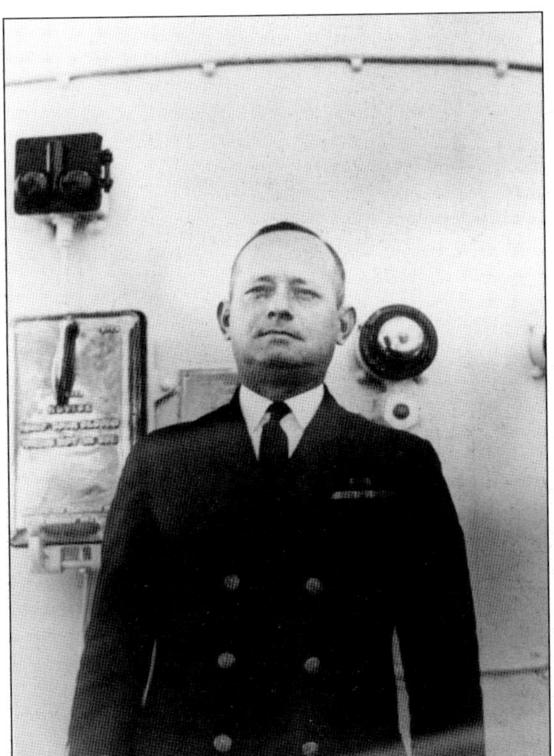

A US Navy warship was said to run on beans, bullets, and black oil. Logistics included supplies, ammunition, and fuel. Logistics win wars, and supply officers run a ship's logistics. This is one of *Houston's* supply officers, Lt. Cdr. James M. Easter. He was aboard in 1934. (USNHHC.)

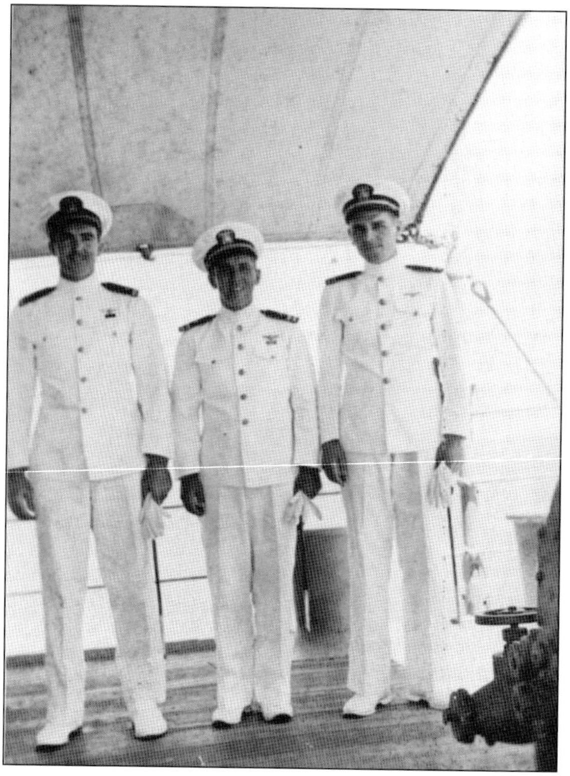

Houston also carried four seaplanes, which meant aviation officers were onboard. These are three of them, from left to right, Ens. Walter G. Winslow, Lt. Jack Lamade, and Lt. Thomas Payne, in late 1941 wearing dress whites. (USNHHC.)

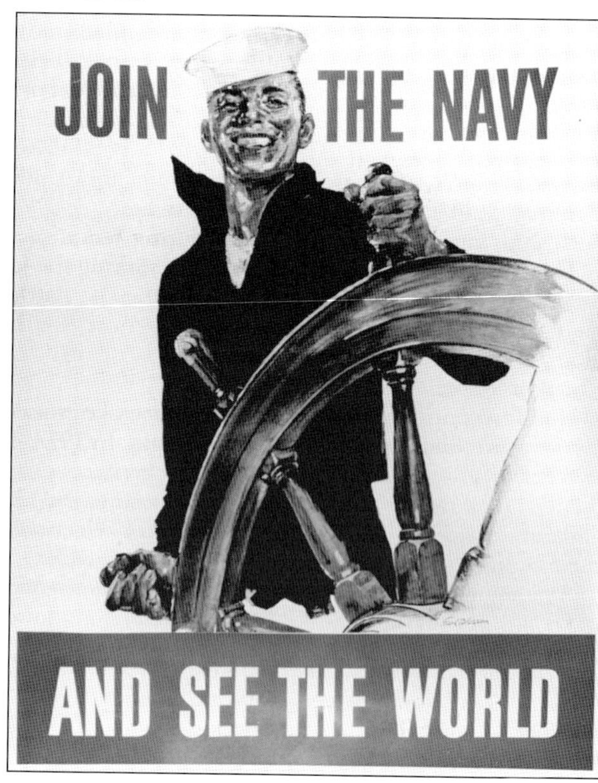

In the early 1930s, the Navy offered steady employment with three hots and a cot thrown in. The Navy also provided adventure. In an age before jumbo jets, most working-class kids could only dream of seeing far-off places. Join the Navy, though, and see the world! (USNHHC.)

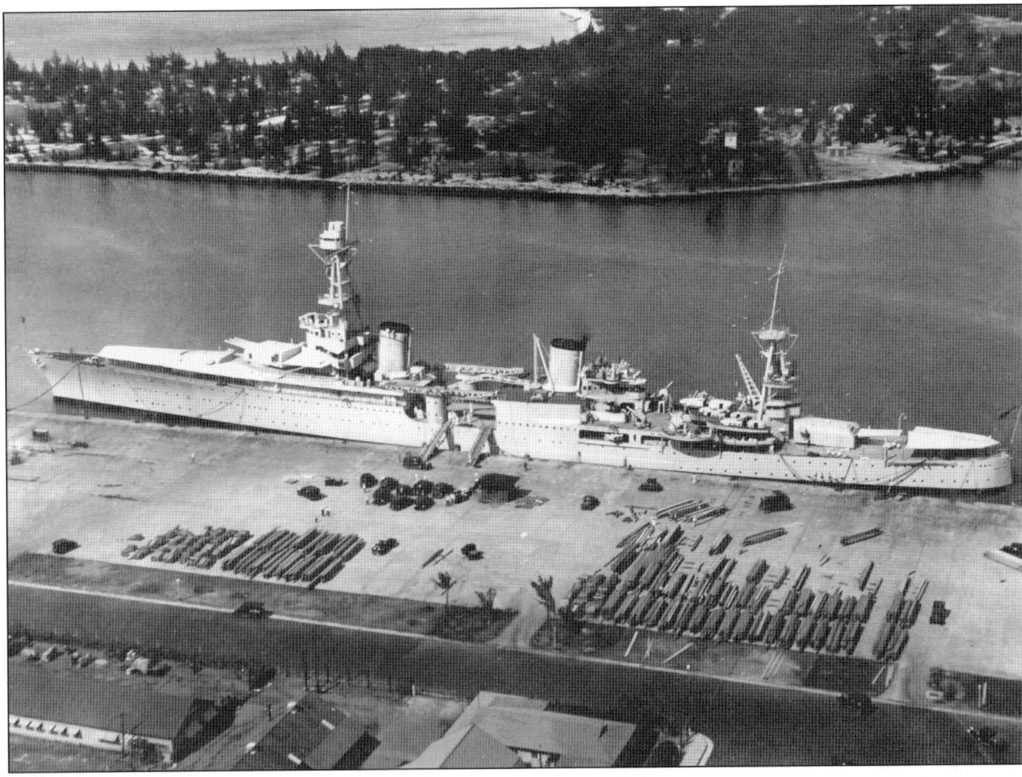

During the 1930s, very few working stiffs got a chance to visit Hawaii. It was an exotic destination, but most of the Navy's warships visited there during that period. Pictured in 1931 is *Houston* docked at Honolulu. This allowed an overnight liberty in Oahu. (NARA.)

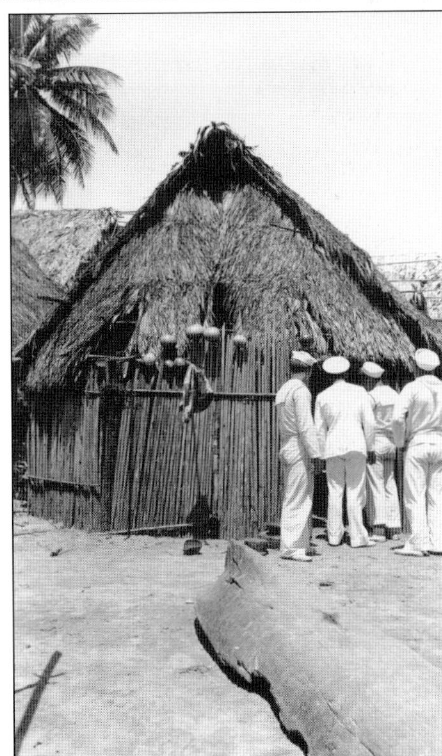

The presidential trips offered opportunities for sightseeing. Here, three sailors and a petty officer from *Houston* take a look at a native hut on Cocos Island. (HMM.)

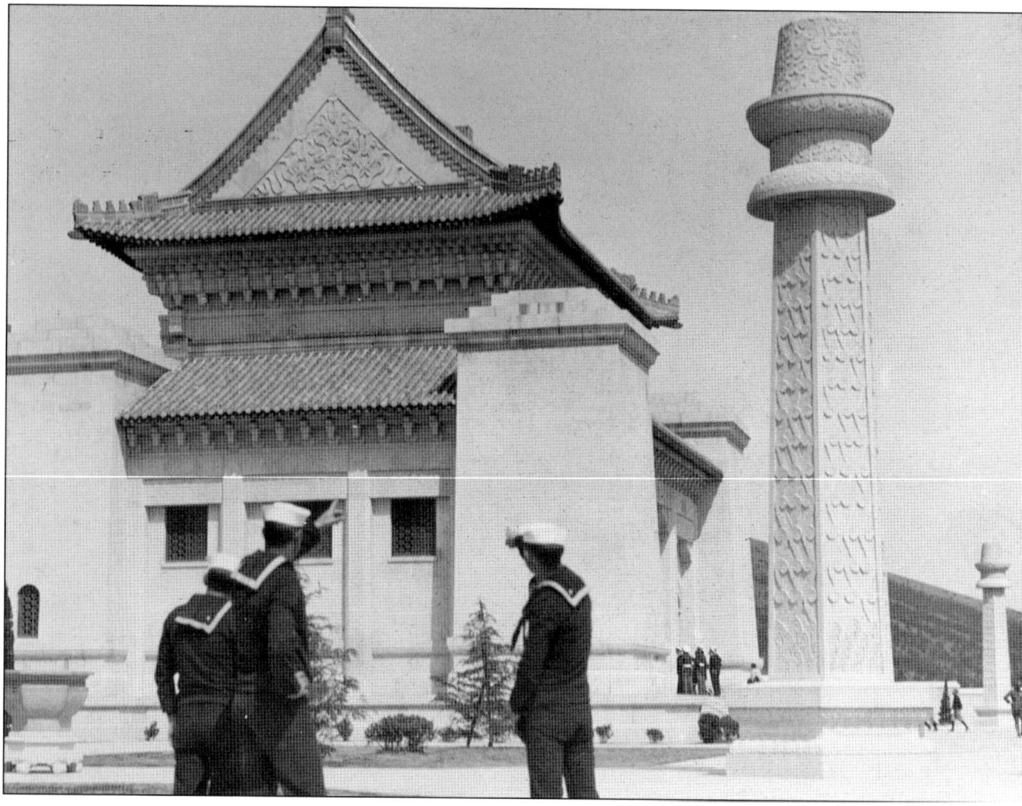

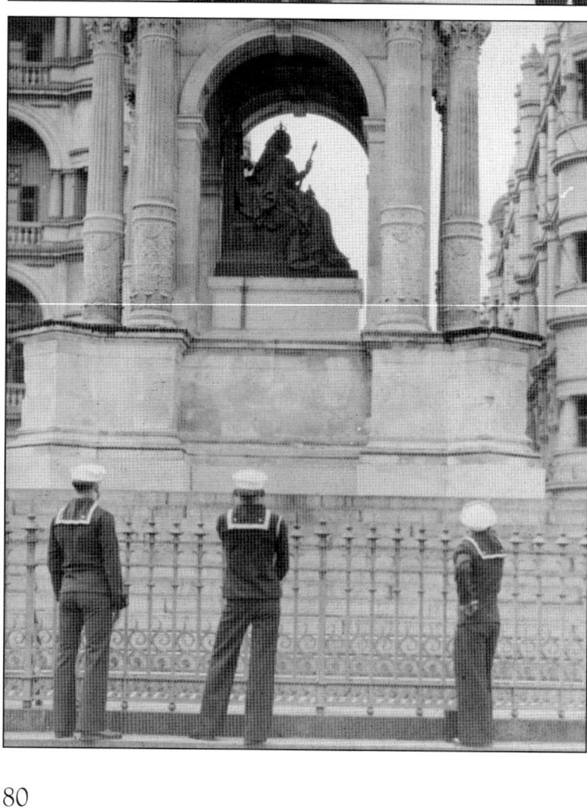

When *Houston* was with the Asiatic Fleet, it gave sailors a real opportunity to play tourist. Here, three crew members stop to look at the Sun Yat-sen Mausoleum in Nanking, China. (USNHHC.)

Taking a break from chasing after booze and babes, three other *Houston* bluejackets sightsee while on liberty in Hong Kong. They are taking in the statue of Queen Victoria at Victoria Park in Hong Kong. The Japanese removed the statue during World War II, but it was restored afterward and is still on display. (USNHHC.)

For any sailors interested in theater, Hong Kong offered opportunities for entertainment that were not available in Kansas. Lt. Gustave Freret, an officer from *Houston* during its 1931–1933 cruise in the Asiatic Fleet, snapped a photograph of this street theater in Hong Kong while he was ashore. (USNHHC.)

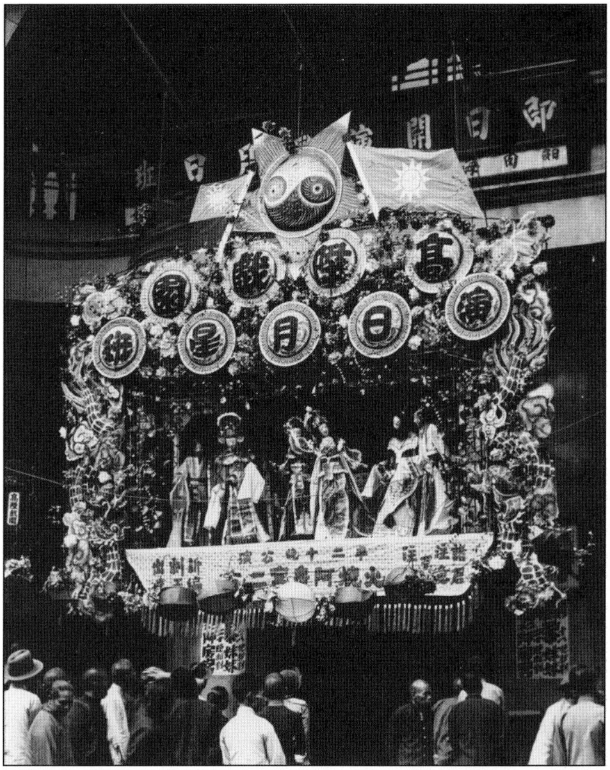

Officers had a busy social circuit when *Houston* was in a foreign port, but the bluejackets were not left out of the fun. The Shanghai chapter of the Fraternal Order of Eagles hosted a dinner for *Houston* crew members in the early 1930s, when the ship was visiting. (USNHHC.)

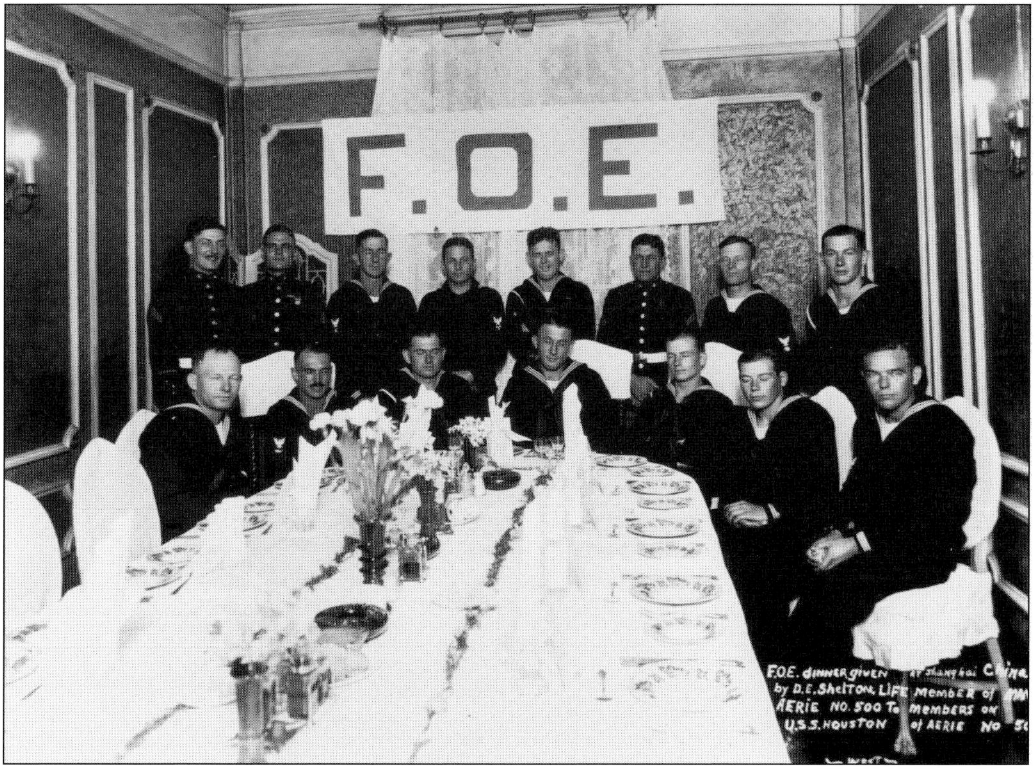

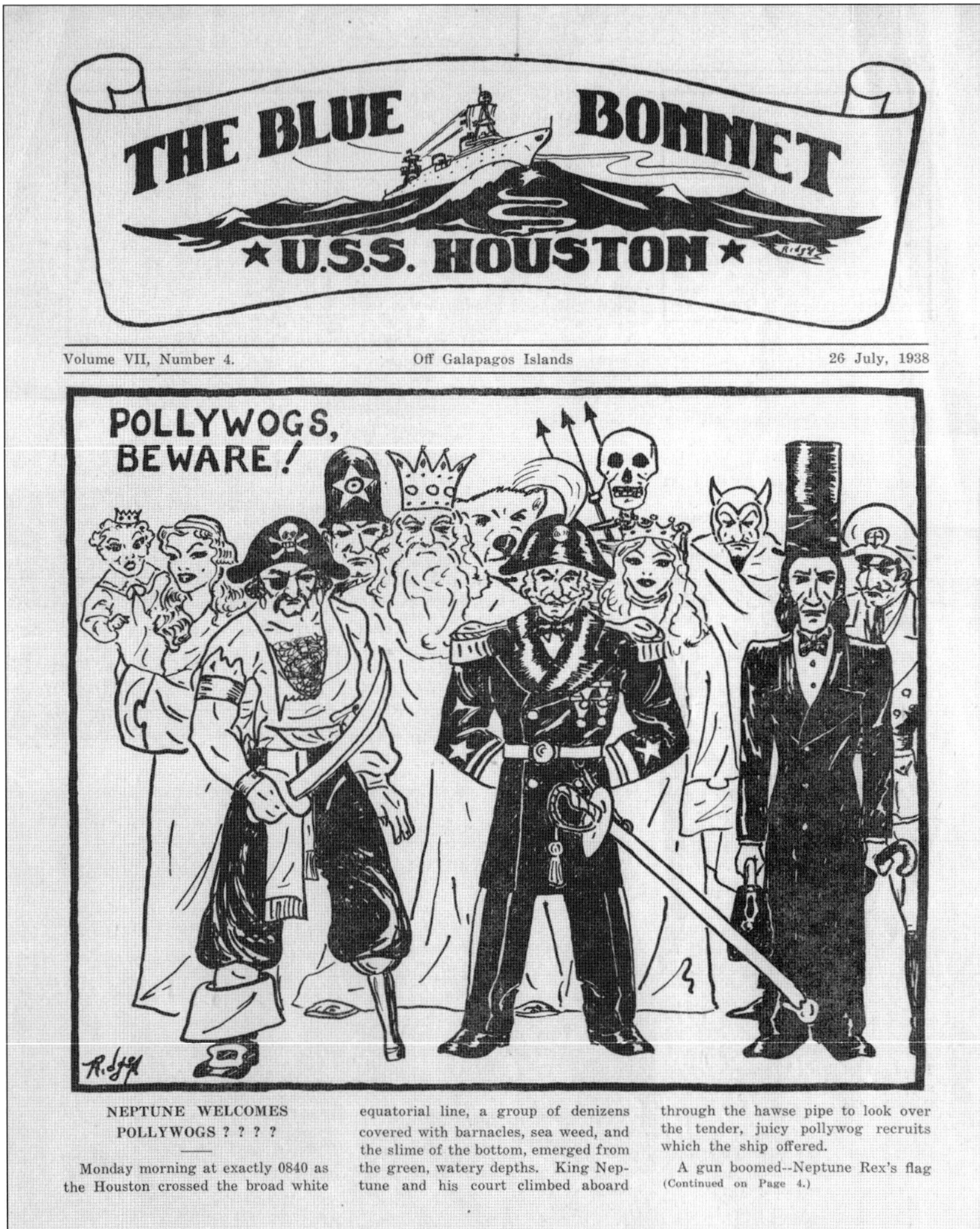

THE BLUE BONNET
★ U.S.S. HOUSTON ★

Volume VII, Number 4. Off Galapagos Islands 26 July, 1938

NEPTUNE WELCOMES POLLYWOGS ? ? ? ?

Monday morning at exactly 0840 as the Houston crossed the broad white equatorial line, a group of denizens covered with barnacles, sea weed, and the slime of the bottom, emerged from the green, watery depths. King Neptune and his court climbed aboard through the hawse pipe to look over the tender, juicy pollywog recruits which the ship offered.

A gun boomed--Neptune Rex's flag

(Continued on Page 4.)

One colorful part of life aboard a Navy warship was the line-crossing ceremony. Carried out when a ship crossed the equator, it allowed the shellback to initiate the polliwogs (sailors who had not already crossed the equator) into the Ancient Order of the Deep. It was an opportunity for some fun. *Houston* crossed the equator numerous times in the 1930s. (UHDL.)

The ceremony started with King Neptune (one of the shellback chiefs or petty officers in costume) boarding *Houston* with his court to preside over the initiation. The king was always piped aboard with all the ceremony due a monarch. (HMM.)

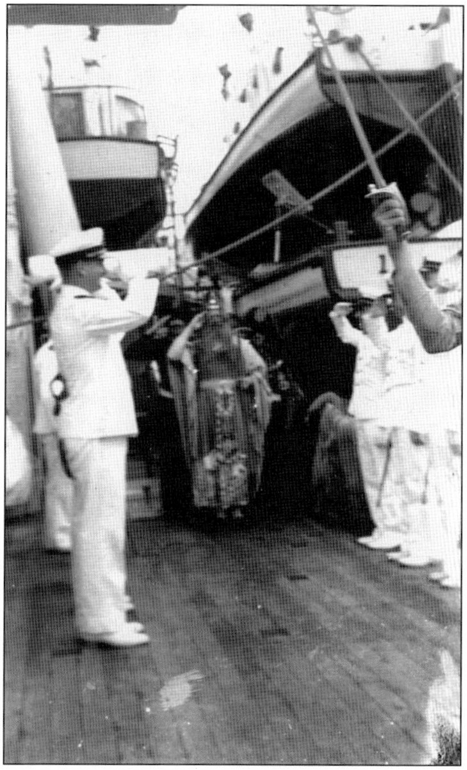

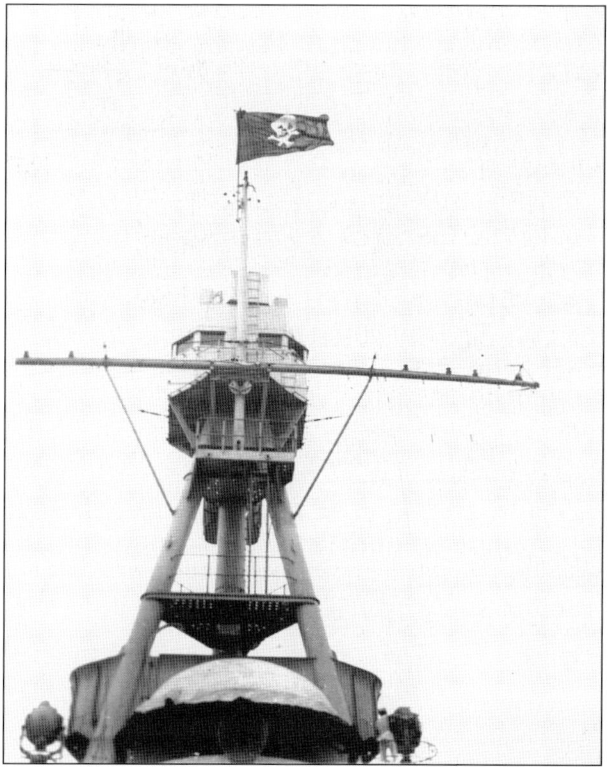

Of course, Neptunus Rex had to have his flag displayed. Hence, after King Neptune came aboard, *Houston* hoisted the Jolly Roger to the peak of the mainmast to signal his royal presence aboard ship. (HMM.)

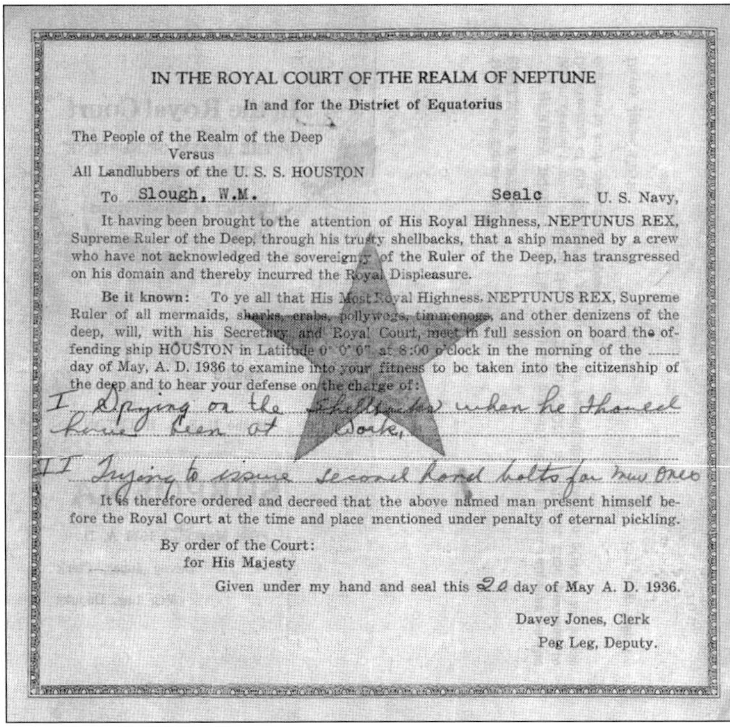

IN THE ROYAL COURT OF THE REALM OF NEPTUNE

In and for the District of Equatorius

The People of the Realm of the Deep
Versus
All Landlubbers of the U. S. S. HOUSTON

To Slough, W.M. Sealc U. S. Navy,

It having been brought to the attention of His Royal Highness, NEPTUNUS REX, Supreme Ruler of the Deep, through his trusty shellbacks, that a ship manned by a crew who have not acknowledged the sovereignty of the Ruler of the Deep, has transgressed on his domain and thereby incurred the Royal Displeasure.

Be it known: To ye all that His Most Royal Highness, NEPTUNUS REX, Supreme Ruler of all mermaids, sharks, crabs, pollywogs, timmenogs, and other denizens of the deep, will, with his Secretary and Royal Court, meet in full session on board the offending ship HOUSTON in Latitude 0° 0' 0" at 8:00 o'clock in the morning of the ...... day of May, A. D. 1936 to examine into your fitness to be taken into the citizenship of the deep and to hear your defense on the charge of:

I Spying on the shellbacks when he should have been at work.

II Trying to issue second hand bolts for new ones

It is therefore ordered and decreed that the above named man present himself before the Royal Court at the time and place mentioned under penalty of eternal pickling.

By order of the Court:
for His Majesty

Given under my hand and seal this 20 day of May A. D. 1936.

Davey Jones, Clerk
Peg Leg, Deputy.

All polliwogs were issued a summons to appear before the royal court of Neptunus Rex. This one was issued to William Sough on his first crossing of the equator on May 20, 1936. (UHDL.)

Polliwogs appeared before the royal court to defend themselves from the specified charges. The court was made up of shellback sailors costumed as fantastic characters. This is the court from *Houston's* summer 1938 line crossing. (The royal nurse is feeding milk to the royal baby.) (USNHHC.)

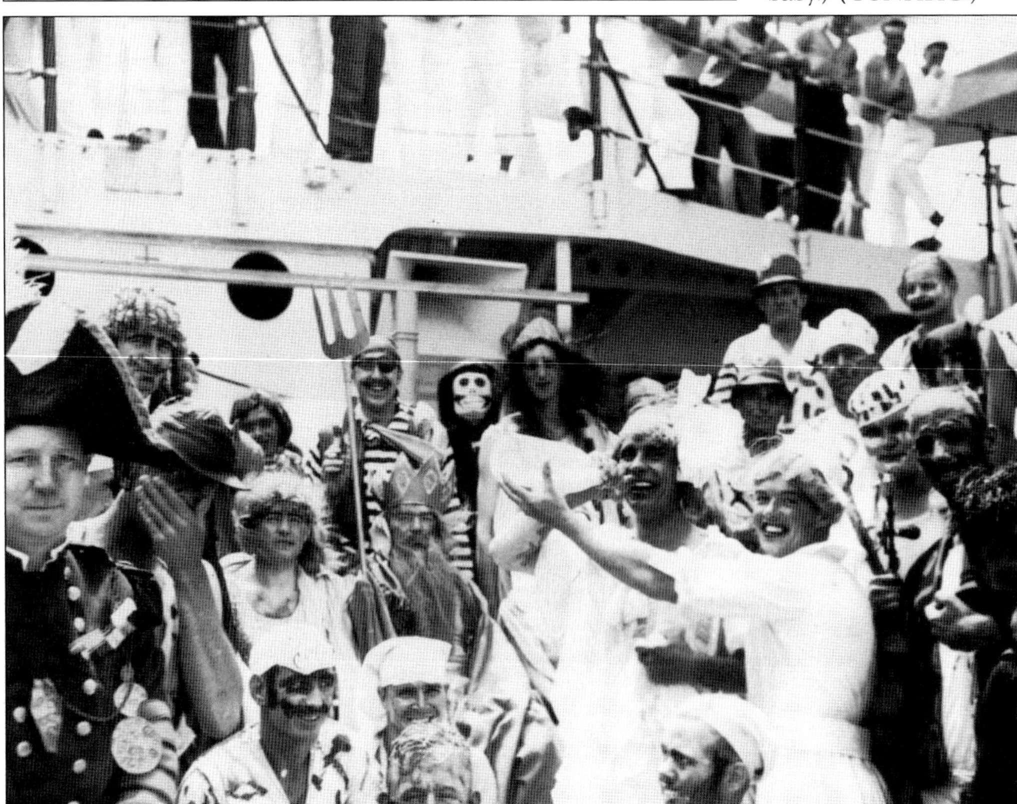

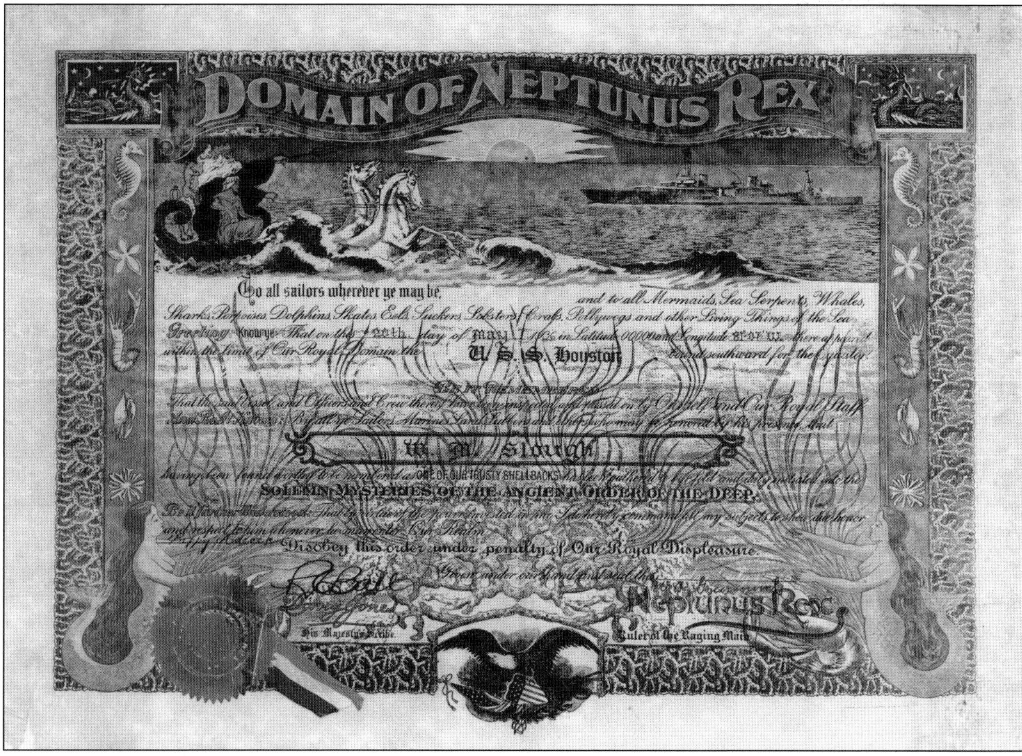

The polliwogs were always found guilty and had to pay a forfeit, which include haircutting, drinking nasty liquids, or partaking in similar indignities. Polliwog officers were allowed to ransom themselves. But at the end, the sailor got a certificate certifying him to be a trusty shellback. It exempted him from further line-crossing indignities, and allowed him to join the royal court next time. (UHDL.)

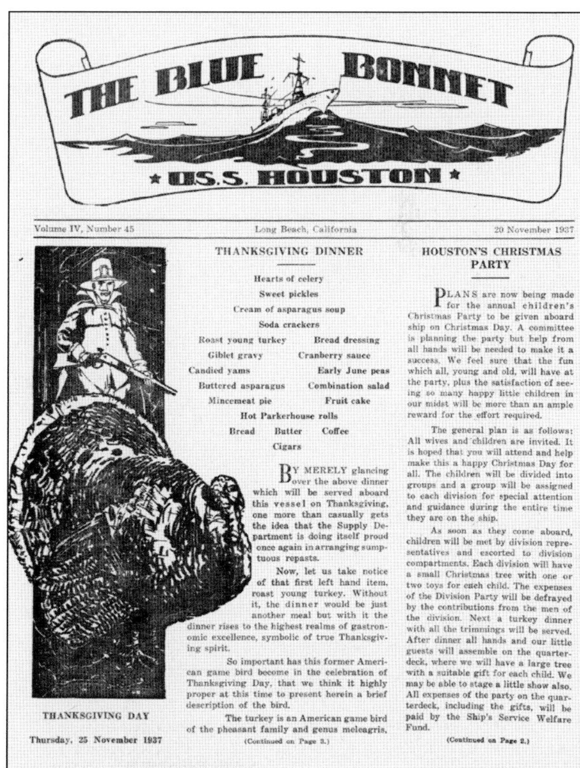

THE BLUE BONNET

★ U.S.S. HOUSTON ★

Volume IV, Number 45 | Long Beach, California | 20 November 1937

THANKSGIVING DAY

Thursday, 25 November 1937

THANKSGIVING DINNER

Hearts of celery
Sweet pickles
Cream of asparagus soup
Soda crackers
Roast young turkey — Bread dressing
Giblet gravy — Cranberry sauce
Candied yams — Early June peas
Buttered asparagus — Combination salad
Mincemeat pie — Fruit cake
Hot Parkerhouse rolls
Bread — Butter — Coffee
Cigars

BY MERELY glancing over the above dinner which will be served aboard this vessel on Thanksgiving, one more than casually gets the idea that the Supply Department is doing itself proud once again in arranging sumptuous repasts.

Now, let us take notice of that first left hand item, roast young turkey. Without it, the dinner would be just another meal but with it the dinner rises to the highest realms of gastronomic excellence, symbolic of true Thanksgiving spirit.

So important has this former American game bird become in the celebration of Thanksgiving Day, that we think it highly proper at this time to present herein a brief description of the bird.

The turkey is an American game bird of the pheasant family and genus meleagris,

(Continued on Page 3.)

HOUSTON'S CHRISTMAS PARTY

PLANS are now being made for the annual children's Christmas Party to be given aboard ship on Christmas Day. A committee is planning the party but help from all hands will be needed to make it a success. We feel sure that the fun which all, young and old, will have at the party, plus the satisfaction of seeing so many happy little children in our midst will be more than an ample reward for the effort required.

The general plan is as follows: All wives and children are invited. It is hoped that you will attend and help make this a happy Christmas Day for all. The children will be divided into groups and a group will be assigned to each division for special attention and guidance during the entire time they are on the ship.

As soon as they come aboard, children will be met by division representatives and escorted to division compartments. Each division will have a small Christmas tree with one or two toys for each child. The expenses of the Division Party will be defrayed by the contributions from the men of the division. Next a turkey dinner with all the trimmings will be served. After dinner all hands and our little guests will assemble on the quarterdeck, where we will have a large tree with a suitable gift for each child. We may be able to stage a little show also. All expenses of the party on the quarterdeck, including the gifts, will be paid by the Ship's Service Welfare Fund.

(Continued on Page 2.)

Holidays were also big aboard *Houston*. An extra effort was made to make the crew happy, especially for days like Thanksgiving and Christmas, which are traditionally spent with family. Elaborate plans were made for meals and parties that were announced in *The Blue Bonnet*. (UHDL.)

Houston's post office even issued special covers for holidays like Valentine's Day, the Fourth of July, and Christmas, as seen here. (HMM.)

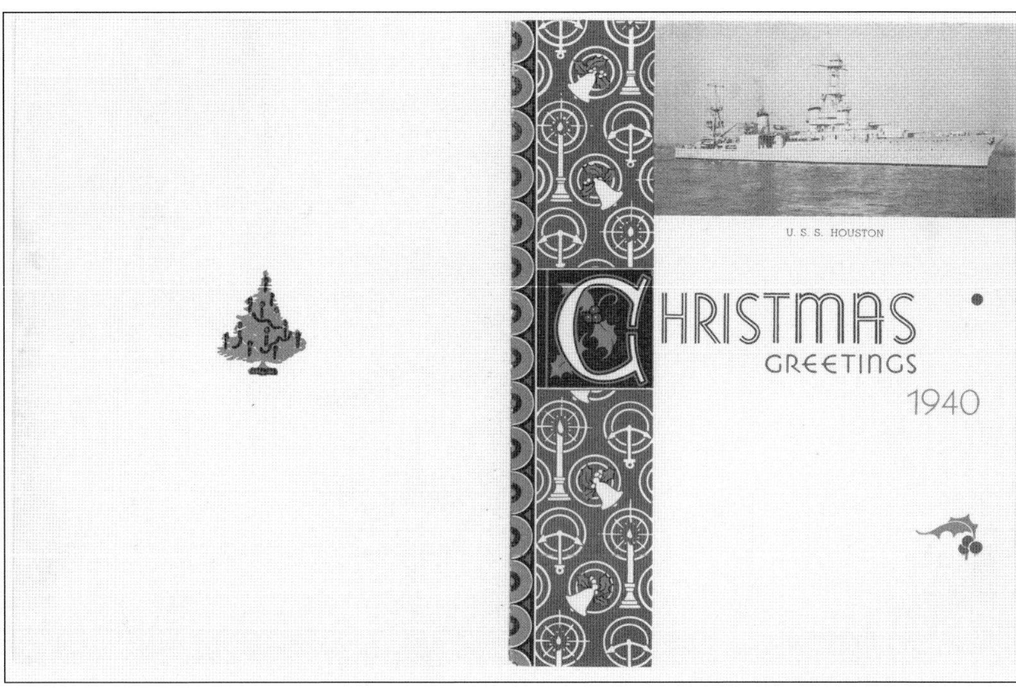

Christmas dinner may have been the biggest holiday event on *Houston*. A special dinner was served along with a dinner card to accompany the meal. This is the outside of the 1940 card. (HMM.)

Inside was the menu. The ingredients really did not differ from those normally served, although special effort was put into the presentation. Note that the menu includes saltine crackers, and closes with cigars and cigarettes. The last two items would be noticeably absent from a Navy Christmas dinner in the 21st century. (HMM.)

MENU

U. S. S. HOUSTON

CHRISTMAS DAY, DECEMBER 25, 1940

FRUIT COCKTAIL

CELERY EN BRANCH SWEET MIXED PICKLES

RIPE OLIVES SALTINE CRACKERS CRANBERRY SAUCE

ROAST RAMONA TURKEY

NUT DRESSING GIBLET GRAVY

PINEAPPLE HAM GLACED

CREAMED WHIPPED POTATOES CREAMED PEAS

ASPARAGUS TIPS

FRESH GARDEN SALAD THOUSAND ISLAND DRESSING

HOT PARKER HOUSE ROLLS

CHERRY PIE NEAPOLITAN ICE CREAM FRUIT CAKE

HARD CANDY NUTS FRUITS CHEESE

CIGARS CIGARETTES

COFFEE LEMONADE ICED

D. H. HANKINSON
Chief Commissary Steward, USN

Sports also played a big role aboard *Houston*, as on all Navy ships. Sports helped develop teamwork. One popular sport was basketball, which could be practiced aboard ship. This is *Houston's* 1940–1941 basketball team. (USNHHC.)

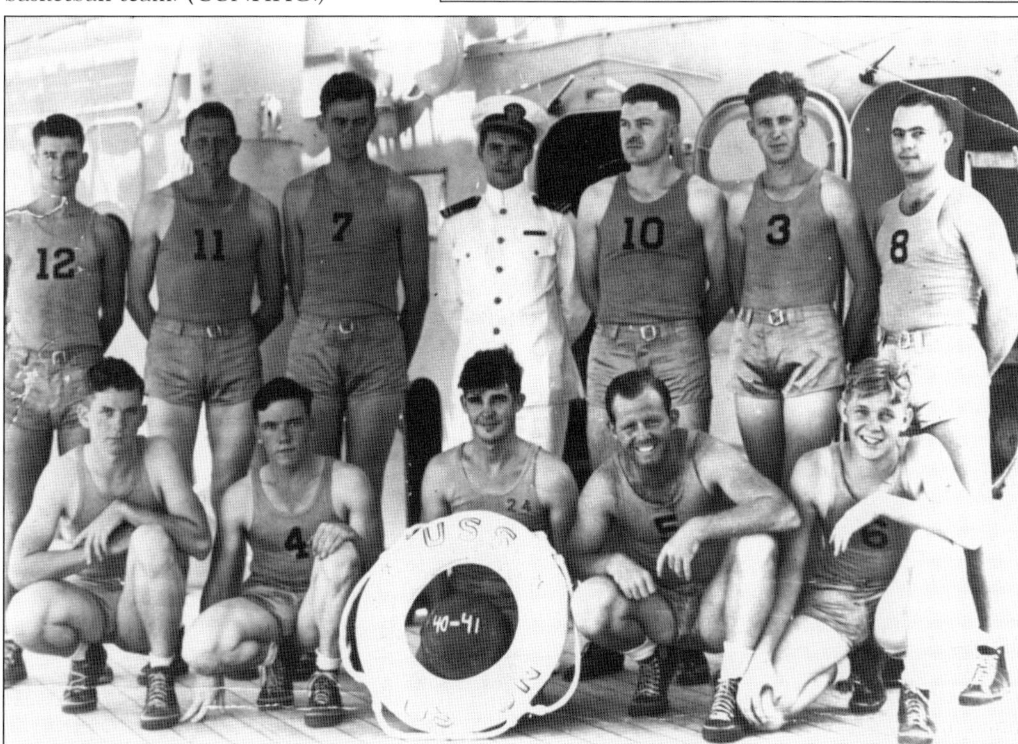

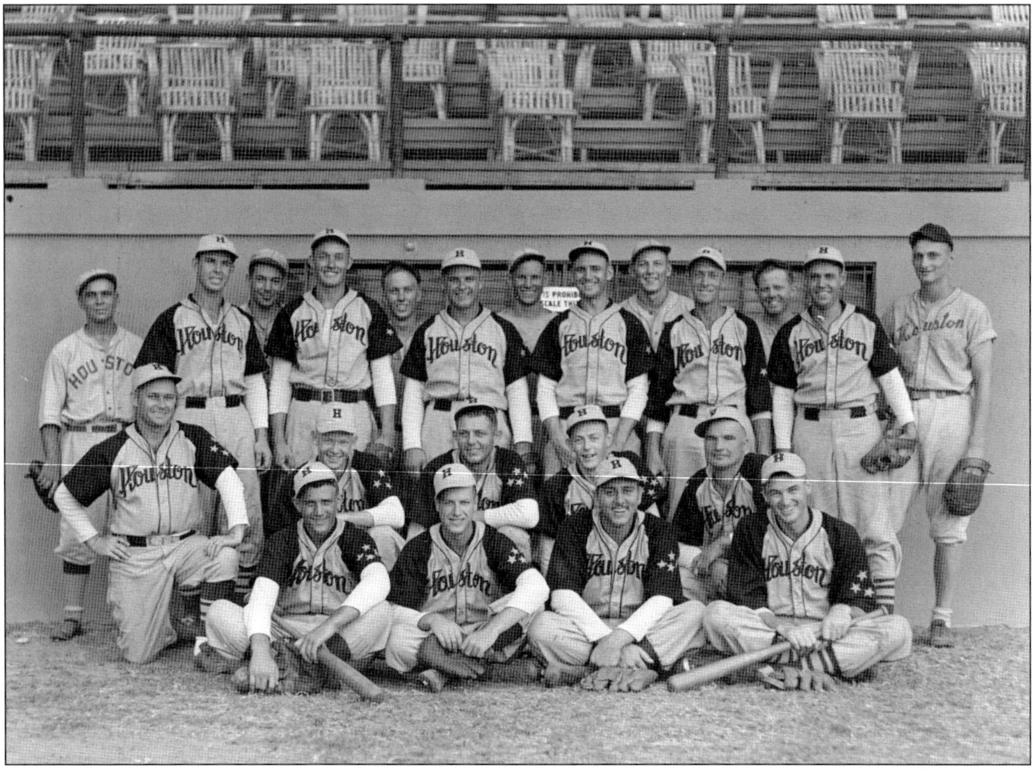

The king of sports in the mid-20th century was baseball, and *Houston* fielded a team. Members are shown in their uniforms at Manila's Rizal Stadium in the Philippines in 1940. (USNHHC.)

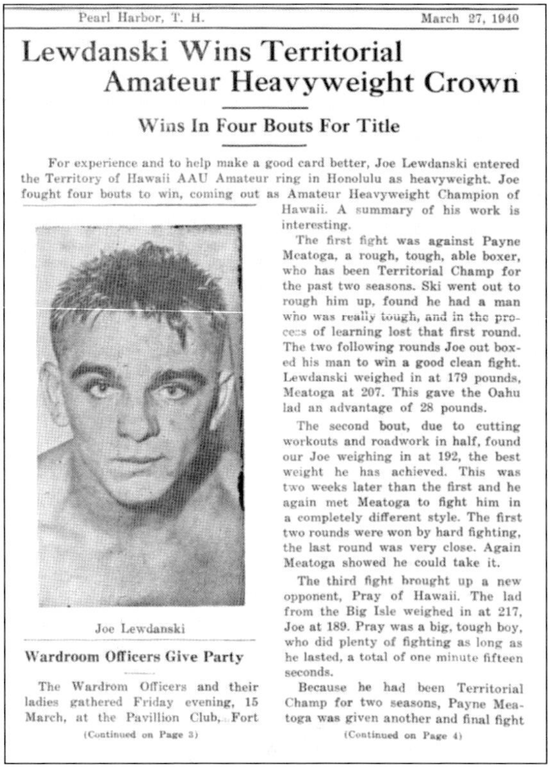

Pearl Harbor, T. H. March 27, 1940

Lewdanski Wins Territorial Amateur Heavyweight Crown

Wins In Four Bouts For Title

For experience and to help make a good card better, Joe Lewdanski entered the Territory of Hawaii AAU Amateur ring in Honolulu as heavyweight. Joe fought four bouts to win, coming out as Amateur Heavyweight Champion of Hawaii. A summary of his work is interesting.

Joe Lewdanski

The first fight was against Payne Meatoga, a rough, tough, able boxer, who has been Territorial Champ for the past two seasons. Ski went out to rough him up, found he had a man who was really tough, and in the process of learning lost that first round. The two following rounds Joe out boxed his man to win a good clean fight. Lewdanski weighed in at 179 pounds, Meatoga at 207. This gave the Oahu lad an advantage of 28 pounds.

The second bout, due to cutting workouts and roadwork in half, found our Joe weighing in at 192, the best weight he has achieved. This was two weeks later than the first and he again met Meatoga to fight him in a completely different style. The first two rounds were won by hard fighting, the last round was very close. Again Meatoga showed he could take it.

The third fight brought up a new opponent, Pray of Hawaii. The lad from the Big Isle weighed in at 217, Joe at 189. Pray was a big, tough boy, who did plenty of fighting as long as he lasted, a total of one minute fifteen seconds.

Because he had been Territorial Champ for two seasons, Payne Meatoga was given another and final fight

(Continued on Page 4)

Wardroom Officers Give Party

The Wardrom Officers and their ladies gathered Friday evening, 15 March, at the Pavillion Club, Fort

(Continued on Page 3)

Individual competitive sports were popular, too. Boxing was particularly popular among the sailors. When Joe Lewdanski, a water tender 2nd class in *Houston's* engine room, won the Territorial Amateur Heavyweight Championship in Hawaii in 1940, the story made the front page of *The Blue Bonnet*, complete with a photograph. (UHDL.)

Five

The Galloping Ghost of the Java Coast

Houston's wartime career lasted three scant months. The war started for the cruiser on December 8 (Hawaii was across the International Date Line from the Philippines). *Houston* had been Asiatic Fleet flagship just over a year, since November 22, 1940. When the war started, *Houston* and light cruiser *Boise* were at Panay. *Marblehead* and Asiatic Fleet destroyers were in Borneo. Adm. Thomas Hart scattered the fleet outside Japanese aircraft range to protect them from attack.

Hart withdrew his badly outnumbered ships to the Java Sea. They combined with the ships of three allied nations forming the American-British-Dutch-Australian (ABDA) Command. They were badly outnumbered by Japanese surface ships and completely outclassed by Japanese air power.

As 1942 started, *Houston* was ABDA Command's most powerful warship. Shuttling between Darwin, Australia, and Dutch East Indies (today's Indonesia) ports, *Houston* escorted convoys carrying troops and supplies to Java.

On February 3, 1942, *Houston* participated in an effort to stop a rumored Japanese landing in the Makassar Strait. Allied naval forces there, including *Houston* and *Marblehead*, were attacked by Japanese bombers. Both US cruisers were damaged. *Houston* had its aft turret destroyed, and *Marblehead* was so badly damaged that it was ordered home.

Houston remained. Over the next three weeks, Japan reported *Houston* sunk so many times that its crew dubbed it "The Galloping Ghost of the Java Coast." On February 27, *Houston* fought at the Battle of the Java Sea, a last-ditch attempt to save Java from invasion. Allied forces were routed, with two cruisers and three destroyers sunk.

The next day, *Houston*, in company with Australian cruiser *Perth*, attempted to escape the Java Sea through the Sunda Strait. The strait was filled by a Japanese fleet, landing troops on Java. Outnumbered and trapped, *Houston* and *Perth* attacked the transports. At least four were sunk, possibly as many as a dozen, before both Allied cruisers were overwhelmed and sunk. Only 372 men survived of the 1,017 men aboard *Houston* when the battle started. They remained prisoners of war for 44 months, and 96 died in captivity.

This chapter captures that struggle. Many images are fuzzy and rough, as there was more interest in fighting a war than photographing it.

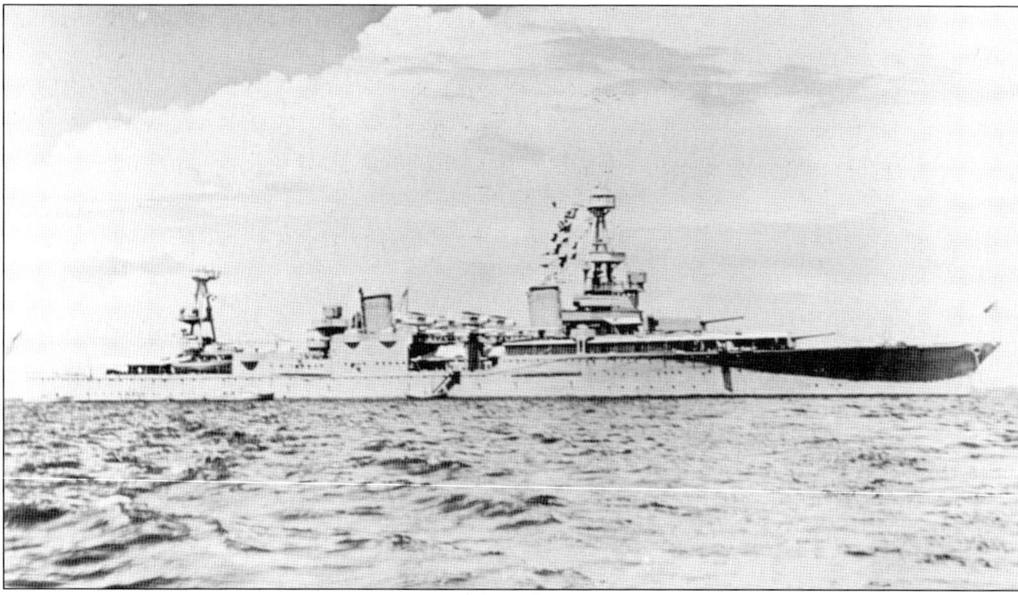

On December 8, 1941, *Houston* was flagship of the Asiatic Fleet and was the most powerful US Navy warship in the Pacific west of the International Date Line. Its 1940 refit doubled the five-inch antiaircraft guns and added numerous 1.1-inch and 20mm antiaircraft guns. Despite this, *Houston* and the Asiatic Fleet would prove badly outgunned. (USNHHC.)

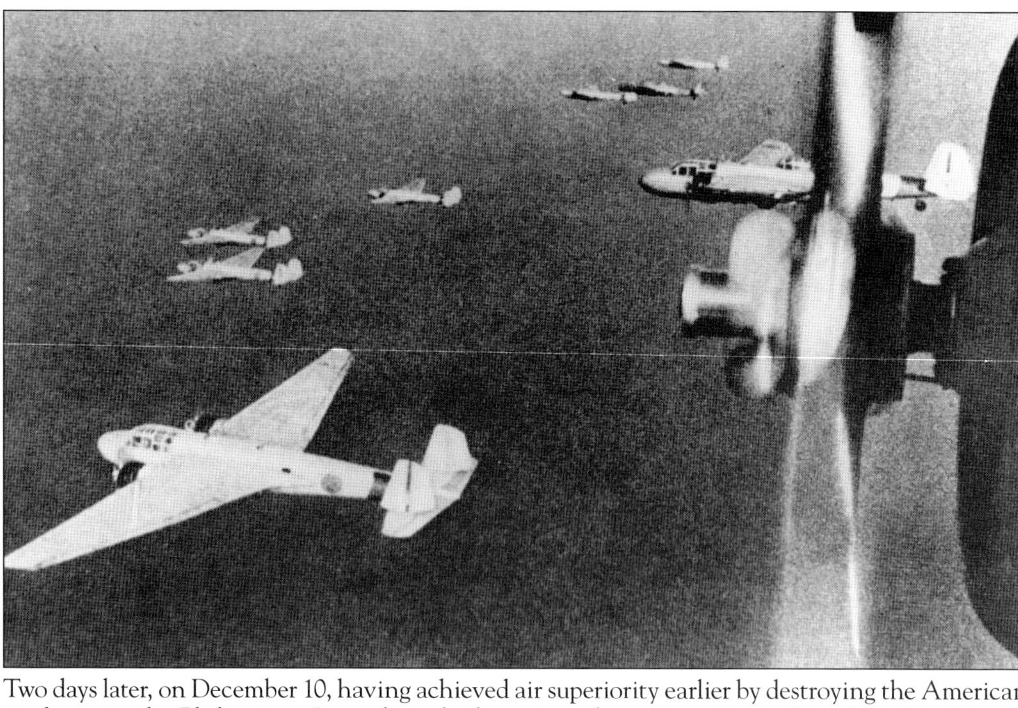

Two days later, on December 10, having achieved air superiority earlier by destroying the American air forces in the Philippines, Japan launched an air strike against Cavite Naval Yard in Manila Bay. Mitsubishi G3M Type 96 attack bombers bombed from 20,000 feet, higher than American antiaircraft guns could reach. (USNHHC.)

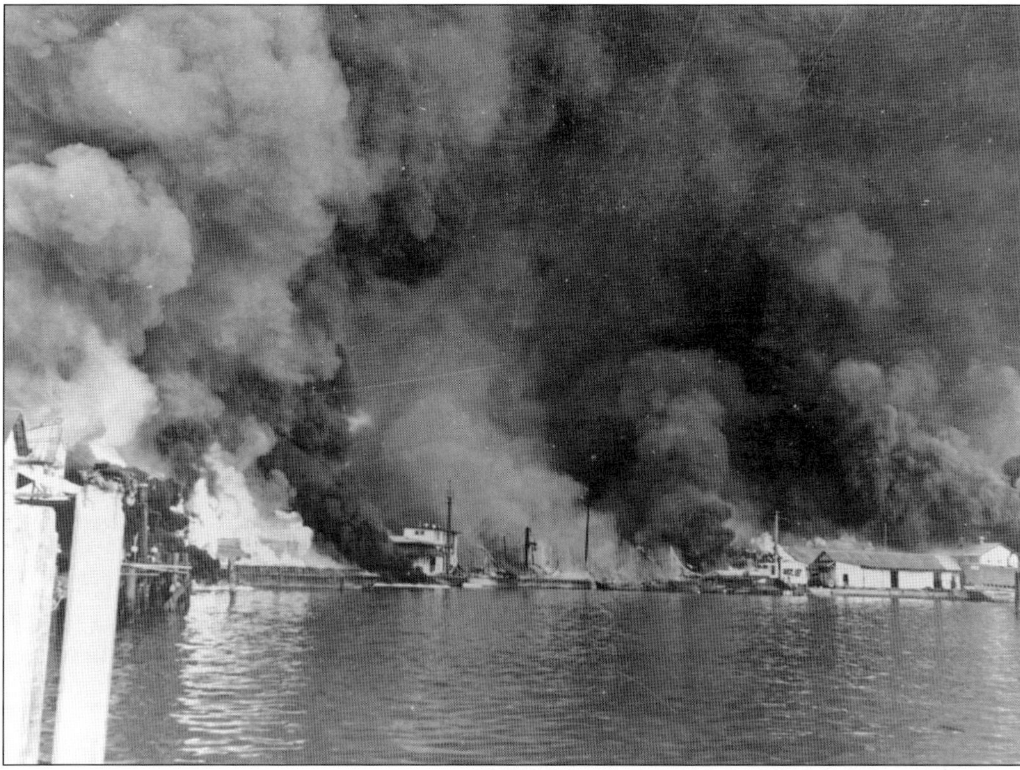

The attack was devastating, destroying most of the base facilities and the submarine *Sealion*, which was in dry dock when the Japanese attacked. (USNHHC.)

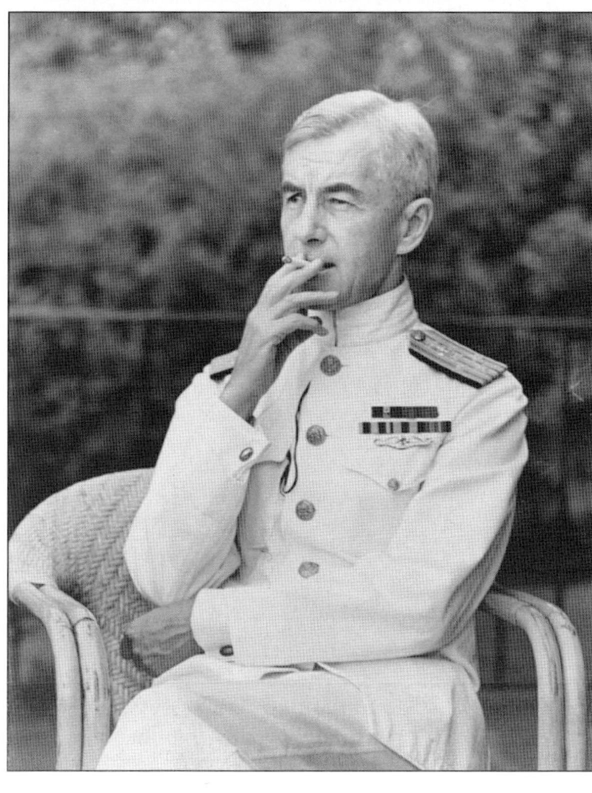

Adm. Thomas Hart commanded the Asiatic Fleet when World War II started. He may have been the most realistic Allied commander in the Far East. He put his fleet on a war footing in November, and after the Japanese attacked Pearl Harbor, he evacuated the Navy surface ships from Manila Bay before the Japanese could trap them in harbor. (USNHHC.)

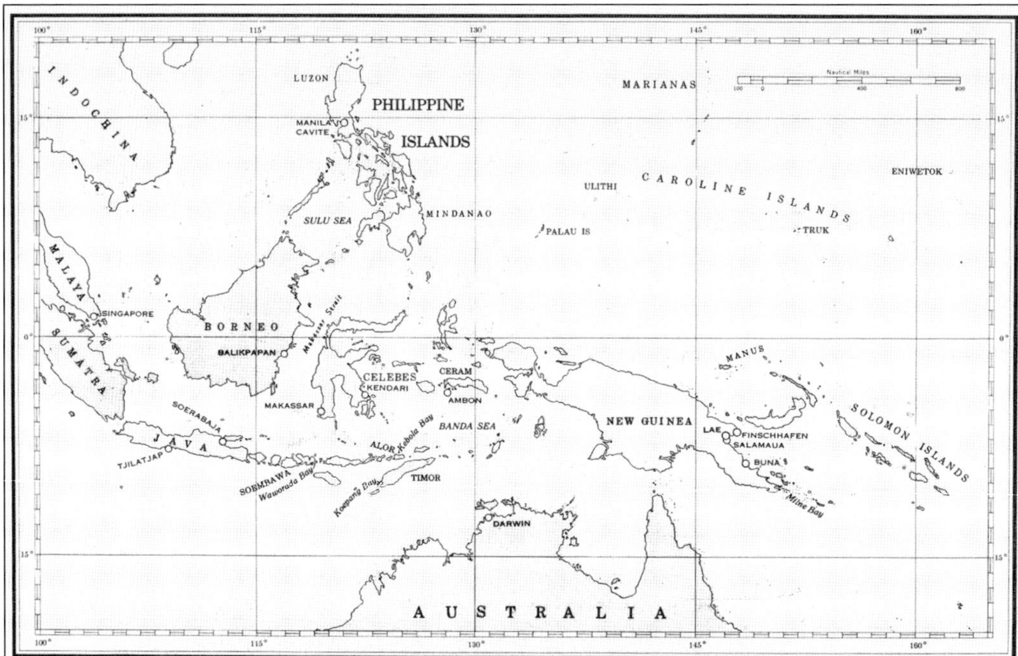

Southwest Pacific, Australia, New Guinea, Borneo.

Over the next three months, from December 8, 1941, through March 1, 1942, the Asiatic Fleet and its British, Dutch, and Australian allies fought an unequal battle against the rampaging Japanese over the area shown on this map. (AC.)

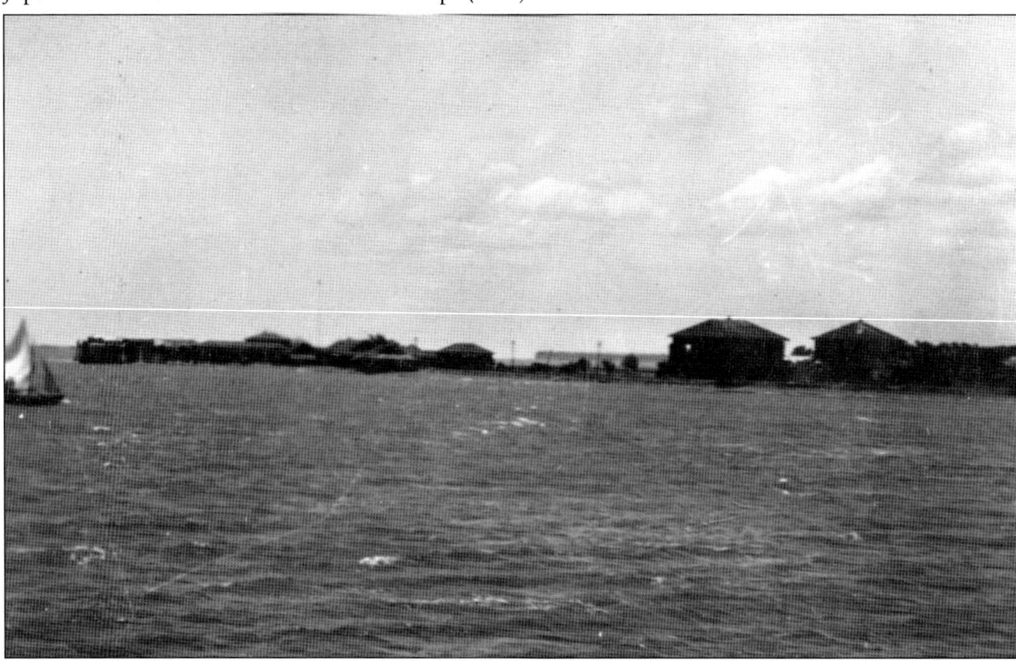

Houston was not in Manila Bay on December 8, 1941. Admiral Hart ordered it to Iloili, a small US Navy anchorage on the island of Panay, nearly 300 miles south of Manila Bay and out of range of Japanese bombers. (USNHHC.)

Admiral Hart's responsibilities kept him in Manila Bay prior to Pearl Harbor. Hart's deputy commander, Rear Adm. William Glassford, was aboard *Houston* in Iloili with his flag flying when the war started. He would be the last flag officer to fly his flag over *Houston*. (USNHHC.)

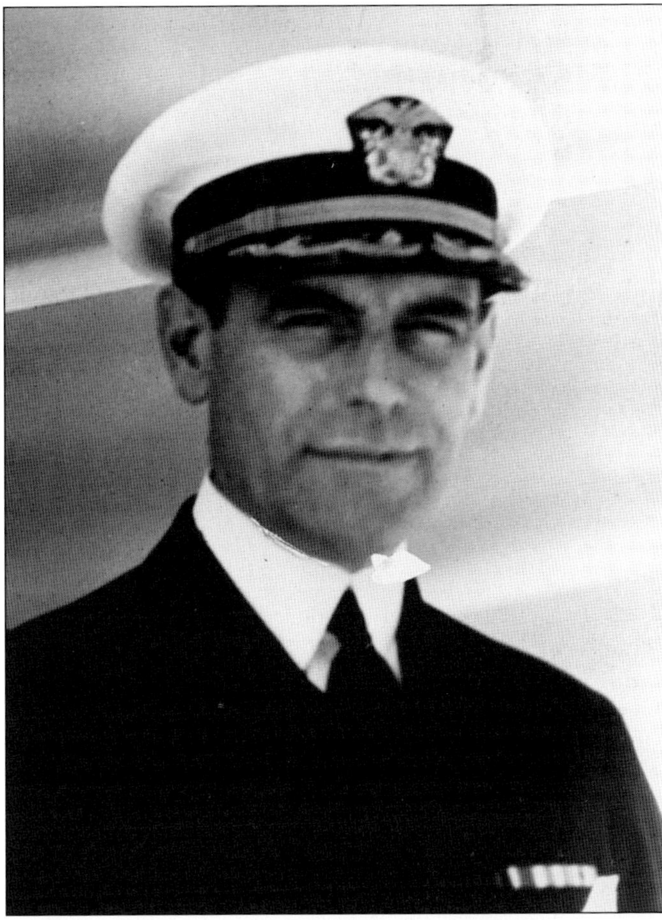

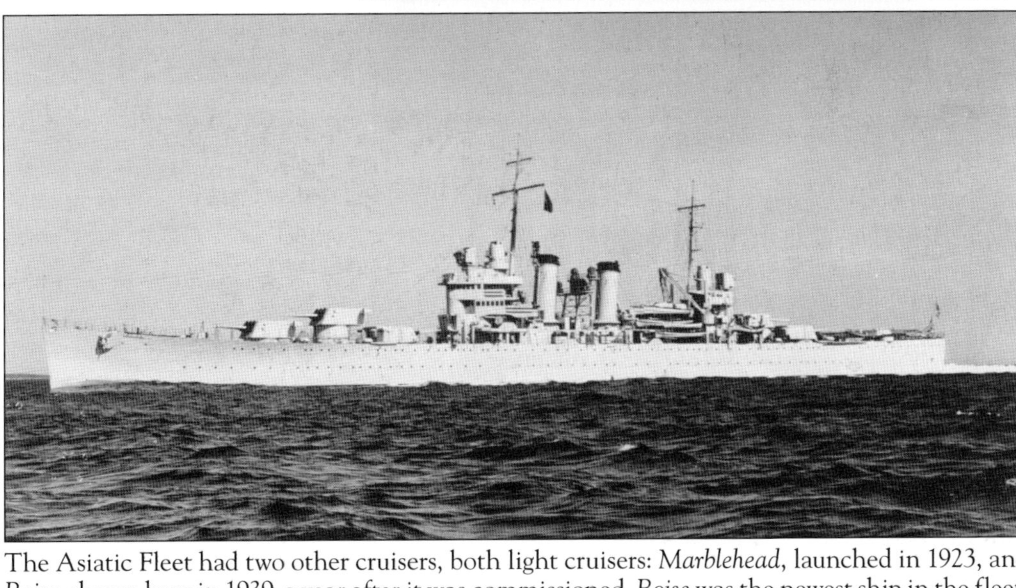

The Asiatic Fleet had two other cruisers, both light cruisers: *Marblehead*, launched in 1923, and *Boise*, shown here in 1939, a year after it was commissioned. *Boise* was the newest ship in the fleet, and it mounted 15 six-inch guns in five triple turrets. (USNHHC.)

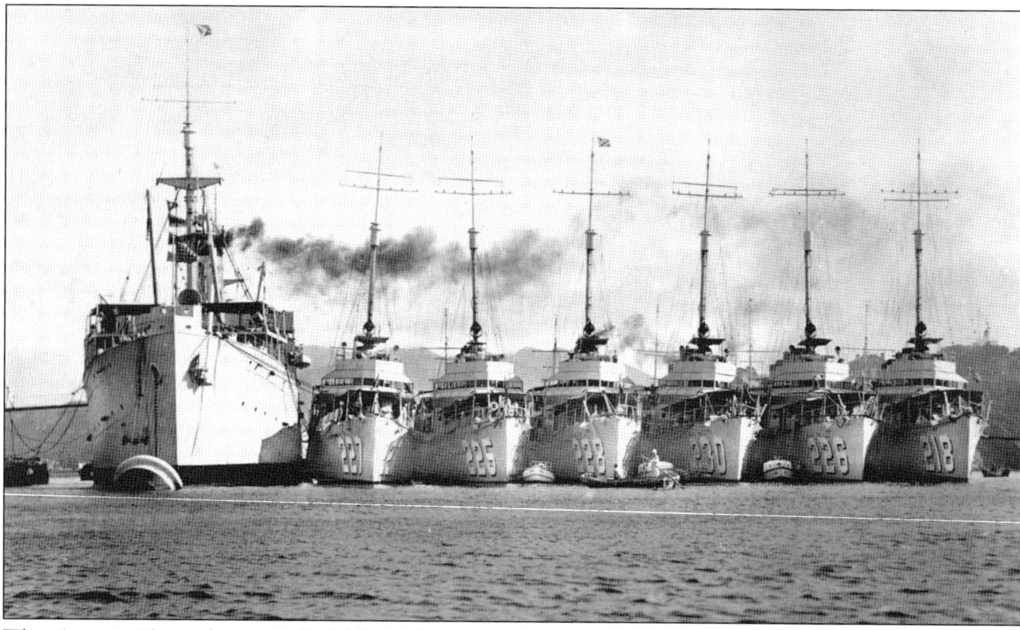

The Asiatic Fleet also included 13 old four-pipe destroyers, built between 1917 and 1923. Six are shown here, tied up to destroyer tender *Black Hawk*. From left to right, they are USS *Pillsbury* (DD-227), USS *Pope* (DD-225), USS *John D. Ford* (DD-228), USS *Paul Jones* (DD-230), USS *Peary* (DD-226), and USS *Parrott* (DD-218). (USNHHC.)

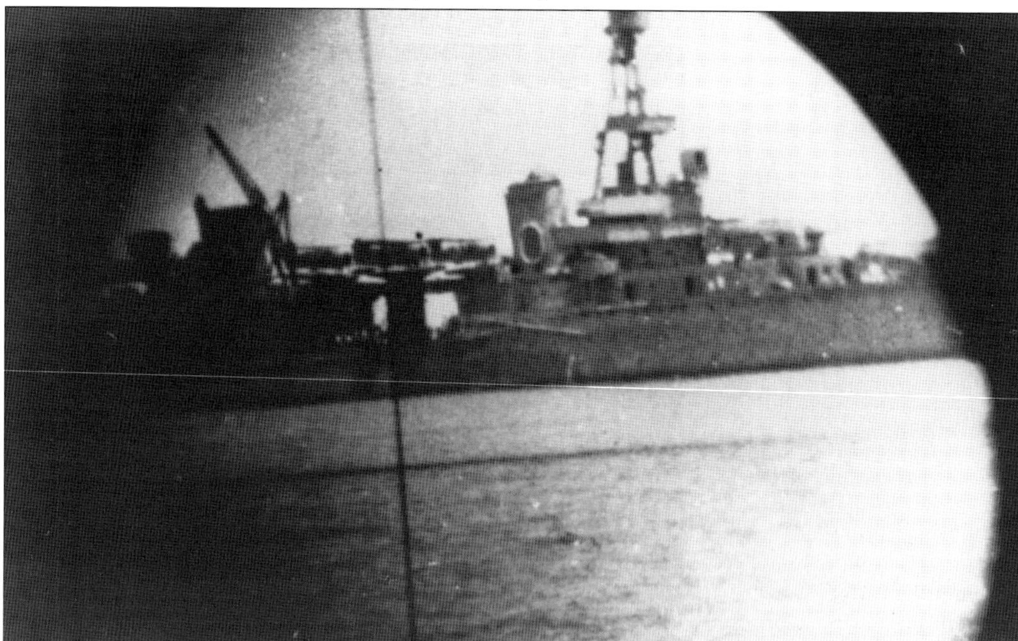

Houston (photographed through the gun sight of an Australian shore battery) and the rest of the Asiatic Fleet found themselves in the crosshairs of the Imperial Japanese armed forces. The advancing Japanese soon forced the US Navy out of the Philippines. They fell back to the Dutch East Indies, where they combined with ships of the Royal Navy, the Royal Netherlands Navy, and the Royal Australian Navy. (USNHHC.)

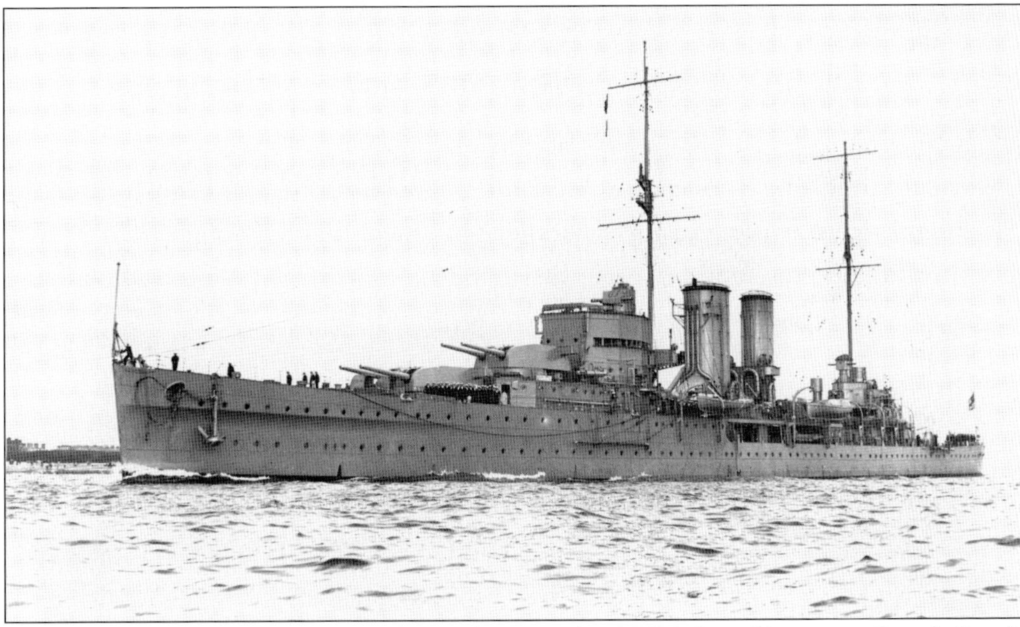

On January 15, 1942, the combined force became the ABDACom (American-British-Dutch-Australian Command). The British contingent contained three destroyers and was led by this ship, heavy cruiser *Exeter*, famous for having helped defeat the German pocket battleship *Graf Spee* at the Battle of the River Plate in 1939. (USNHHC.)

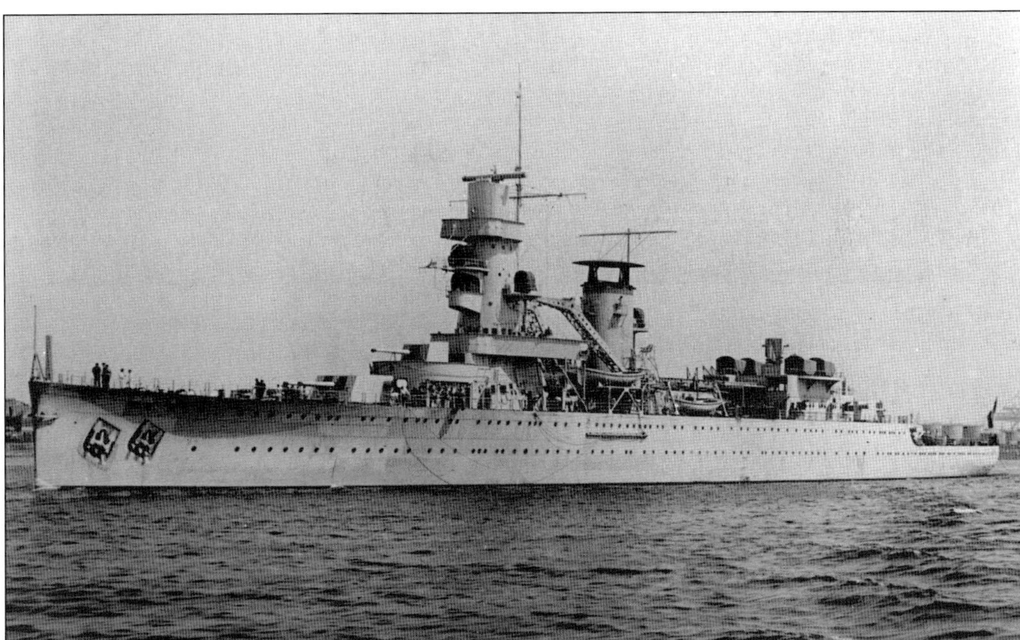

The Dutch contingent consisted of three light cruisers and seven destroyers. The flagship was the *de Ruyter*, shown here. Commissioned in 1936, it was modern, but weakly armed and poorly protected. Two cruisers, including *de Ruyter*, and all seven destroyers were lost defending the Dutch East Indies. (RNDM.)

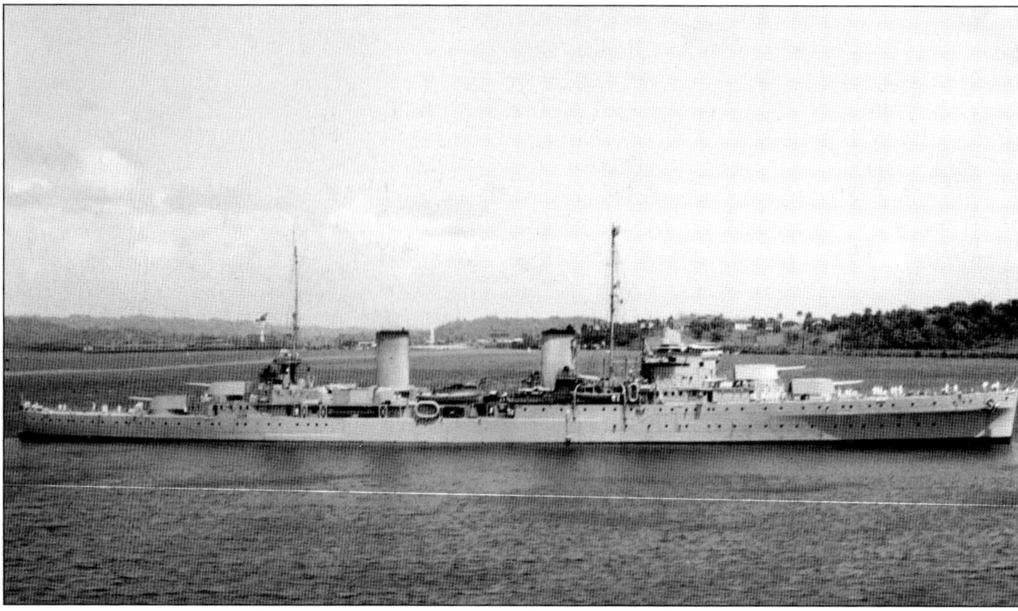

Australia contributed light cruisers *Hobart* and *Perth*. *Hobart* was withdrawn in late February, but *Perth*, pictured in 1940, remained, taking part in the Battle of the Java Sea and fighting beside *Houston* at the Battle of Sunda Strait. (USNHHC.)

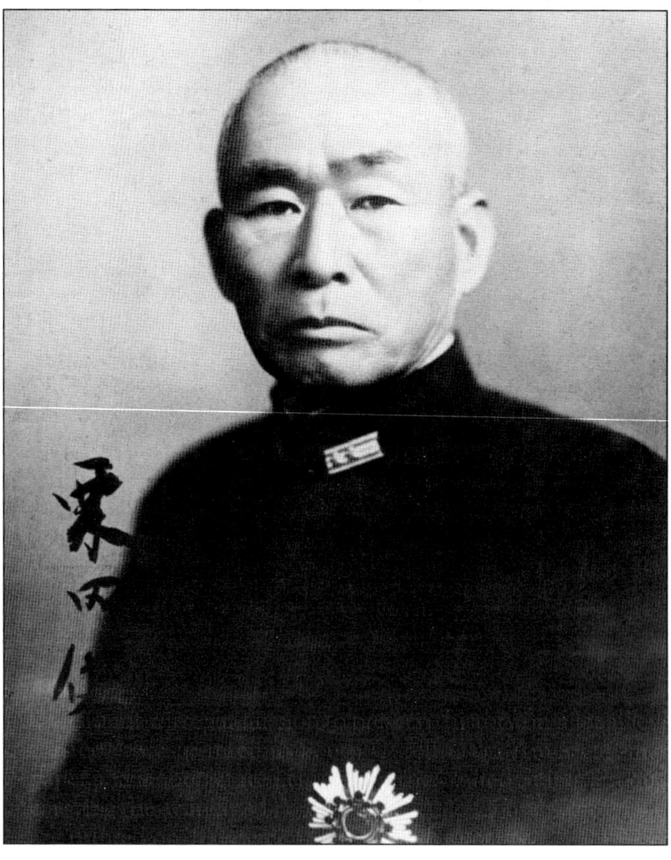

In addition to an overwhelming superiority in aircraft, the Japanese badly outgunned the ABDA fleet. Divided into three groups, the Japanese committed two light aircraft carriers, eight heavy cruisers, six light cruisers, and nearly 50 destroyers to the capture of the Dutch East Indies. Adm. Takeo Kurita commanded the western attack force, which fought at the Battle of Sunda Strait. (USNHHC.)

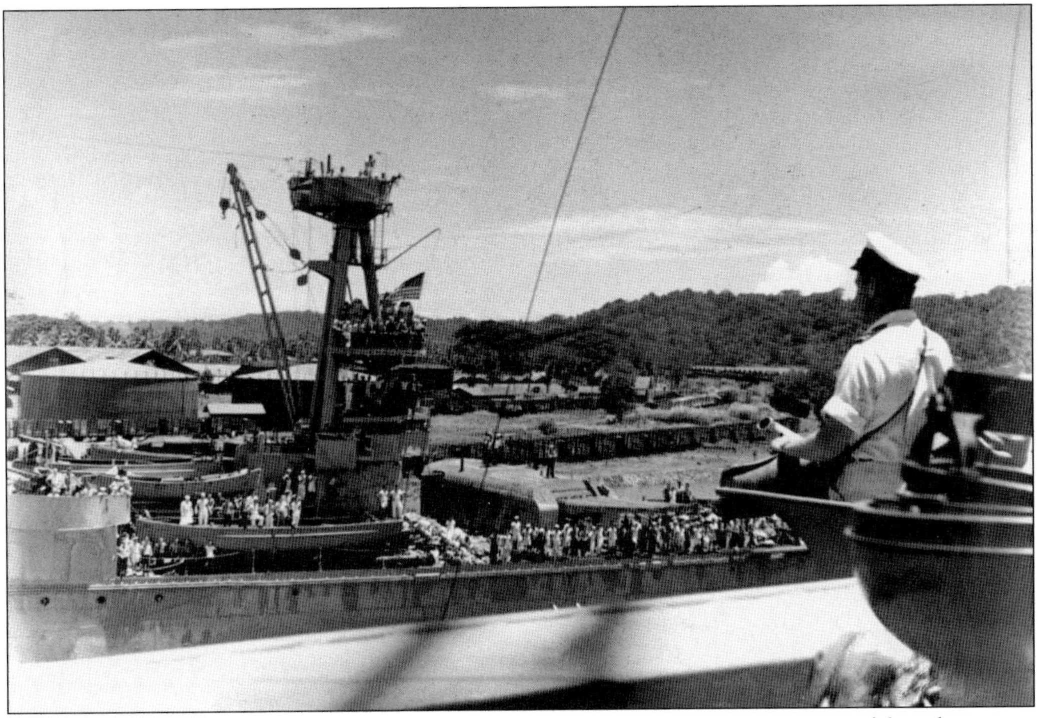

Three weeks after ABDA was formed, *de Ruyter*, *Tromp*, *Marblehead*, *Houston*, and four destroyers steamed into the Makassar Strait to stop a Japanese invasion fleet. Sixty Japanese bombers found the Allied fleet and attacked. In the ensuing Battle of Makassar Strait, *Houston* shot down four Japanese aircraft, but *Houston* and *Marblehead* were hit by bombs. *Houston's* aft turret was knocked out, and 48 members of its crew killed. The dead were buried at Tjilatjap. (USNHHC.)

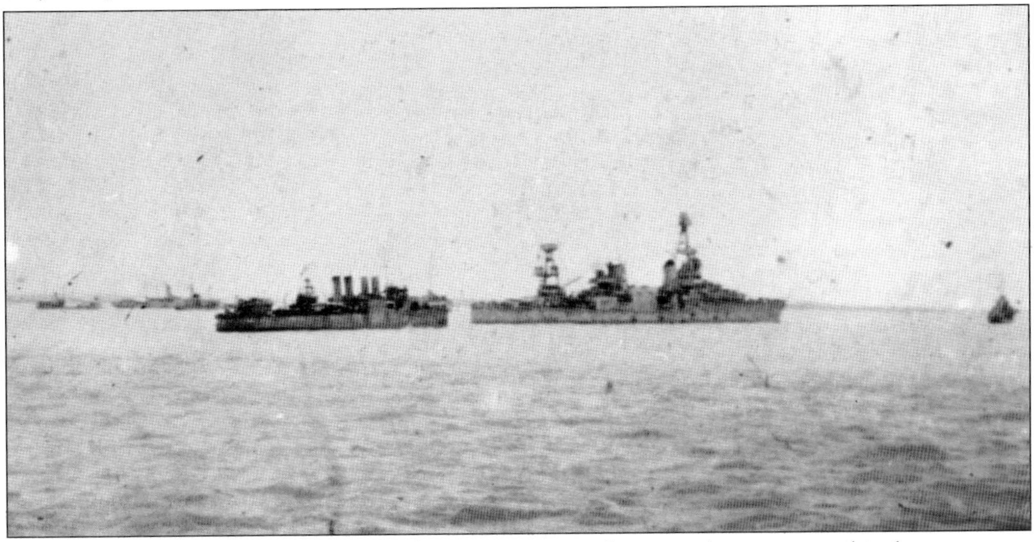

Marblehead, badly damaged, was sent home. *Boise* was also gone, having ripped its bottom open on a coral head. *Houston*, with one turret out, was still the most powerful ship left in ABDA. Captain Rooks opted to keep fighting. This grainy image shows *Houston* at Darwin, Australia, in February 1942, returning to the fight, leading a convoy to Timor. It was one of the last photographs of *Houston*. (USNHHC.)

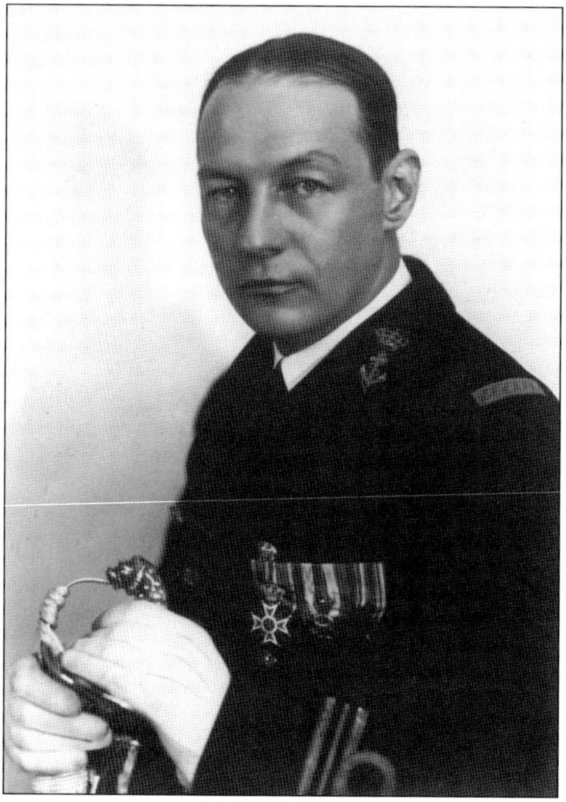

On February 27, 1942, Dutch rear admiral Karel Doorman led the remaining ships of ABDACom, two heavy cruisers, three light cruisers, and nine destroyers, against a superior Japanese fleet. In the seven-hour Battle of the Java Sea, the Allies lost two light cruisers and three destroyers. *Exeter* was badly damaged, and 2,300 sailors killed. The Japanese had one destroyer lightly damaged and 36 dead. (RNDM.)

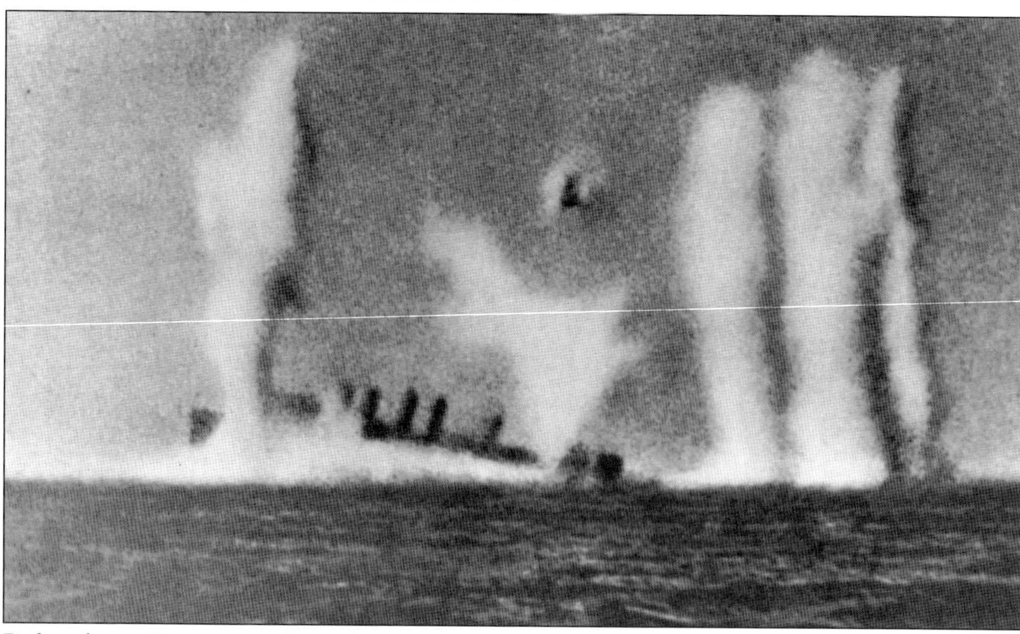

Before dying, Doorman ordered the surviving ships to escape. Few did. *Exeter*, along with escorts destroyers HMS *Encounter* and USS *Pope*, were caught by the Japanese as they fled west and sunk. This picture, taken aboard a Japanese heavy cruiser, shows *Pope* struck by a salvo of Japanese shells. (USNHHC.)

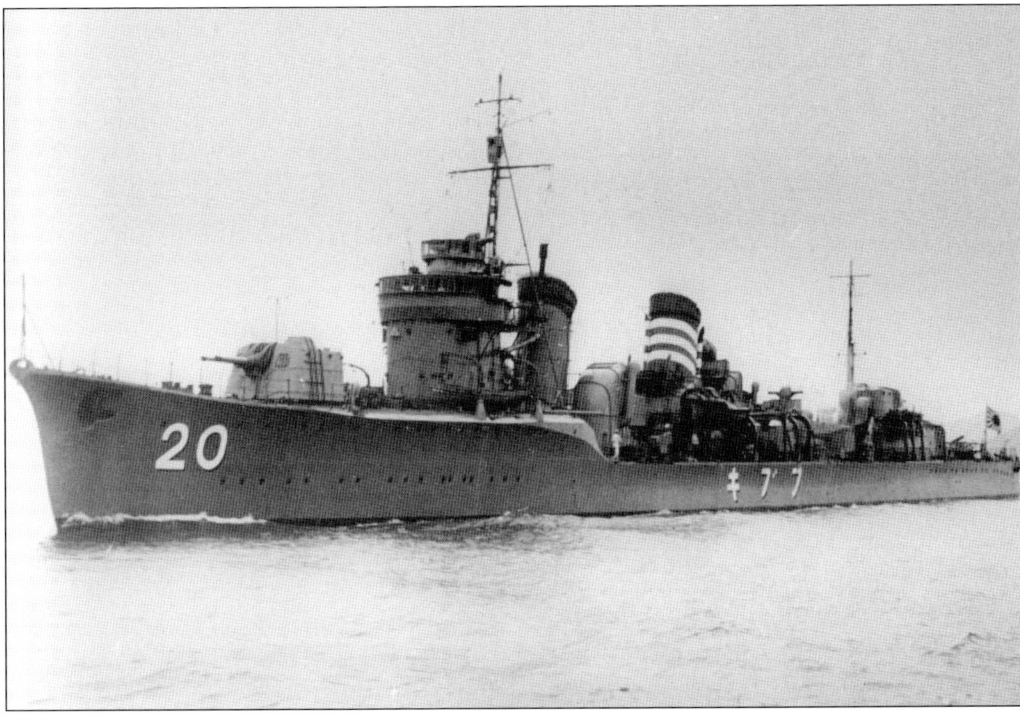

Houston and *Perth* attempted to escape the Java Sea through the Sunda Strait, between Sumatra and Java. They were low on ammunition and fuel, and damaged. As the two ships crept through the night of February 28–March 1, they were spotted by the Japanese destroyer *Fubuki*, shown here. (AC.)

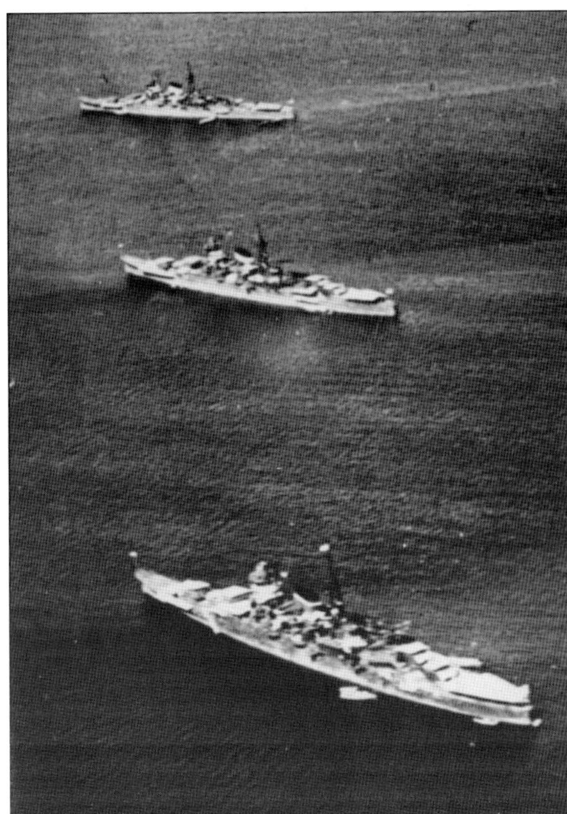

The Japanese were landing an invasion force at Bantam Bay, near the mouth of the Sunda Strait. In addition to *Fubuki*, the 58 troopships there were guarded by 11 other destroyers, and five cruisers of the 7th Cruiser Squadron, including *Mogami*, *Mikuma*, and *Kumano*, shown in this prewar photograph. (USNHHC.)

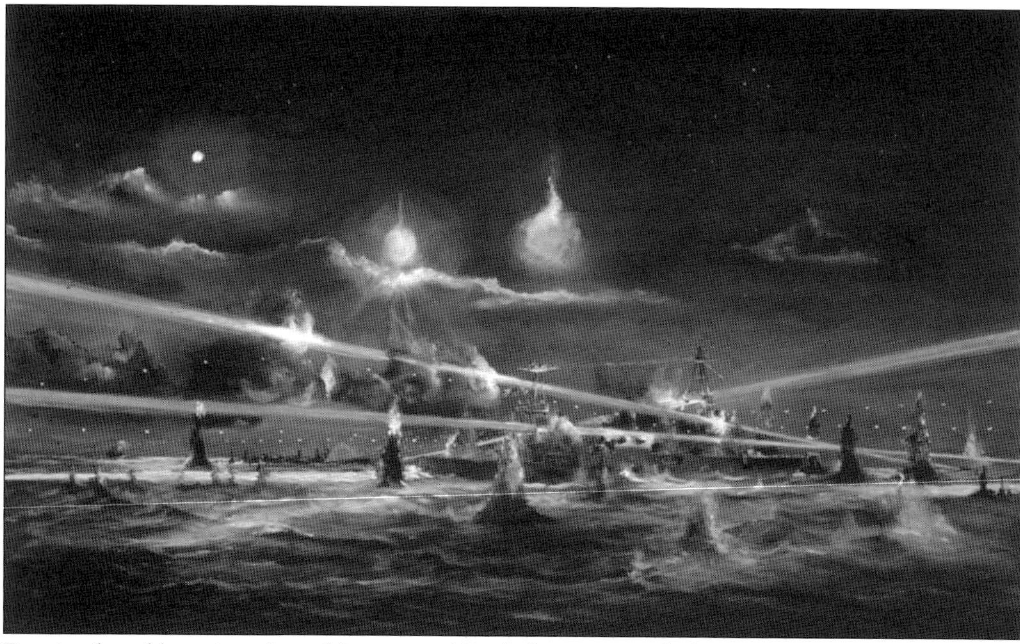

Despite the odds against them, *Houston* and *Perth* chose to attack the transports rather than escape through the Sunda Strait. Both Allied warships fired until they ran out of ammunition. Meanwhile, the Japanese opened up with both guns and Long Lance torpedoes. *Perth* was soon mortally wounded by torpedoes, while *Houston* was struck by a hurricane of gunfire. (USNHHC.)

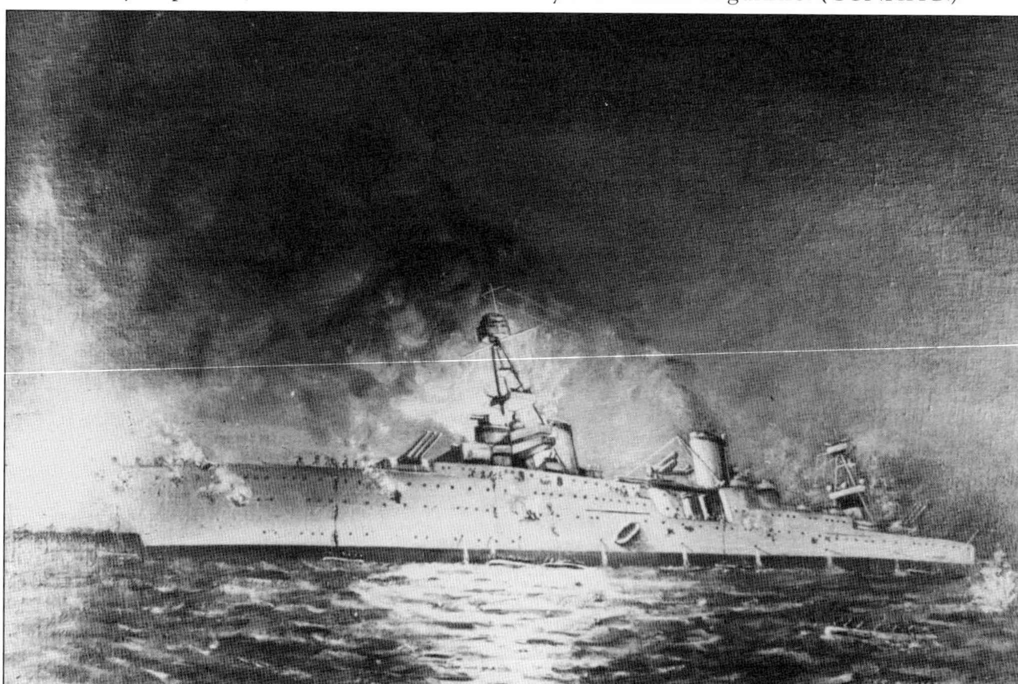

Houston fought on alone, but damage quickly accumulated. The No. 2 eight-inch turret was hit and destroyed. The engines were damaged. Ammunition ran out. Finally, at 12:45 a.m. on March 1, 1942, just 99 minutes after *Perth* reported seeing an enemy ship, *Houston* sank. (USNHHC.)

At 12:25 a.m., 20 minutes before *Houston* sank, Captain Rooks had ordered her abandoned. He then left the signal bridge to go to the communications deck when he was hit by flying shrapnel. The wound proved fatal within minutes. (USNHHC.)

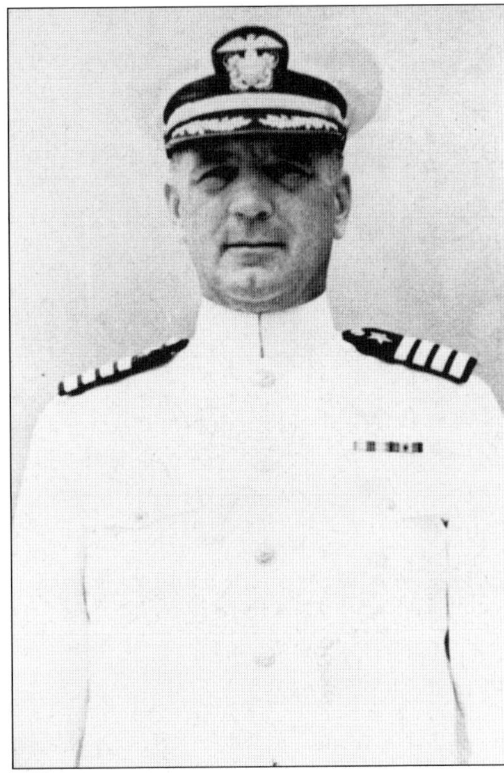

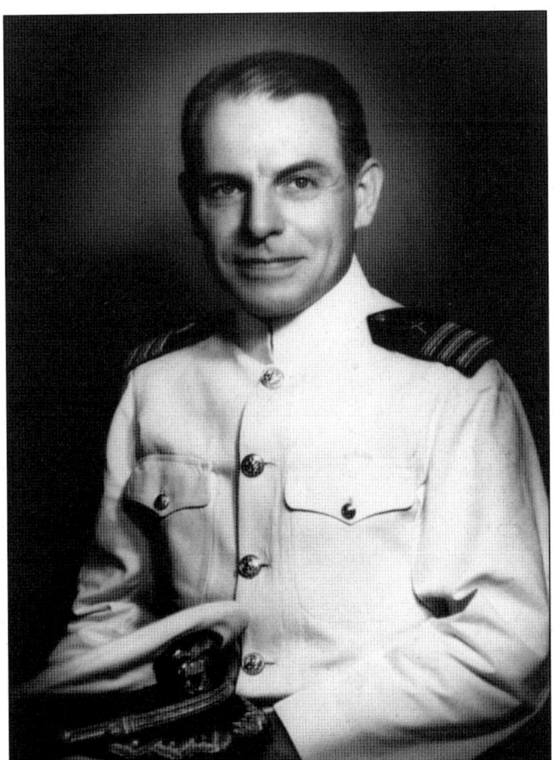

Houston's chaplain, George Snavely Rentz, survived the sinking but drowned after giving his life jacket to another survivor without one. *Houston* survivors spent up to 18 hours in the water before being washed ashore or getting picked up by the Japanese. Rentz was posthumously awarded a Navy Cross after the war, when survivors told of his sacrifice. (USNHHC.)

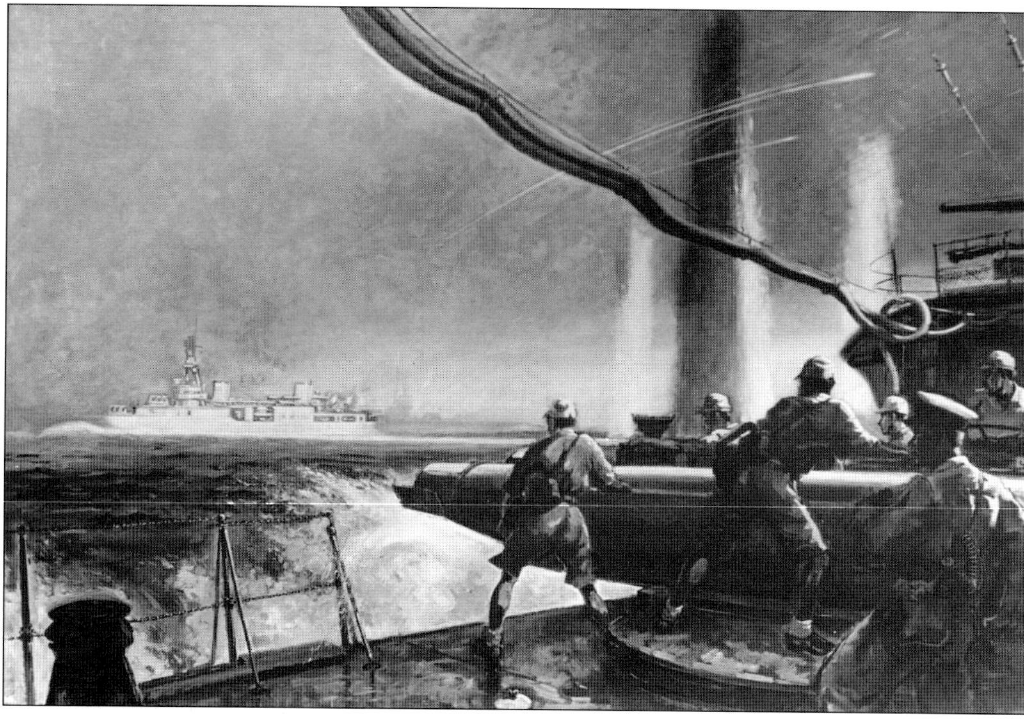

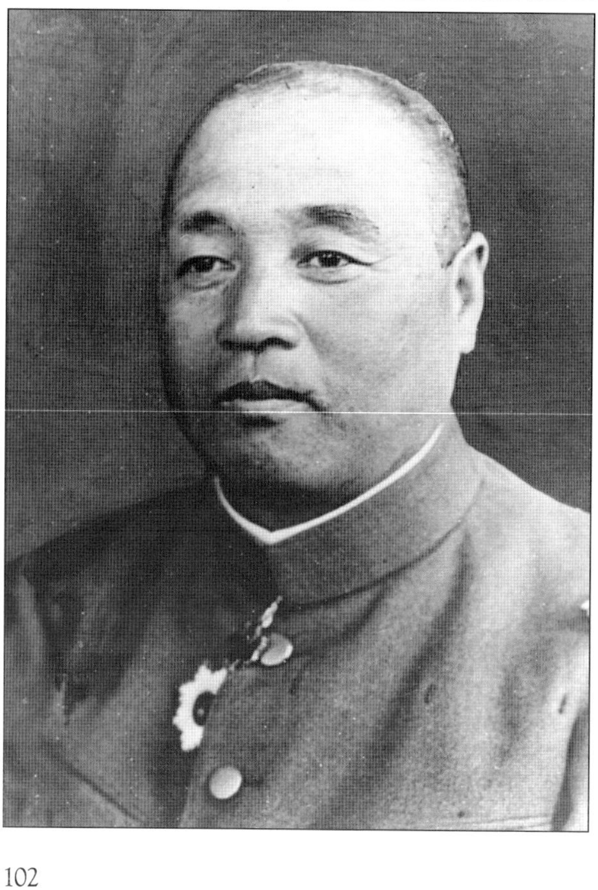

The Japanese wrote up their victory in fulsome terms, advertising how their destroyers sank two much bigger enemy cruisers without loss. They published artwork, such as this piece, illustrating their glorious victory. In it, *Houston* is shown apparently undamaged with a full battery of nine 8-inch guns and two sets of torpedo tubes. (USNHHC.)

In reality, at least five Japanese ships were sunk, one patrol boat and four troopships. Numerous others were damaged by Allied gunfire. Gen. Hitoshi Imamura, commander of the invasion troops, ended up in the water after his ship was torpedoed and sunk. Ironically, the torpedoes were fired by Japanese destroyers, which had missed the Allied cruisers. (USNHHC.)

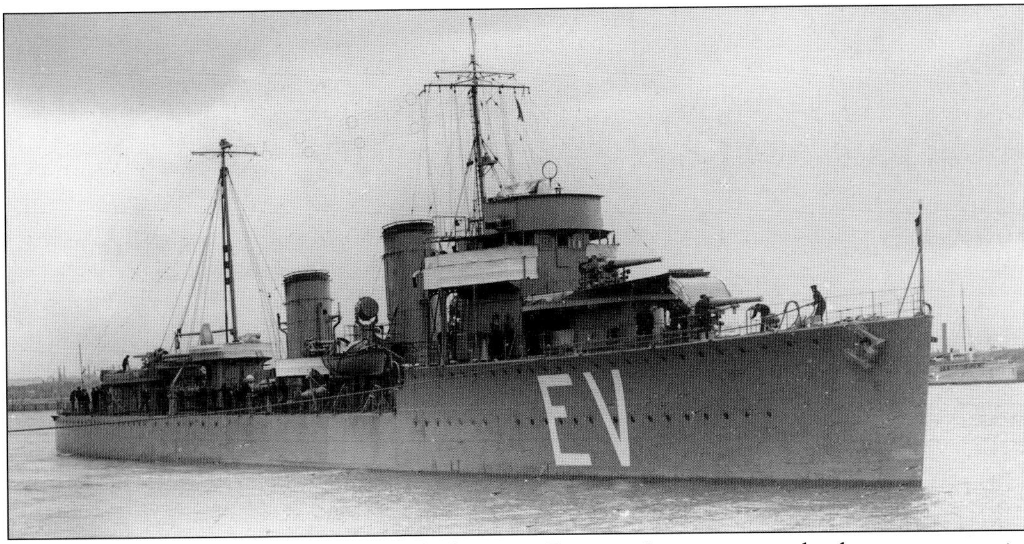

The battle's final casualty was the Dutch destroyer *Evertsen*. It was supposed to have accompanied *Perth* and *Houston*, but left port late. It saw the battle from a distance and attempted to escape the Java Sea while the Japanese were busy fighting the cruisers. It reached the Sunda Strait but was caught by two Japanese destroyers and forced aground. (RNDM.)

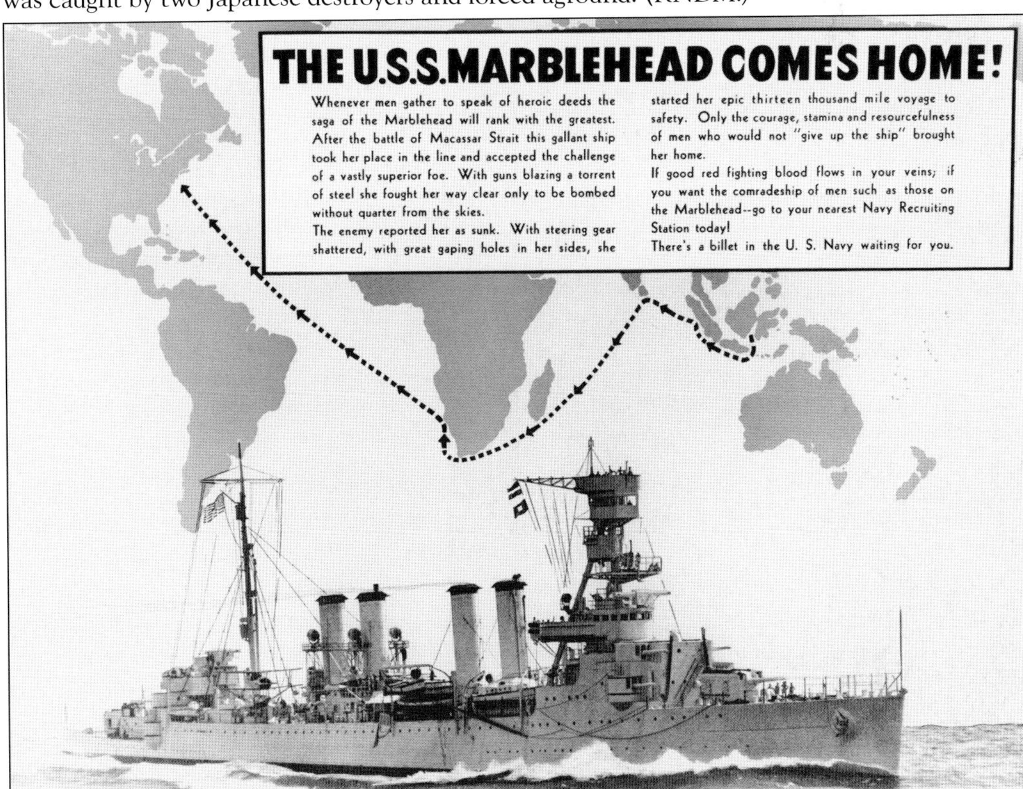

Marblehead made it home and served as a recruiting tool. But darkness closed around *Houston* and the other ships sunk at *Sunda Strait*. No word reached the Navy about the fate of *Houston* or its crew until the end of World War II. (USNHHC.)

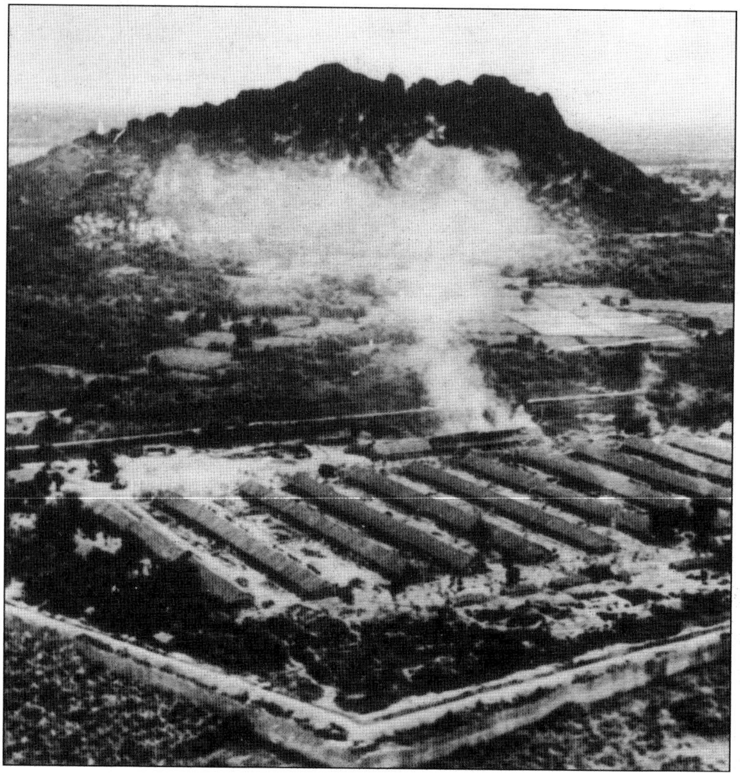

Of the 1,017 men aboard *Houston* at the Battle of Sunda Strait, only 372 survived. All were taken prisoner by the Japanese within days of the battle. The officers captured were sent to Japan. Most of the men ended up in prisoner-of-war camps in Thailand or Burma, where they were used as laborers. (HMM.)

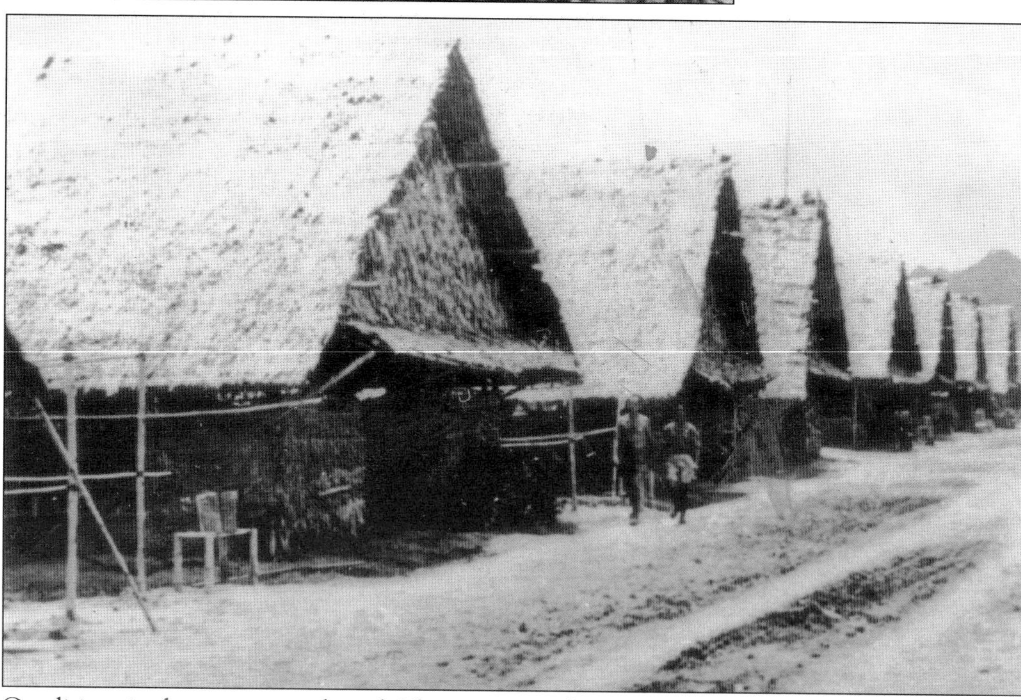

Conditions in the camps were brutal. The men were ill-fed and provided inadequate housing and medical care. Ninety-six survivors died while Japanese prisoners. Only one-quarter of the men aboard *Houston* on December 8, 1941, lived to return to the United States. (HMM.)

Navy Department
BUREAU OF NAVAL PERSONNELL
Washington, D. C.

30 June 1943

Mrs. Mildred A. Felix
4730 11th. N. E.
Seattle, Washington

My dear Mrs. Felix:

This Bureau when communicating with you on 10 March 1943 relative to your husband, Irving Arthur Felix, Yoeman first class, U. S. Navy was so hopeful that it would soon have definite favorable news of him for transmittal to you.

However, there is herewith quoted a short wave broadcast which was intercepted by the official Monitors of the Federal Communication Commission and transmitted to this Bureau. This broadcast is alleged to have emanated from the American prisoners of war on Java and sent by Ensign Herbert A. Leavitt, U.S. Navy, who has been reported and identified as a known of prisoner of war, through the medium of the International Red Cross.

"This is written from Headquarters USSHOUSTON DETACHMENT, ~~Java, April 30, 1943 to Mrs. I. A. Felix, 1528 East Third Street~~ Bend, Oregon. My dear Mrs. Felix it is with the deepest regret that I must inform you that on Easter Sunday last your husband, Irving A. Felix, Yoeman first class, United States Navy, left port for the last time to rejoin his ship, the Cruiser Houston, his Captain and some six hundred of his shipmates at their final anchorage. He was buried in the Bintambelen Cemetery, Batavia, Java with full military honors accorded him by his shipmates and friends. I know that little I can say or do at this time will assuage the grief of your bereavement. However, I offer my sincerest condolences and wonder if the thought that he made the supreme sacrifice in the service of his country can in any way mitigate hisloss. Respectfully yours, Herbert A. Leavitt, Ensighn United States Navy, Commanding."

"Headquarters USS HOUSTON Detachment, Java, April 26, 1943 to Bureau of Navigation, Navy Department, Washington, D. C. Subject---Report of Death, Yoeman first class Irving A. Felix United States Navy, Service Number unknown, Died this date of Pulmonary Tuberculosis and other causes at the Military Hospital Java. His remains are interred in plot 116 Bintabelen Cemetery Batavia. His next of kin are notified unofficially through the same channels. Signed Herbert A. Leavitt, Ensign U. S. Navy, Commanding. Please forward this letter to the people concerned"

For the families, it was as if their loved ones had disappeared. Japan released no information on the fate of *Houston* crewmen, and only a few dribs of information leaked through Japan's Bamboo Curtain. During the war, families dreaded receiving letters like this one. (HMM.)

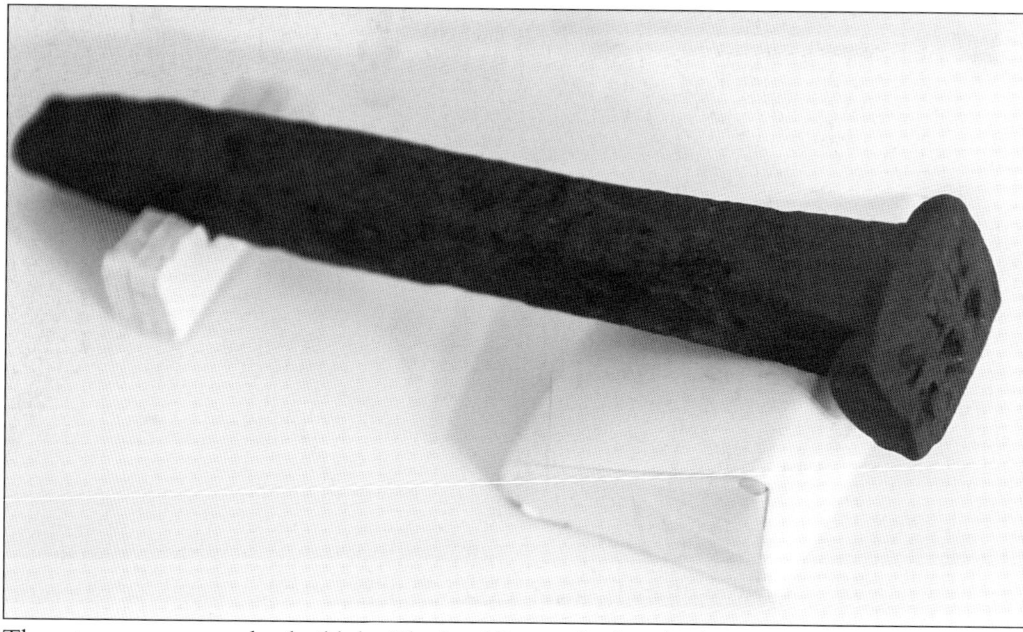

The prisoners were used to build the Thailand-Burma Railroad. This was the railroad featured in *The Bridge over the River Kwai.* So many POWs died building the railroad it became known as the Death Railroad. This spike came from the railroad, kept by a *Houston* survivor after liberation. (WL.)

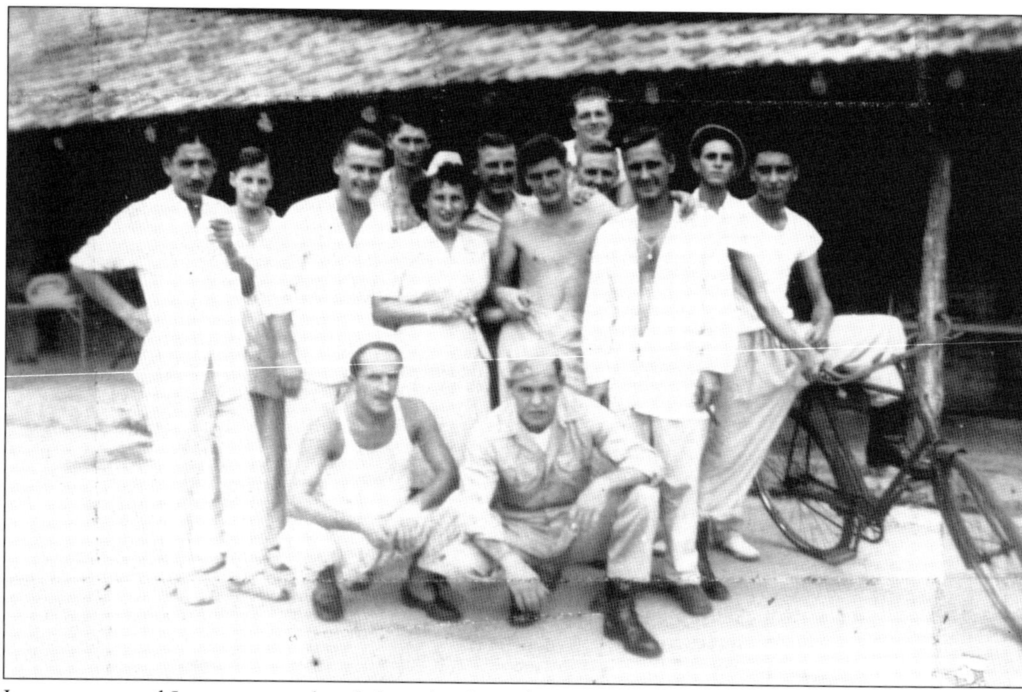

It was not until Japan surrendered that the fate of *Houston's* crew was discovered. The survivors, when discovered, were quickly evacuated to Allied territory. Here, a dozen *Houston* survivors are photographed in Calcutta, India, along with a nurse and an orderly (far left) at a rehabilitation camp in September 1945. (HMM.)

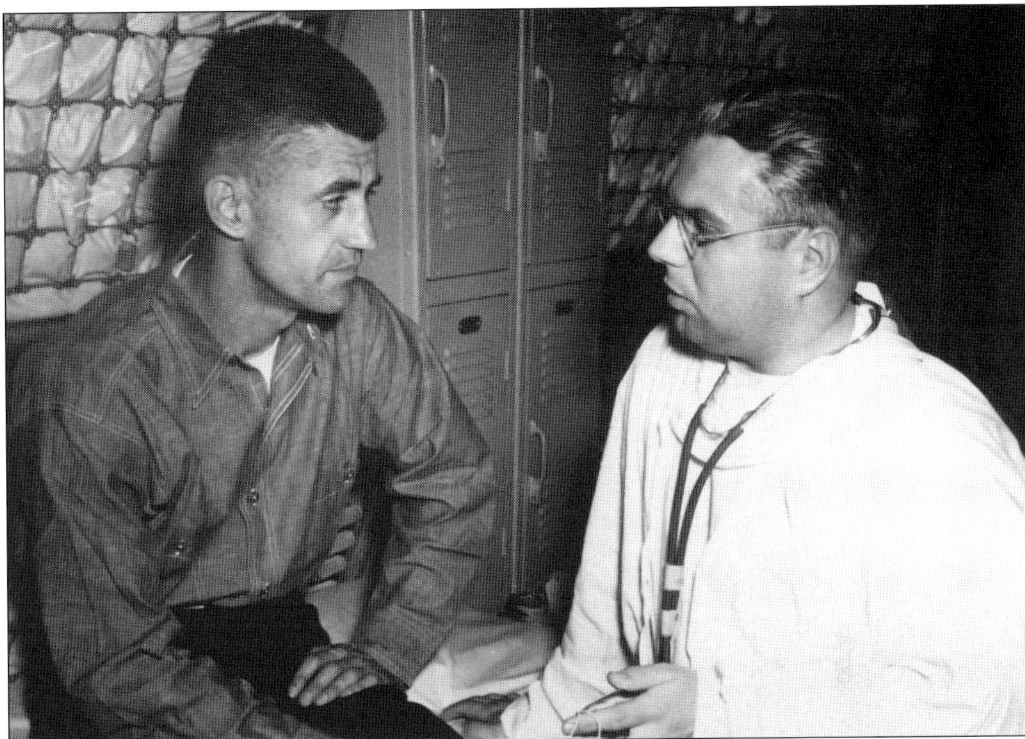

The senior survivor was Cdr. Arthur Maher, *Houston's* gunnery officer. He is being checked by a medical officer after his liberation. Maher became senior officer at the Omori Camp No. 8 outside Tokyo. After liberation, he witnessed the formal surrender of Japan aboard USS *Missouri* at Admiral Nimitz's invitation. (NARA.)

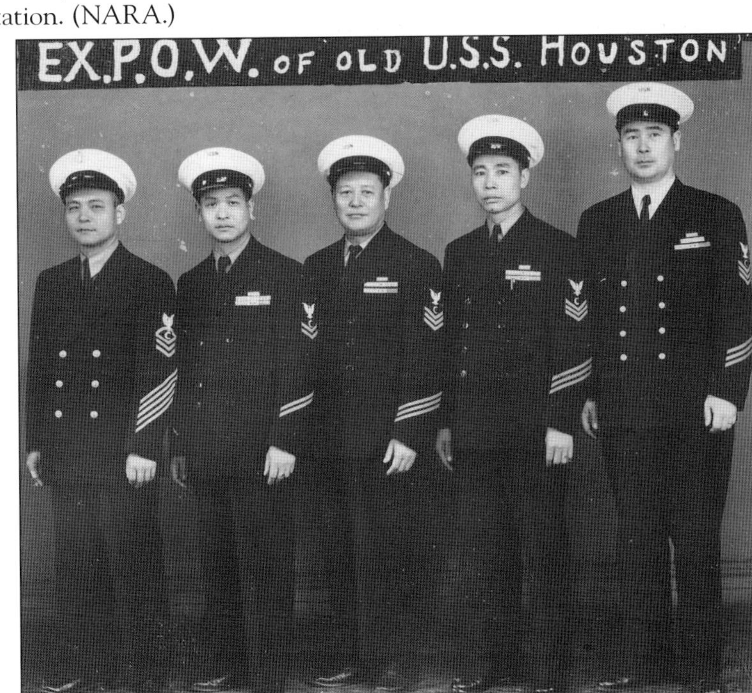

Five *Houston* survivors were Chinese American. They had joined at Hong Kong and served as mess stewards and cooks. They resumed their Navy careers after liberation, several gaining US citizenship. This picture was taken after the war. From left to right, they are Chief Steward Marco Su, Steward 2nd Class Shun Ching Kei, Steward 1st Class Yu Kun, Steward 1st Class Ah Chie, and Steward 1st Class Chu Lin Tsao. (USNHHC.)

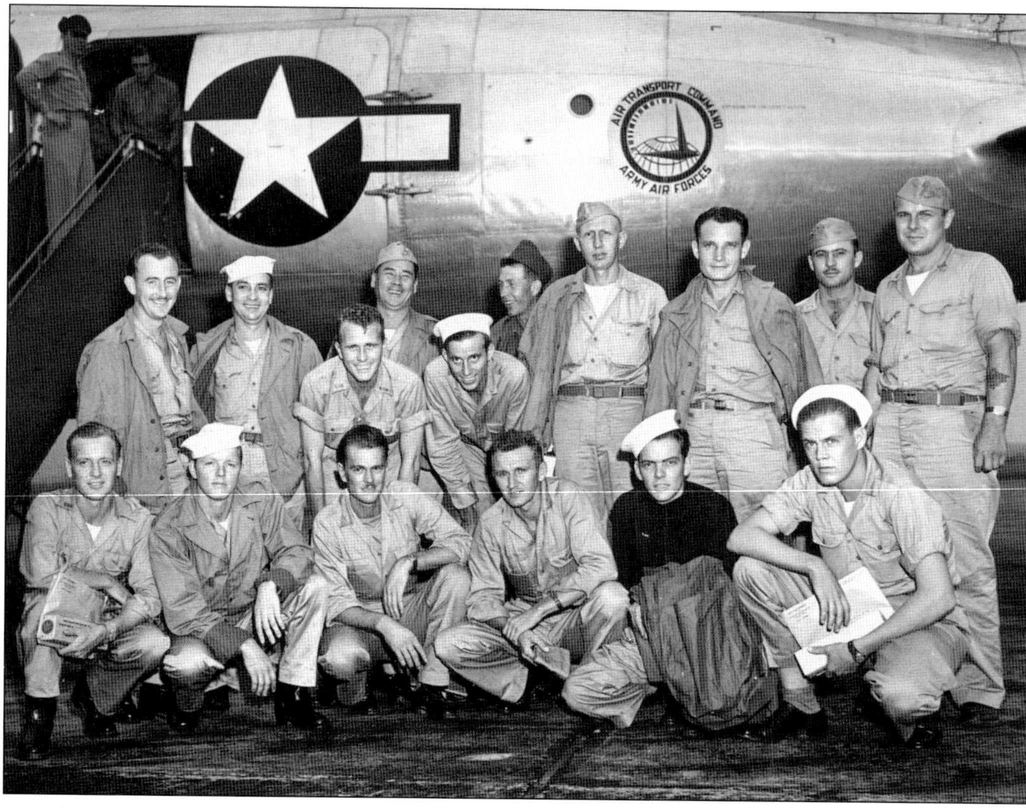

The survivors were repatriated to the United States as soon as possible. This photograph captures the September 18, 1945, Washington, DC, arrival of 15 *Houston* survivors and another former POW, who had been captured by the Japanese at Corregidor in the Philippines. They were all transported via an Air Transport Command aircraft. (USN.)

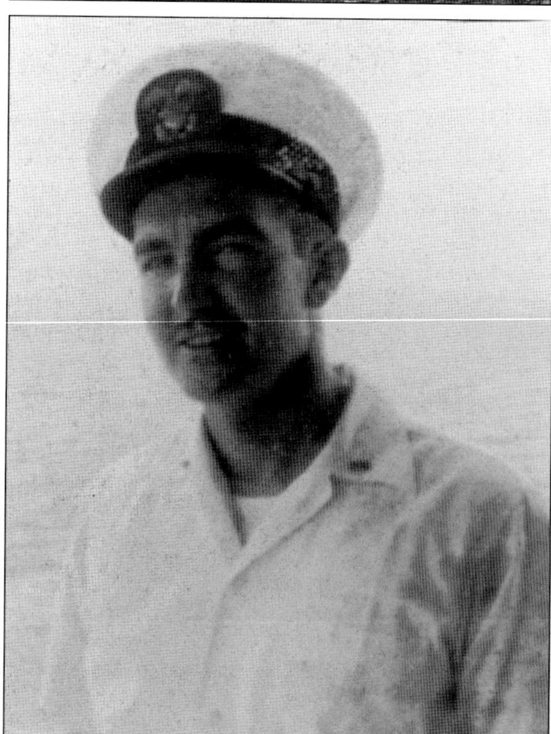

Another survivor was Walter G. Winslow. An ensign when he reported aboard *Houston* in 1941, he was a member of *Houston's* aviation section. He continued his career in the US Navy, retiring as a commander. He also wrote one of the first published accounts of the Battle of Sunda Strait, which appeared in the *United States Naval Institute Proceedings* in February 1949. (USNHHC.)

Six

REMEMBRANCE

The cruisers were initially "missing" when they failed to report the next day. By March 14, when it was obvious they were not simply late arriving in Australia, *Houston's* status was changed to "missing and presumed lost."

In Houston, loss of its namesake created disbelief, shock, grief, anger, and finally, determination. The city was determined to avenge the loss, and started a drive to replace the *Houston*—both ship and crew. In May 1942, a recruiting drive started seeking 1,000 Houstonians to join the Navy, replacing the men lost aboard *Houston*. By the end of the month, 1,650 men had volunteered, with the first 1,000 designated the Houston Volunteers.

That was not enough. The city started a bond drive to buy a new cruiser *Houston*. It ended on December 21, 1942. By then, it had raised $85 million—enough to buy a new cruiser (USS *Houston*, CL-82), with enough left over to buy a light aircraft carrier (USS *San Jacinto*, CVL-30). Both ships saw combat in the Pacific during World War II, under arduous conditions.

The Navy remembered in its own way, sinking the Japanese ships that fought at the Battle of Sunda Strait. The first one was sunk during the Battle of Midway, one month before the date Japan officially claimed to have sunk *Houston*: July 2, 1942. The Navy also named warships after *Houston* crew members who went down with the ship, most notably Captain Rooks and Chaplain Rentz.

Houston continued remembering its namesake cruiser, especially after the war ended when the mystery surrounding its loss was peeled away. In 1972, divers discovered the location of *Houston* and *Perth*. Three collections of *Houston* artifacts exist in three Houston locations, the M.D. Anderson Library at the University of Houston, the Heritage Society Museum at Sam Houston Park, and the Houston Maritime Museum. Collections include items donated by survivors and their families and objects recovered from the wrecks.

A monument to the Houston Volunteers was erected where they were sworn in, and a monument to the cruiser was erected in 1995. *Houston's* memory grows in stature, even as it grows more distant in time.

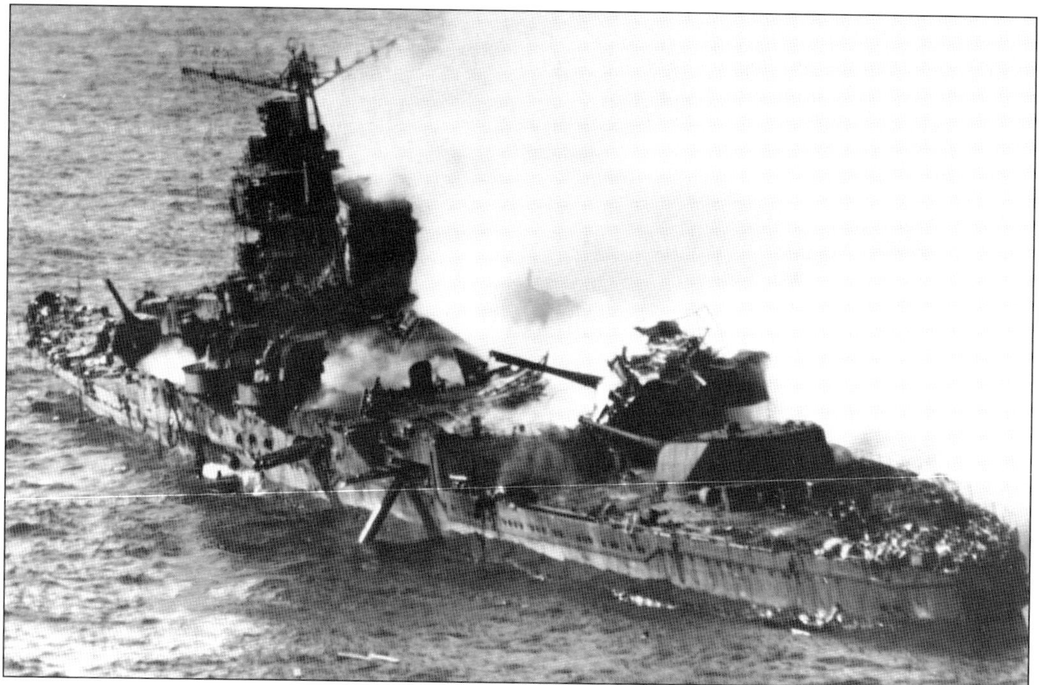

Only two Japanese ships at the Battle of Sunda Strait survived World War II. The first one to go down was heavy cruiser *Mikuma*, shown here shortly before being sunk by US Navy aircraft at the Battle of Midway. *Fubuki* was sunk at the Battle of Cape Esperance in October 1942. (USNHHC.)

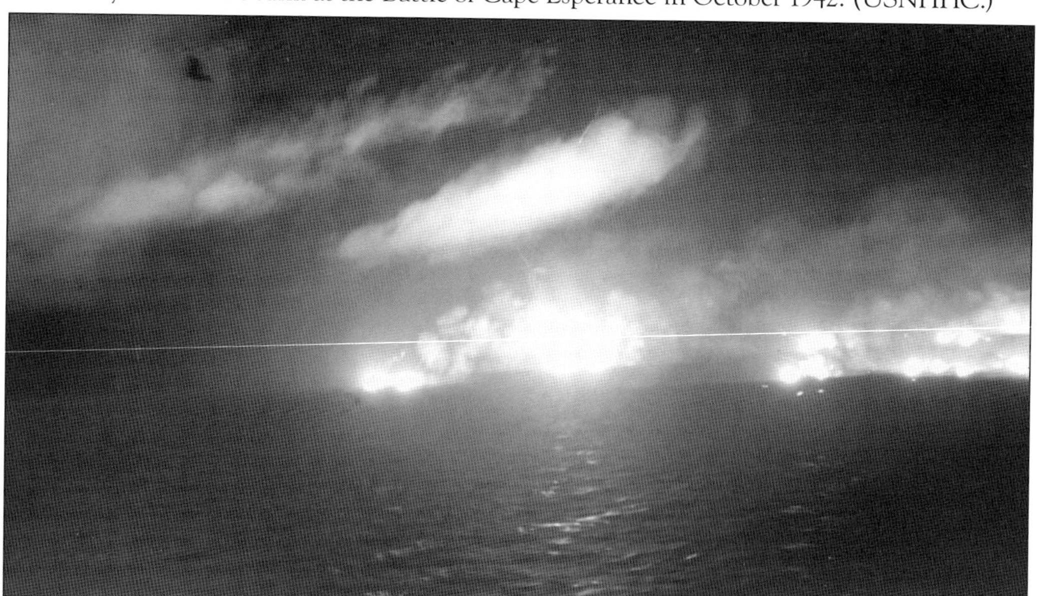

Jesse Oldendorf, *Houston's* next-to-last commander, achieved a special piece of payback on October 25, 1944. Then a rear admiral, he commanded US Navy forces covering Surigao Strait. A Japanese fleet attempted to force the passage, and Oldendorf destroyed them in a night action, the last surface fleet action of World War II. Among the Japanese ships sunk was the *Mogami*, another Sunda Strait veteran. Shown is a broadside from Oldendorf's flagship *Pennsylvania* during the battle. (USNHHC.)

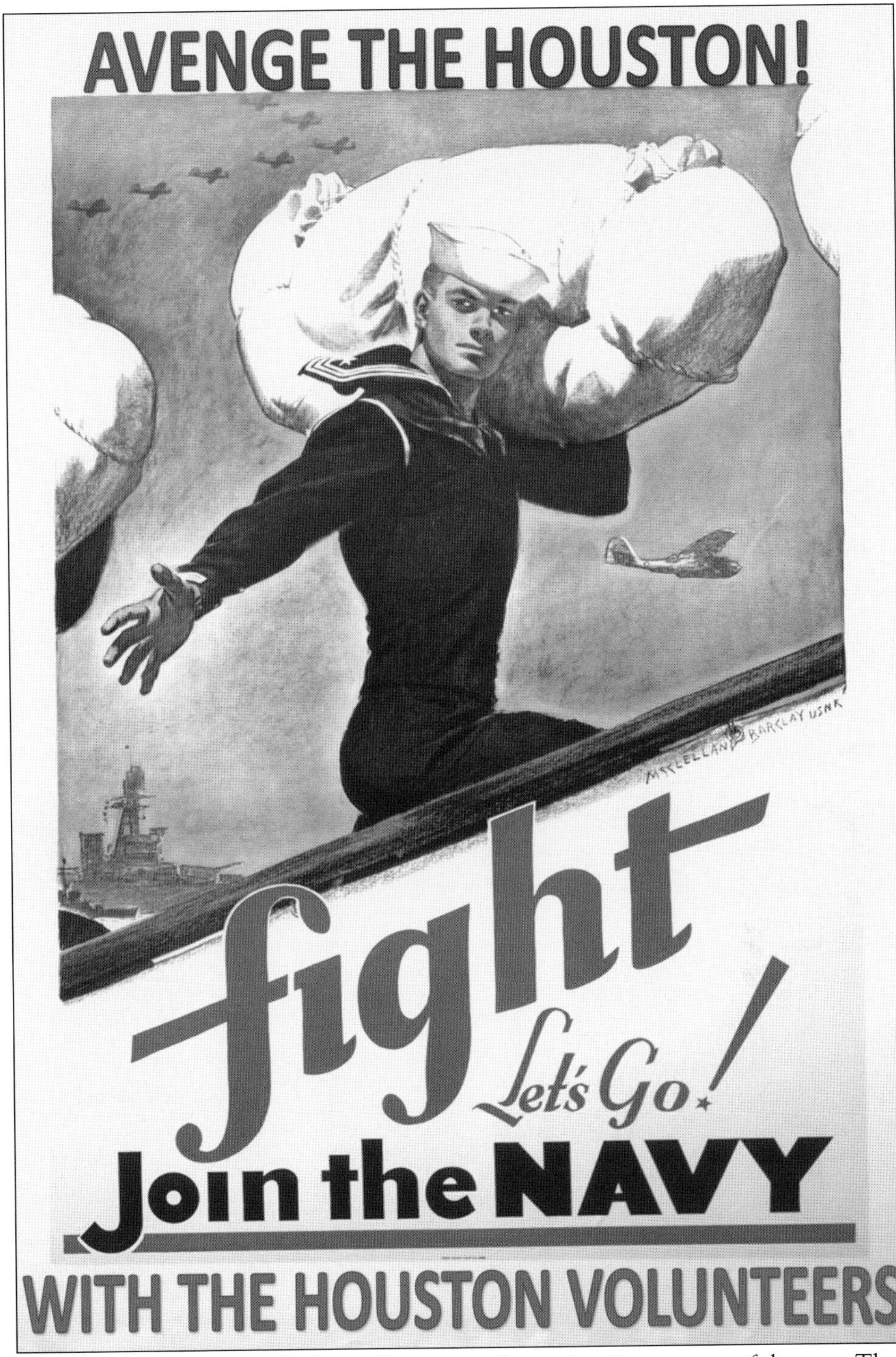

Houston turned its grief at the loss of its namesake cruiser into purposeful anger. The city organized a recruiting drive aimed at recruiting 1,000 volunteers to replace the cruiser's crew. A Navy recruiting poster, shown in this recreation, was modified to add the inscription "Avenge the *Houston* with the Houston Volunteers." (AC.)

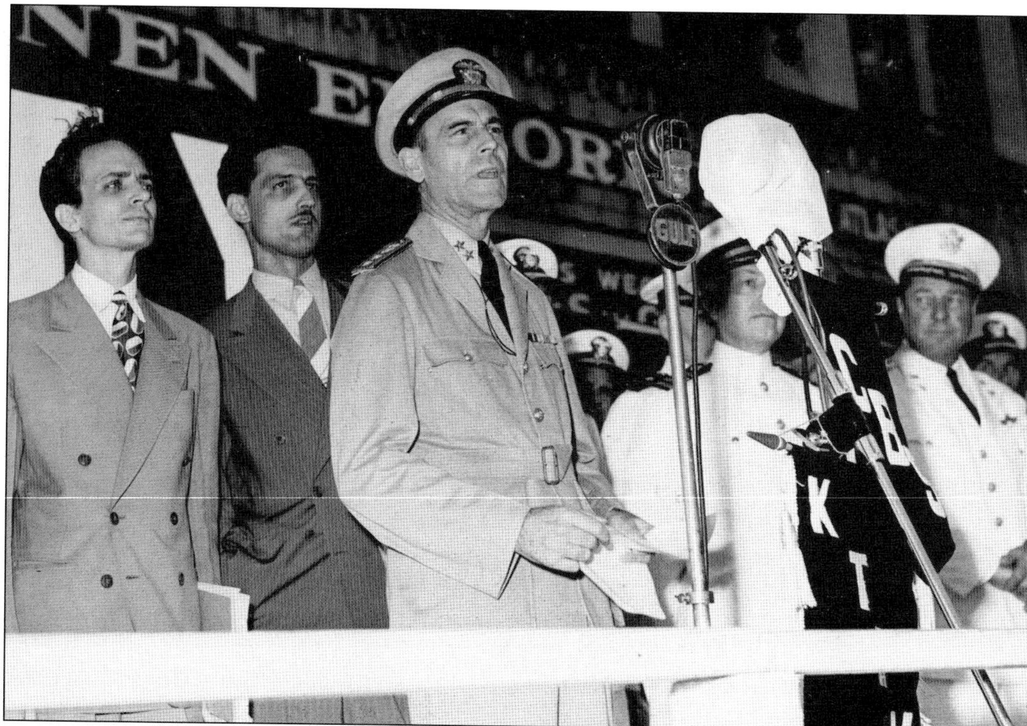

The drive netted 1,650 volunteers. On Memorial Day 1942, ninety days after *Houston's* sinking, 1,000 of these men were sworn in as the Houston Volunteers in a ceremony attended by over 100,000. Rear Adm. William Glassford, the last admiral to use *Houston* as a flagship, administered the Navy Oath to the recruits. (USN.)

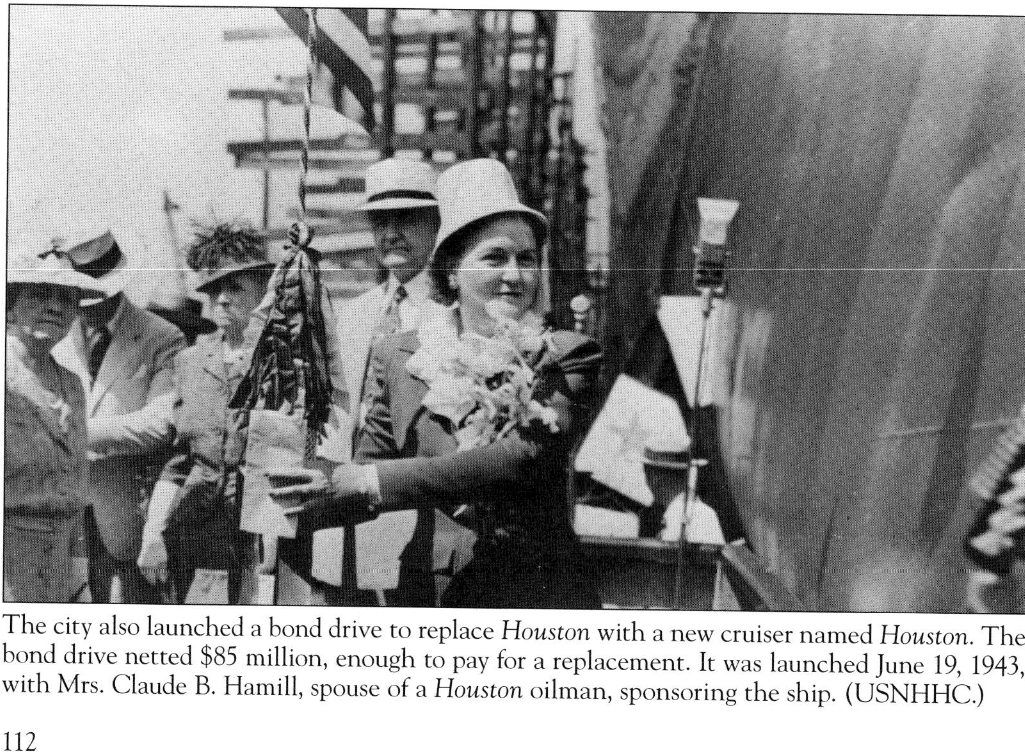

The city also launched a bond drive to replace *Houston* with a new cruiser named *Houston*. The bond drive netted $85 million, enough to pay for a replacement. It was launched June 19, 1943, with Mrs. Claude B. Hamill, spouse of a *Houston* oilman, sponsoring the ship. (USNHHC.)

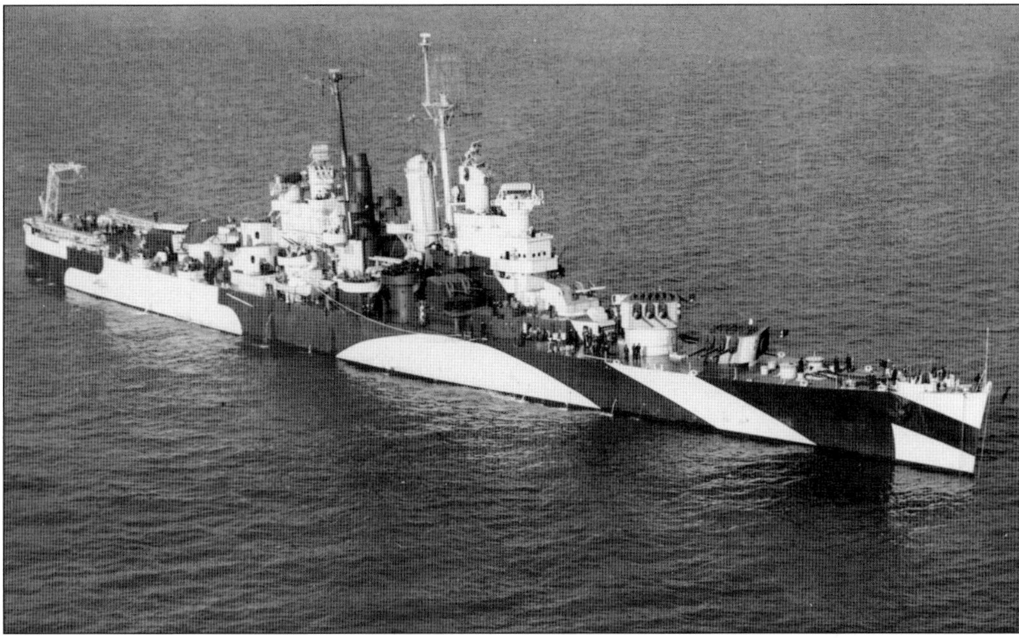

This *Houston* (CL-81) was a *Cleveland*-class light cruiser, armed with 12 six-inch and 12 five-inch guns. It was 2,000 tons bigger than the previous *Houston*. It fought at the Battle of the Philippine Sea and supported the invasion of Palau. Only one member of the Houston Volunteers served on this ship. (USNHHC.)

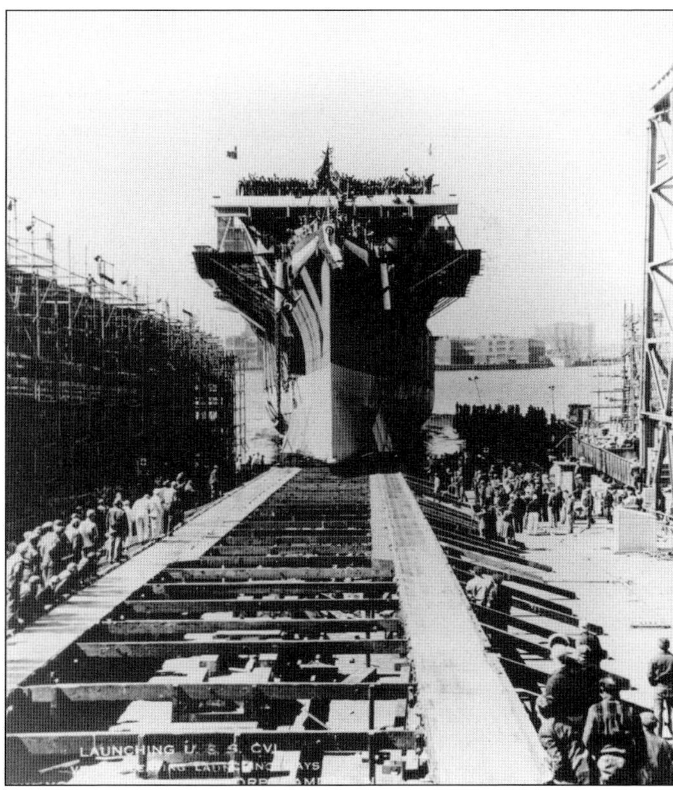

The bond drive more than paid for a new cruiser. There was enough money left over to pay for an aircraft carrier, too. As a result, the Navy launched USS *San Jacinto* (named for the Texas War of Independence battle fought just east of Houston) on September 26, 1943. (USNHHC.)

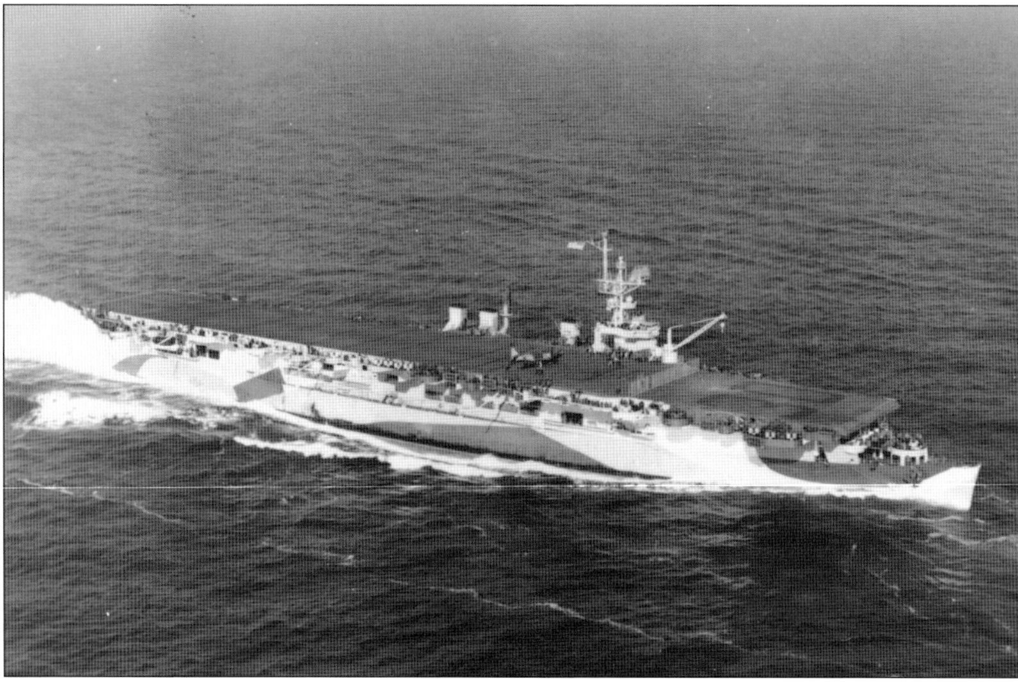

San Jacinto (CVL-30) was an *Independence*-class light aircraft carrier. Built on the hull of *Cleveland*-class cruisers, they were smaller than the *Essex*-class fleet carriers and carried 45 aircraft. *San Jacinto* joined the Fast Carrier Task Force of the Pacific Fleet in early 1944. (USNHHC.)

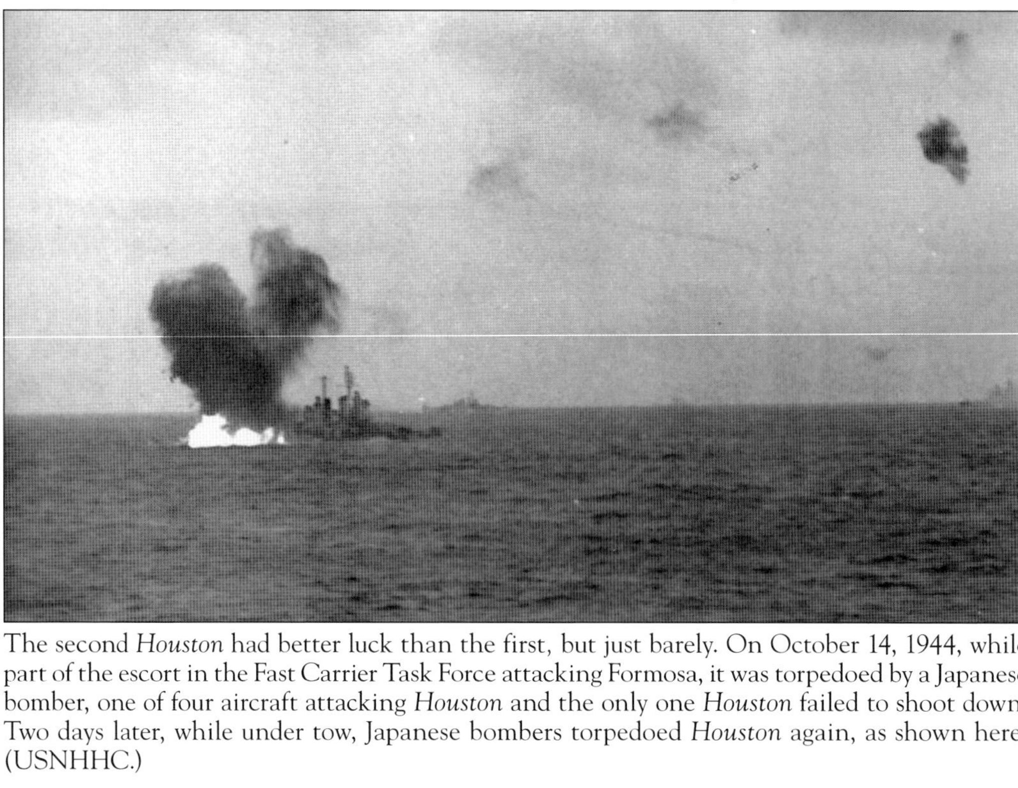

The second *Houston* had better luck than the first, but just barely. On October 14, 1944, while part of the escort in the Fast Carrier Task Force attacking Formosa, it was torpedoed by a Japanese bomber, one of four aircraft attacking *Houston* and the only one *Houston* failed to shoot down. Two days later, while under tow, Japanese bombers torpedoed *Houston* again, as shown here. (USNHHC.)

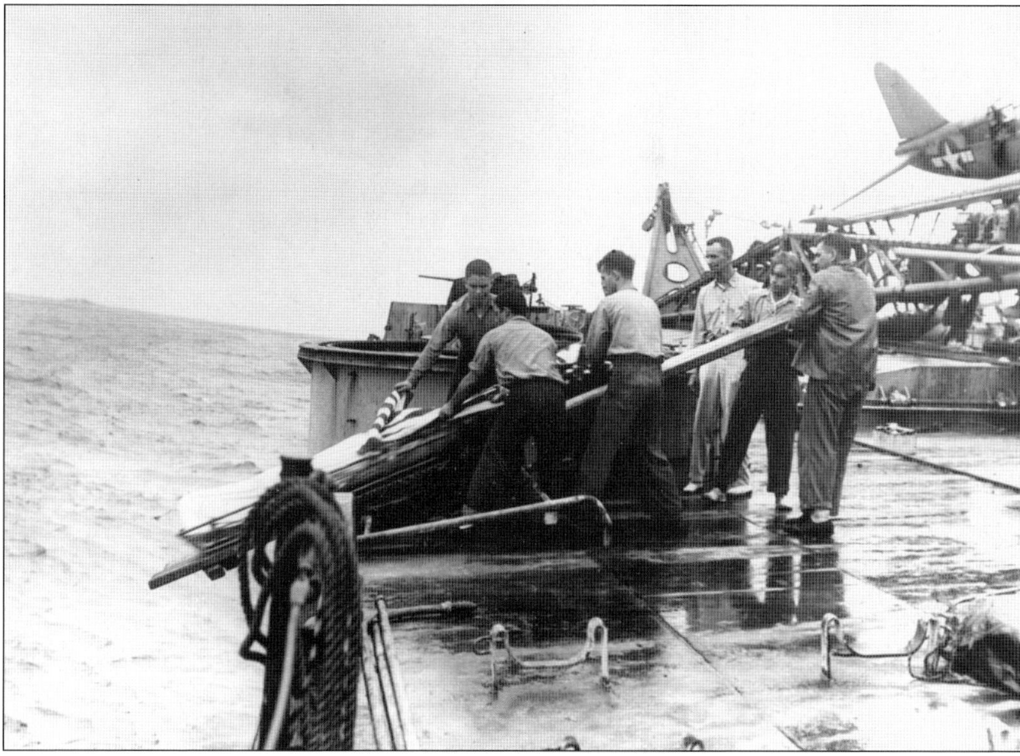

It was an echo of the Battle of Makassar Strait when a bomb killed 48 men in the heavy cruiser's No. 3 turret. The second *Houston* lost 55 crew members in the first torpedo hit. They were buried at sea on October 16, as shown here. Despite being hit by a second torpedo the next day, *Houston* made it back to the states and was repaired before the war ended. (USNHHC.)

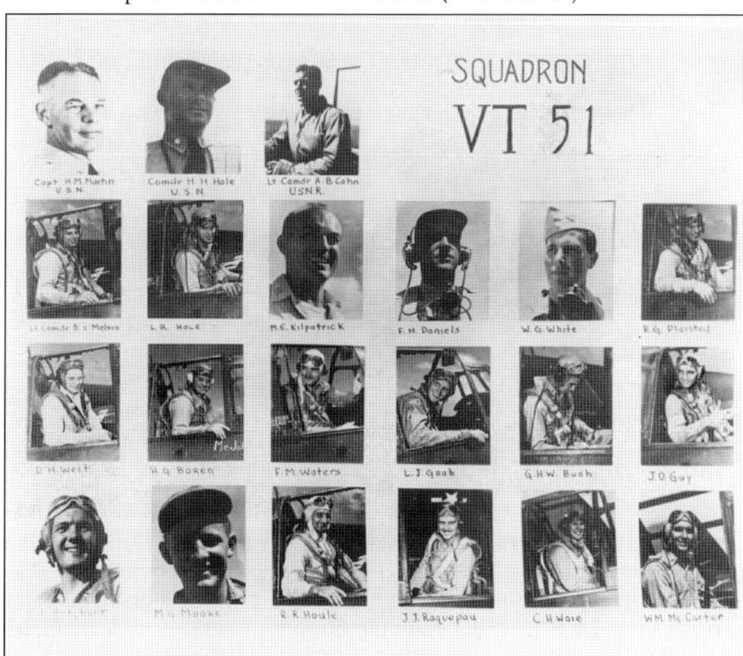

San Jacinto had an easier war, although it participated in every major carrier action after April 1944. Its biggest claim to fame was one of its aviators, a torpedo bomber pilot named George Herbert Walker Bush, shown second from the right and second from the bottom in this collage of Squadron VT-51's pilots. He went on to become the 41st president of the United States and, later, called Houston home. (USNHHC.)

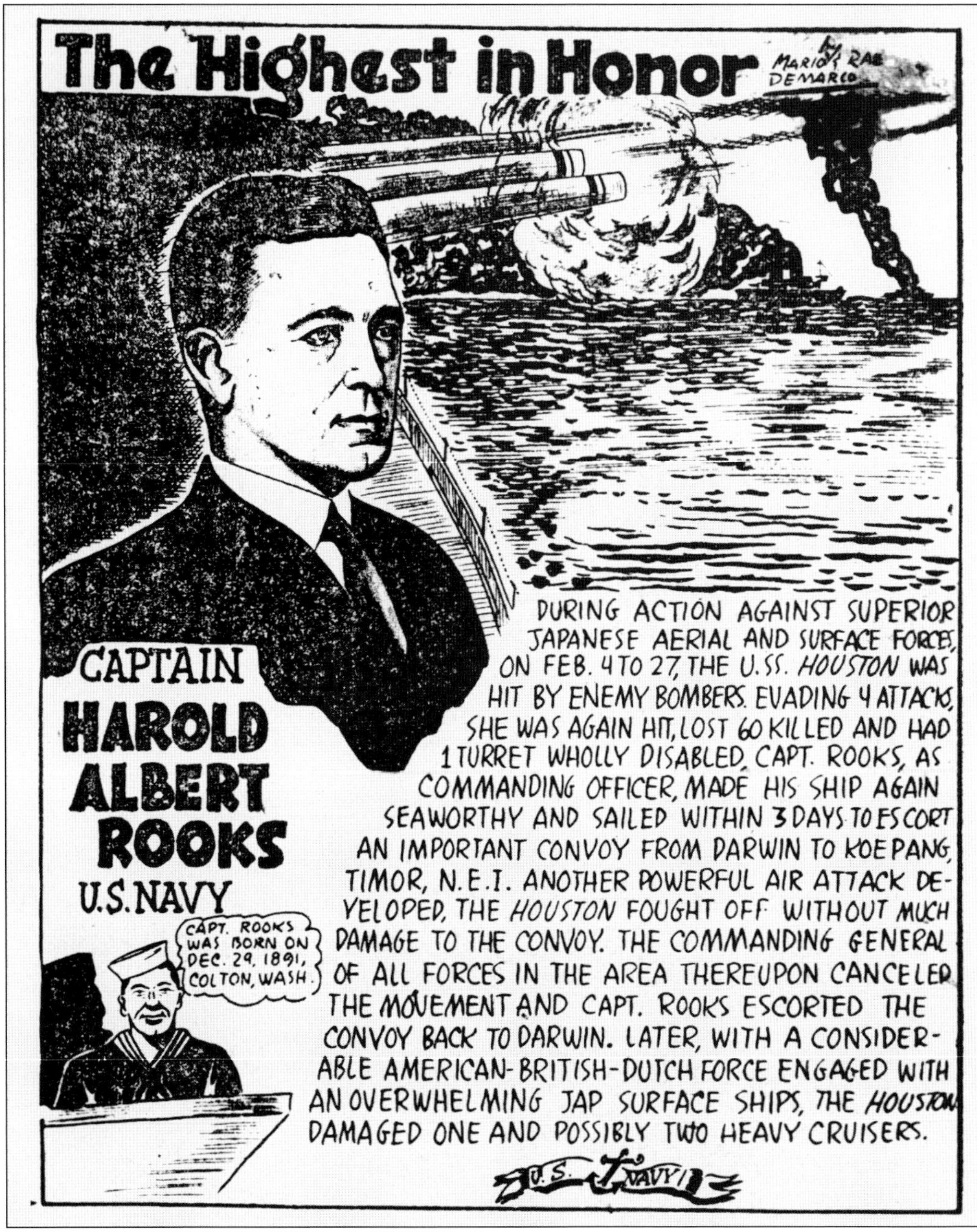

After World War II, the Navy remembered the sacrifices made by the men of the first cruiser *Houston*. Capt. Albert Rooks was awarded a posthumous Medal of Honor. The citation, shown here in a vignette published in *Navy Times* on October 23, 1954, was written before the Navy learned about Rook's actions during the Battle of Sunda Strait. (USNHHC.)

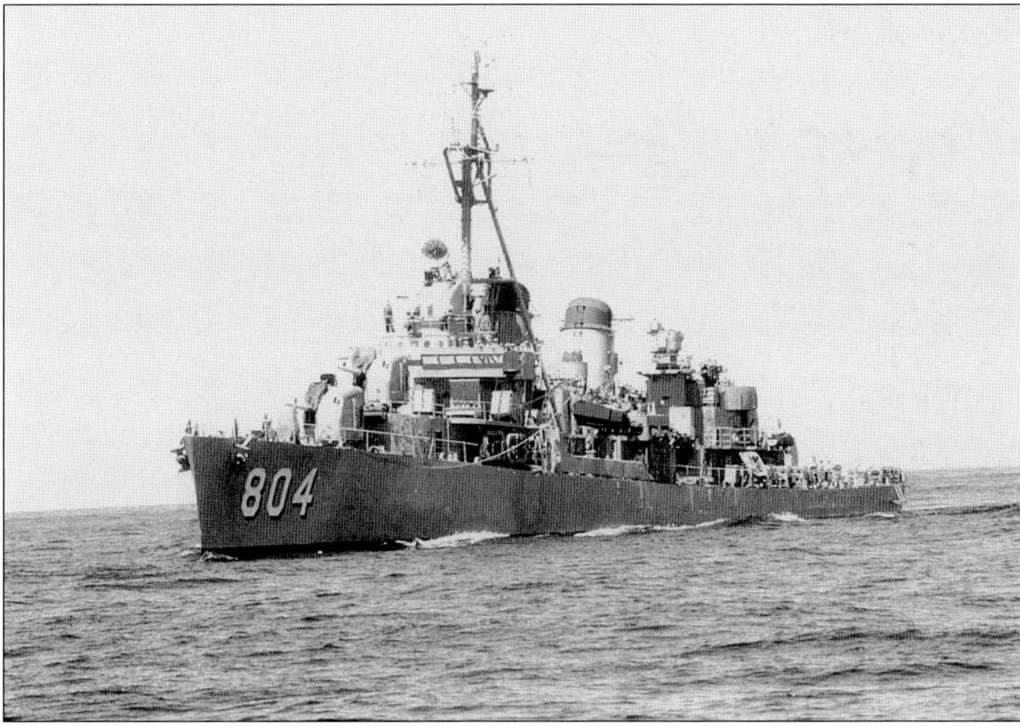

The Navy named a *Fletcher*-class destroyer for Captain Rooks, USS *Rooks* (DD-804). It was launched on June 6, 1944. Rooks's widow, Edith R. Rooks, sponsored the ship. USS *Rooks* fought at Iwo Jima and Okinawa, earning three battle stars for World War II services and two battle stars for service in the Korean conflict. This picture shows *Rooks* in 1955. (USNHHC.)

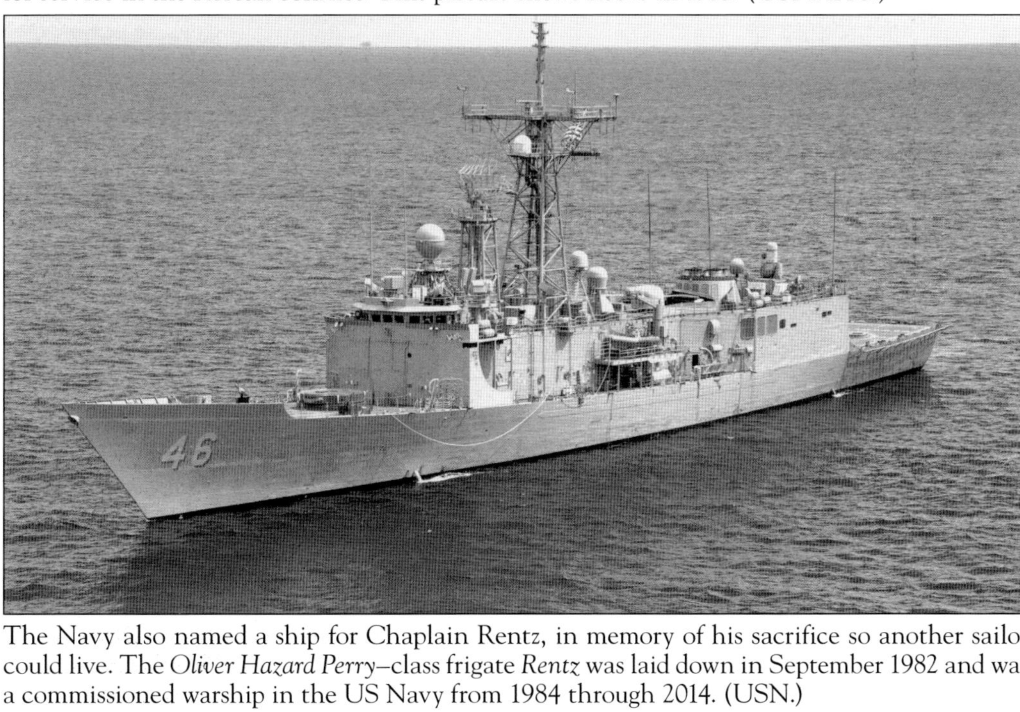

The Navy also named a ship for Chaplain Rentz, in memory of his sacrifice so another sailor could live. The *Oliver Hazard Perry*–class frigate *Rentz* was laid down in September 1982 and was a commissioned warship in the US Navy from 1984 through 2014. (USN.)

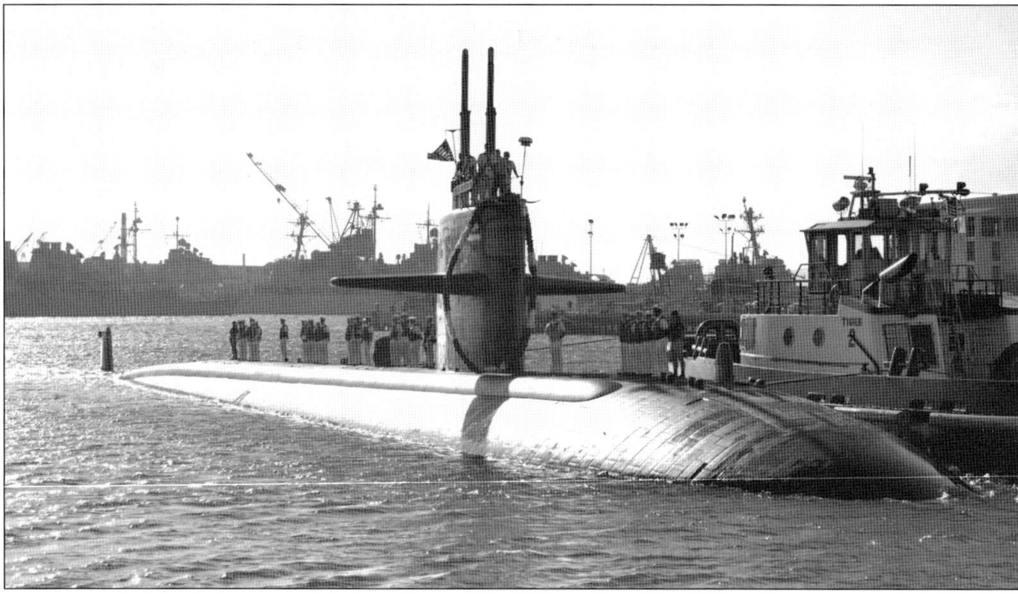

The light cruiser *Houston* was scrapped in 1959. The Navy named a third warship for the City of Houston. In 1982, the Navy commissioned USS *Houston* (SSN-713), a *Los Angeles*–class nuclear attack submarine. The ship remained in service until decommissioned in 2016. It appeared in the movie *The Hunt for Red October*. (USN.)

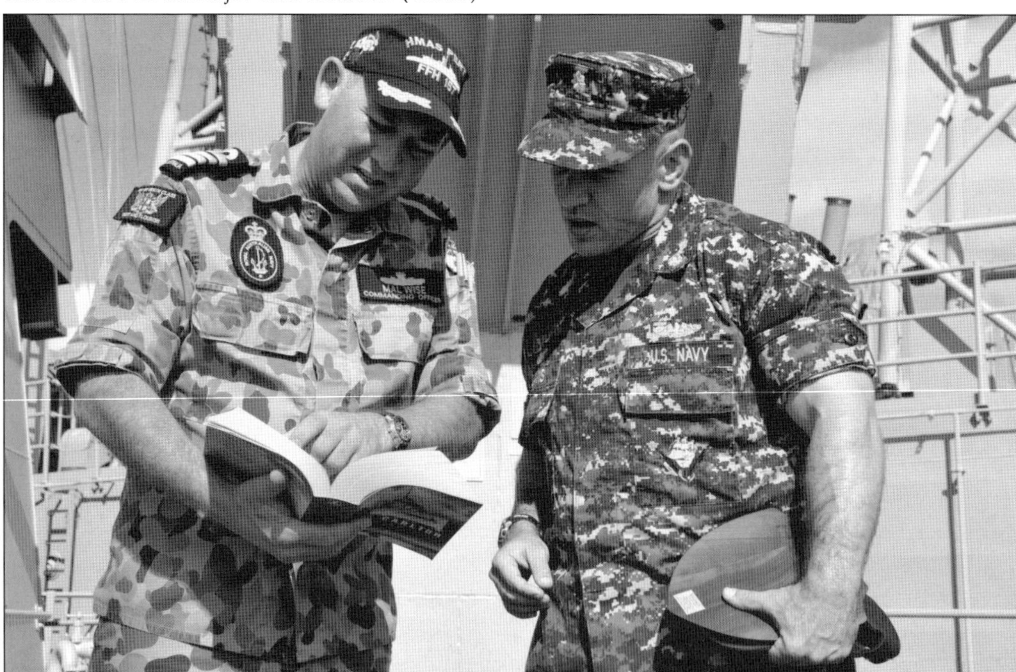

Nor did Australia forget *Perth*. The Royal Australian Navy has named two ships for *Perth*. The most recent is an ANZAC-class frigate launched in 2006. In 2012, Malcolm Wise, captain of that *Perth*, met Cdr. Paul Davis, commanding USS *Houston*, and presented Captain Davis with a book titled *Cruiser: The Life and Loss of HMAS* Perth to commemorate the 70th anniversary of the Battle of Sunda Strait. (USN.)

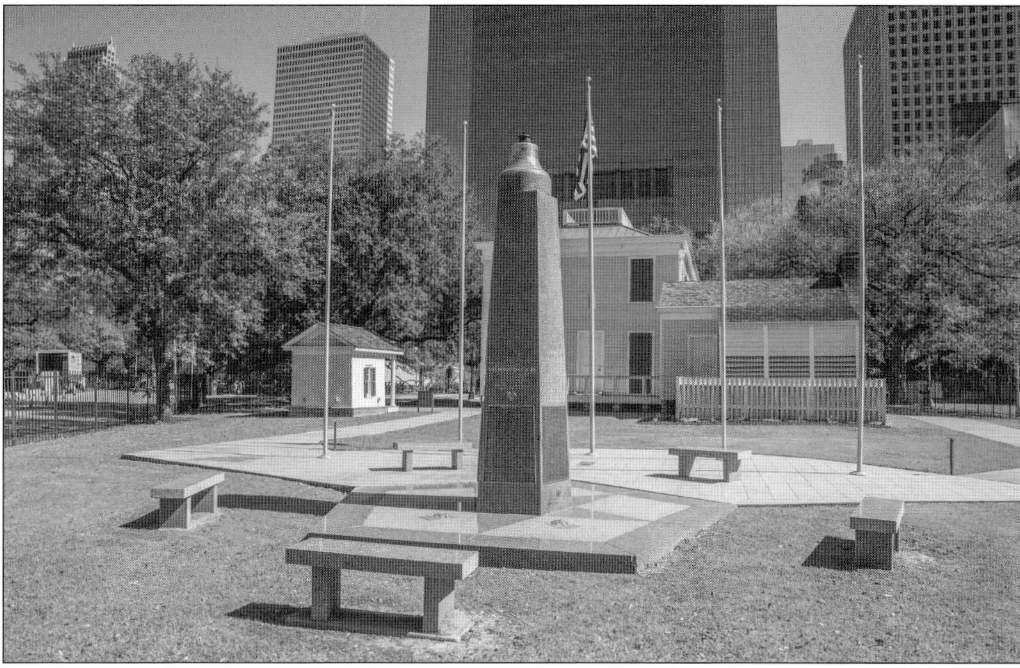

The City of Houston remembers the cruiser *Houston* in many ways. In 1998, citizens erected a monument to the ship in Sam Houston Park in downtown Houston. The names of its crew are inscribed on plaques on the five sides of the obelisk. Every year, on the Saturday closest to March 1, a memorial service is held there. (WL.)

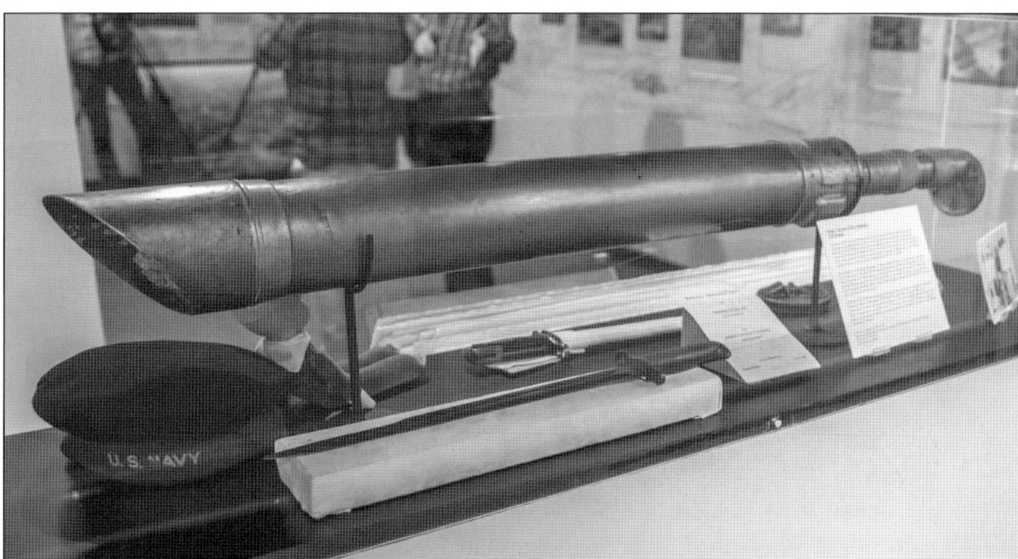

The Heritage Society Museum at Sam Houston Park contains a display of *Houston* artifacts. Among them is this bridge telescope. It was recovered from the wreck during a 1973 dive sanctioned by the Indonesian government. (WL.)

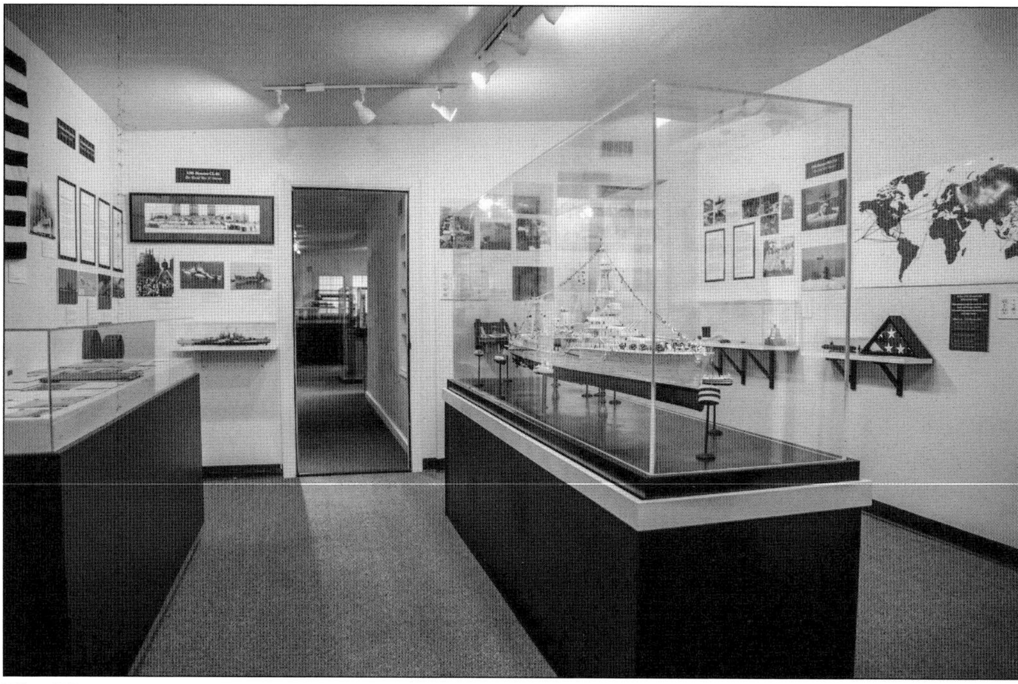

The Houston Maritime Museum recently opened a *Houston* room, dedicated to all four naval vessels that bore the name. Pride of place is given to the second *Houston*, the heavy cruiser launched in 1929. (WL.)

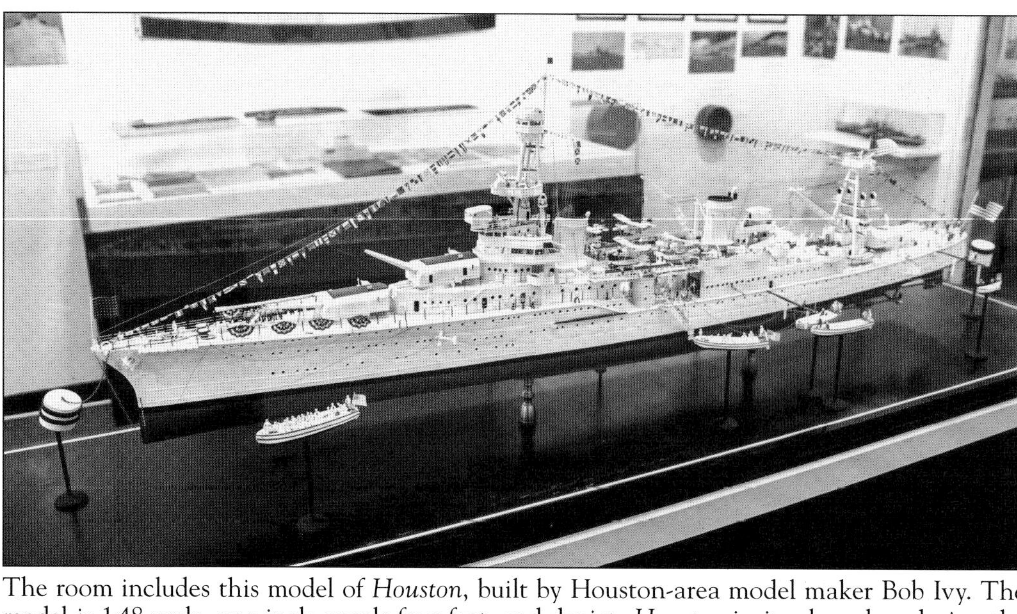

The room includes this model of *Houston*, built by Houston-area model maker Bob Ivy. The model is 1:48 scale, one inch equals four feet, and depicts *Houston* in its glory days during the 1930s. (WL.)

Also on display are artifacts donated by survivors from *Houston's* crew. This includes items like this locket, brought back by a member of the crew after his captivity as a POW. (WL.)

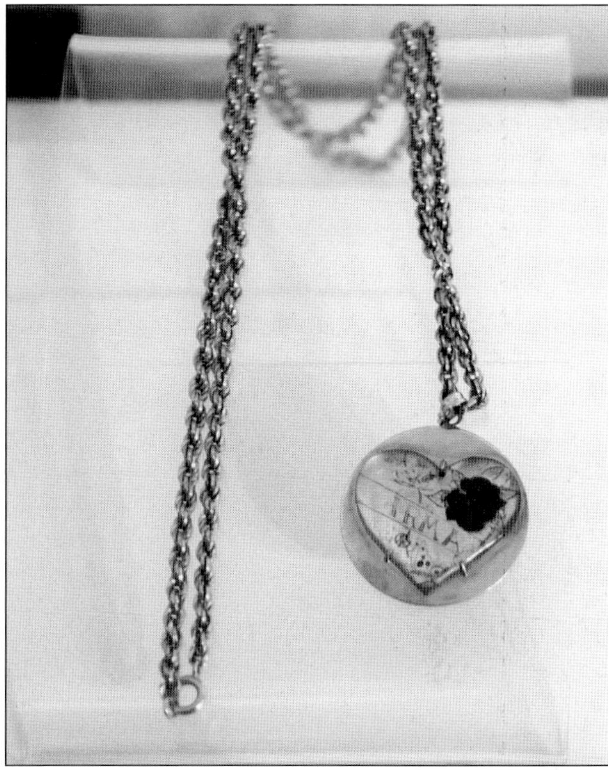

Another collection of *Houston* artifacts can be found on the third floor of the M.D. Anderson Library at the University of Houston. There are two sets of display cases on the walls and several stand-alone displays, which showcase uniforms and a model of *Houston*. The flag was made by members of the *Houston's* crew while prisoners of war in Thailand; they successfully kept it hidden from the Japanese during the war. (AC.)

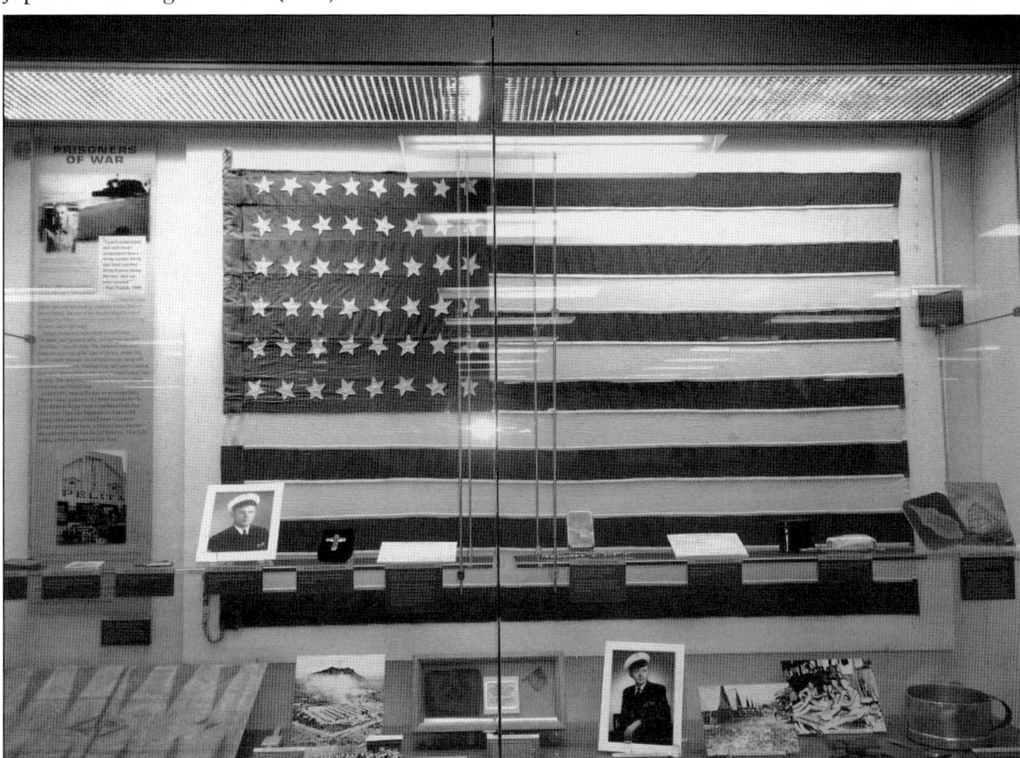

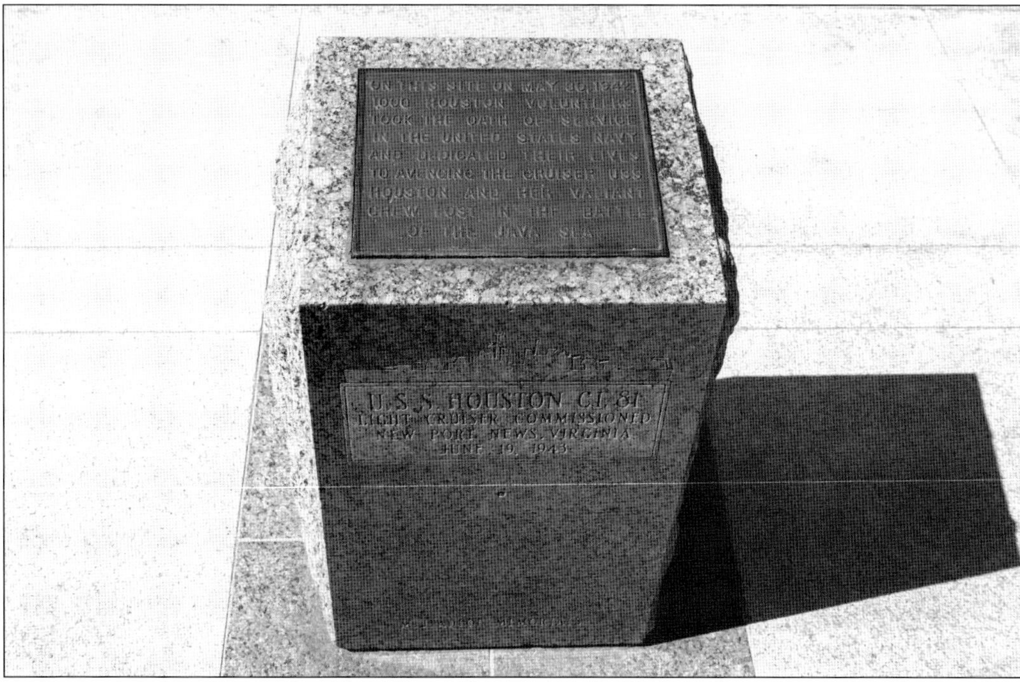

The Houston Volunteers are remembered, too. This monument to these men now stands at the site where they were sworn in to the Navy, at Main Street near McKinney Avenue in downtown Houston. (WL.)

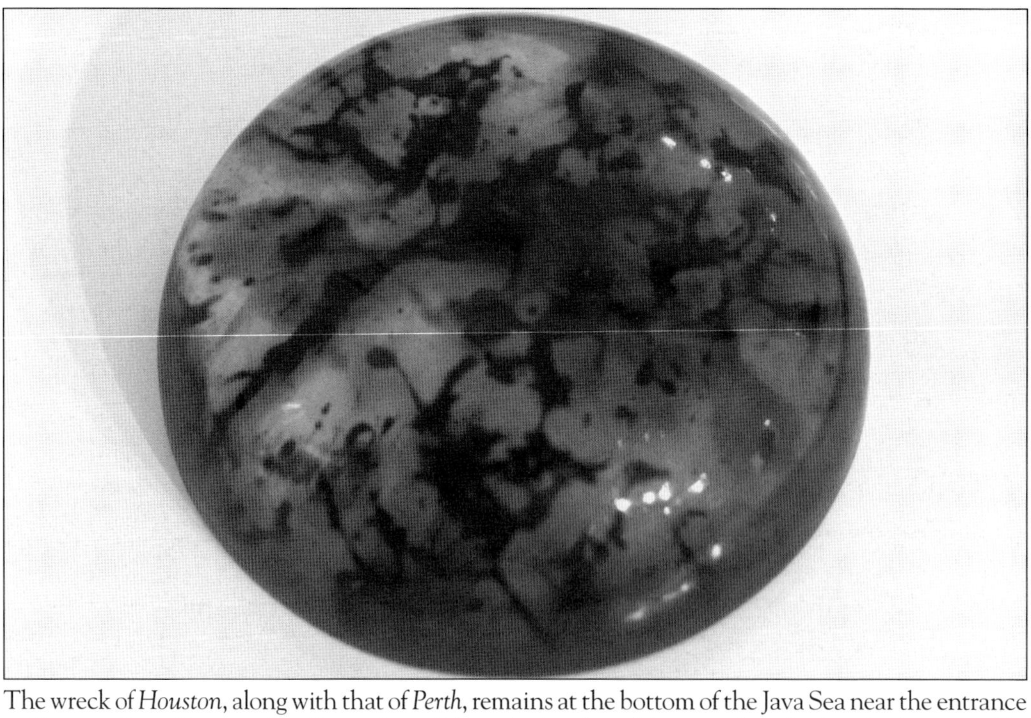

The wreck of *Houston*, along with that of *Perth*, remains at the bottom of the Java Sea near the entrance to Bantam Bay. *Houston* is still seeping oil from its bunkers 75 years after the battle. Preserved in this plastic hemisphere, some of the oil is on display at the Houston Maritime Museum. (WL)

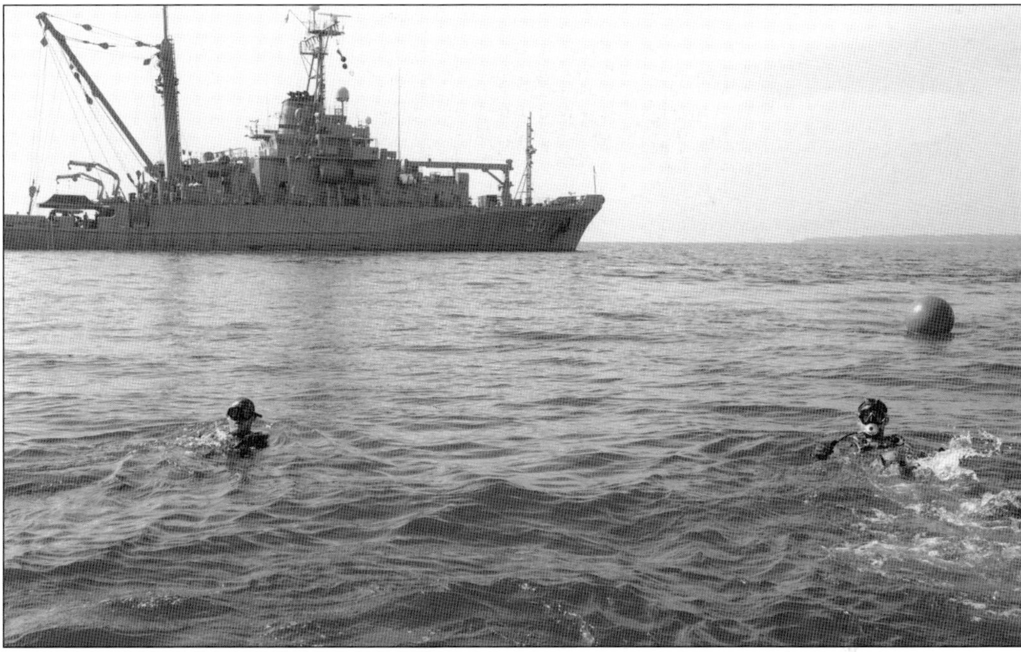

In 2014, the US Navy decided to combine underwater training with a wreck assessment of the *Houston* and *Perth* by sending the dive team of the rescue and salvage ship USNS *Safeguard* to investigate the condition of these ships on the ocean bottom. It was motivated in part by reports salvagers were illicitly stealing parts from World War II naval wrecks. (USN.)

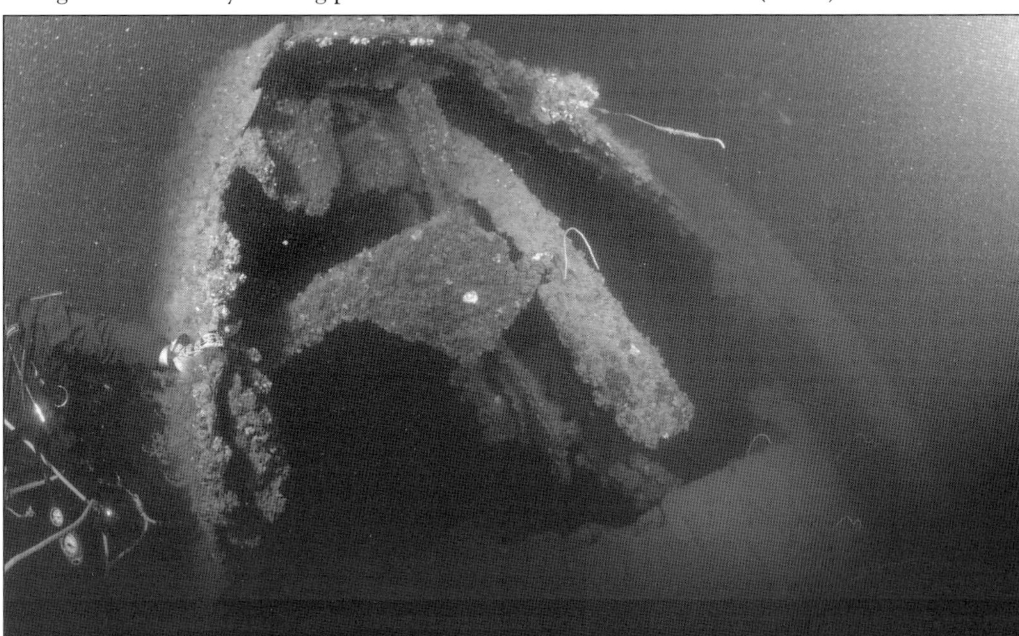

The condition of the two ships was recorded and cataloged by Navy divers. They were found to be largely intact; however, there was evidence that artifacts had been illegally removed from both ships. This is a photograph of the *Perth*, taken during the survey. (USN.)

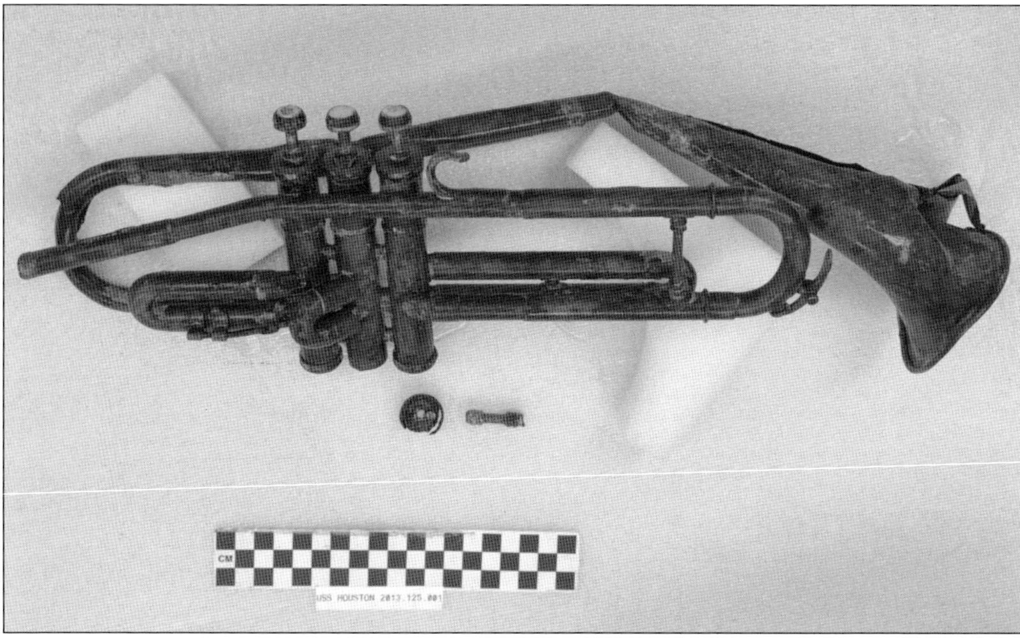

Among the objects recovered illegally from *Houston* was this brass trumpet. Taken by an Australian diver in 2013, it was subsequently voluntarily turned over to the US Naval Attaché in Canberra. The trumpet is believed to have belonged to a member of *Houston's* band. The serial number indicates that it was manufactured between 1933 and 1934. (USNHHC.)

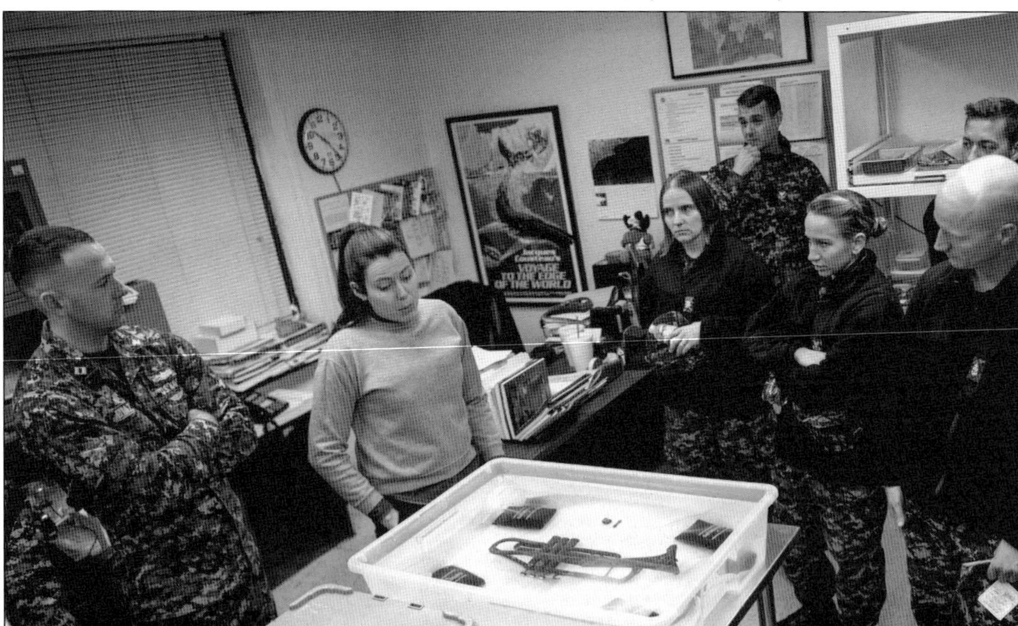

The trumpet went through an extensive conservation process removing recent corrosion and stabilizing it from further deterioration. Kate Morrand, archaeological conservator at Naval History and Heritage Command's Underwater Archaeology Branch, briefs Navy personnel on the preservation treatment of the trumpet at the Naval History and Heritage Command's laboratory of archaeology and conservation at the Washington Navy Yard. (USN.)

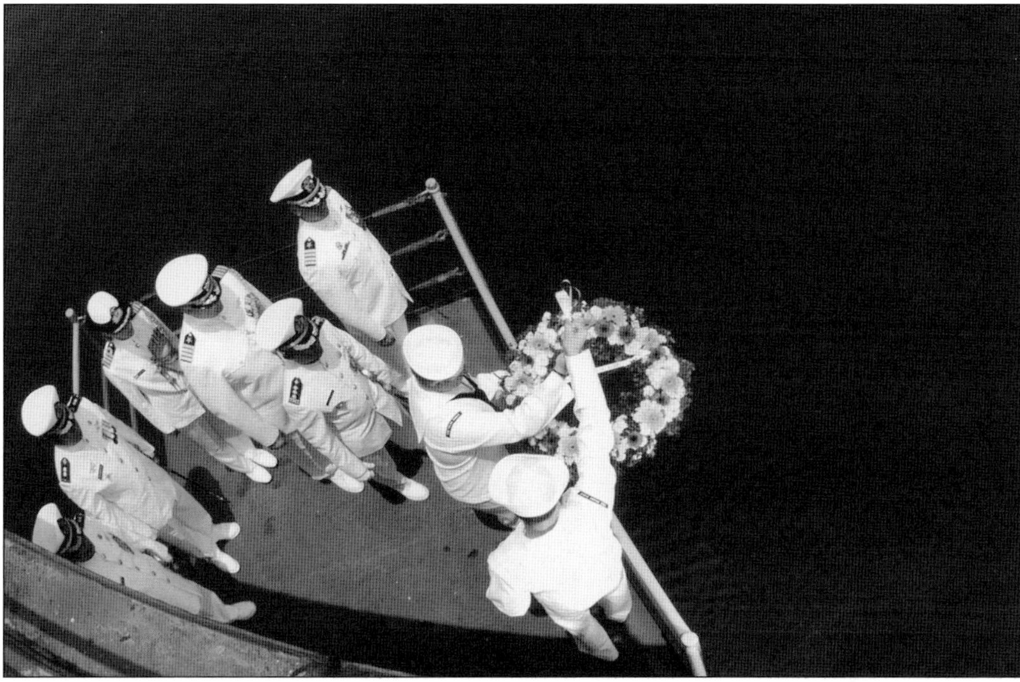

At the end of the 2014 expedition, a wreath was laid in the waters near where the two cruisers sank in memory of the sailors who died aboard these ships. Naval officers from Australia, Indonesia, and the United States participated in the ceremony. (USN.)

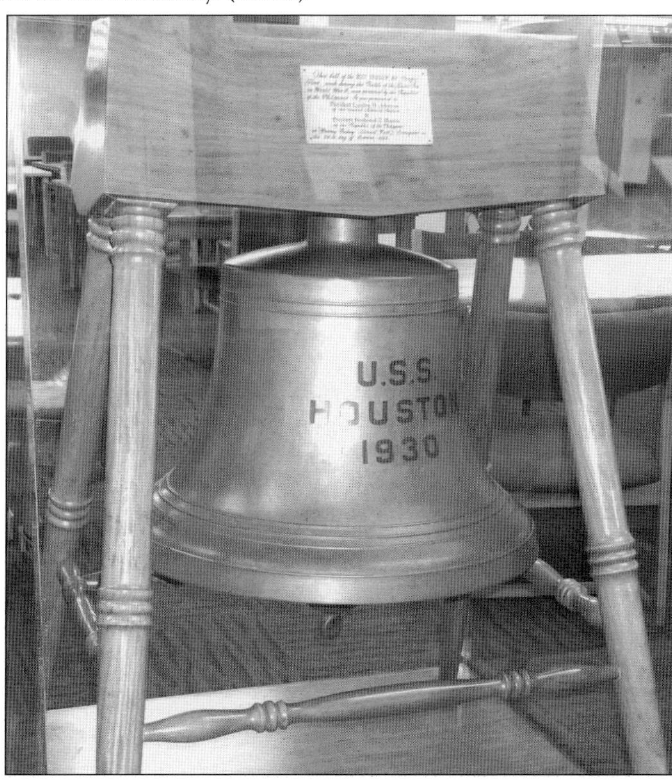

Houston had two ship's bells during its existence. This is *Houston's* original bell. It cracked in 1940 and was replaced. Sold at auction by the Navy in 1941, it disappeared during World War II. In 1966, after being found, it was presented by Philippine president Ferdinand Marcos to Pres. Lyndon Johnson. It was subsequently placed on long-term loan to the University of Houston and is on display at M.D. Anderson Library. (AC.)

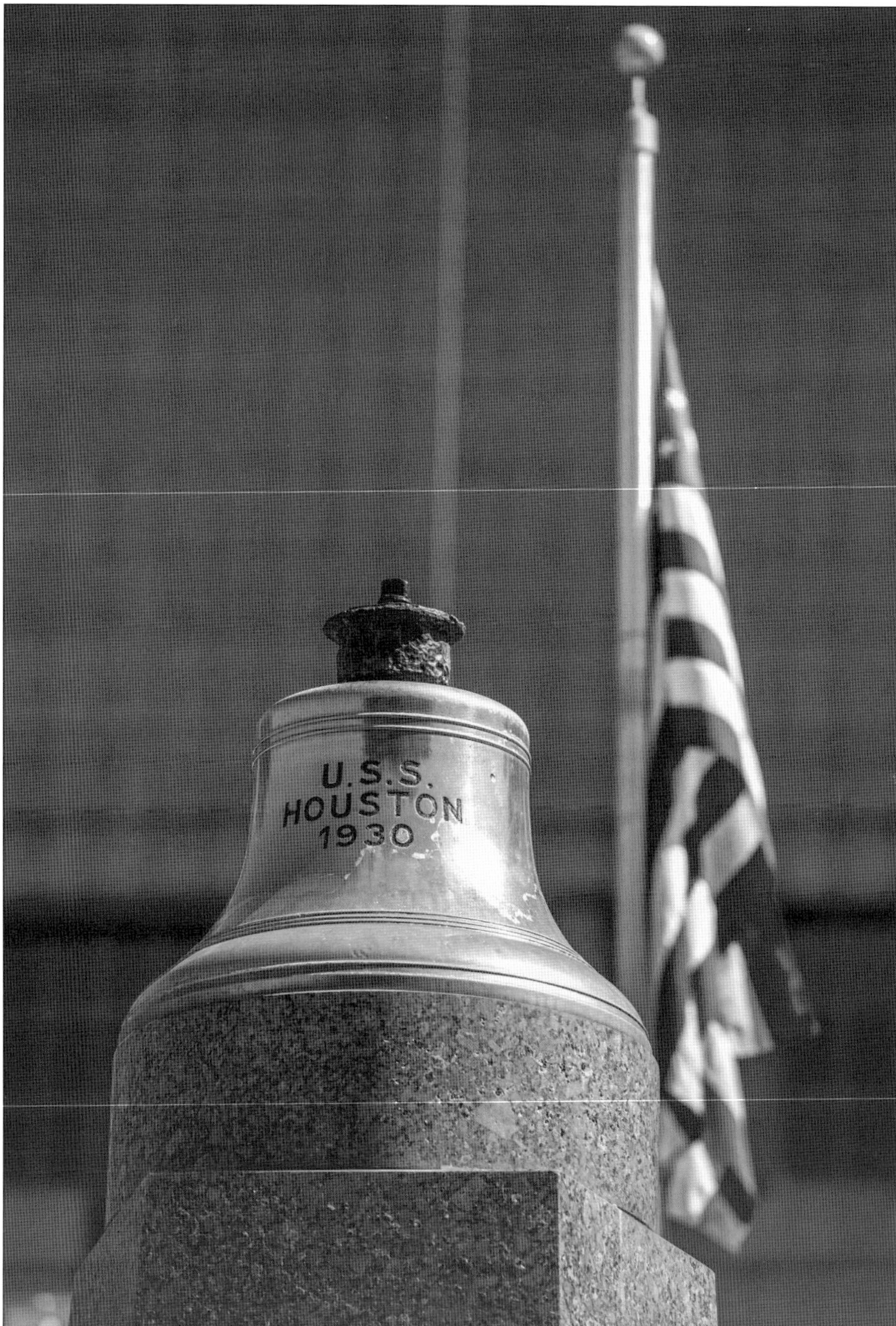

This is the replacement bell aboard *Houston* when the ship fought at the Battle of Sunda Strait. It was also recovered in July 1973 in the first dive expedition to the *Houston*. The expedition turned over the bell on behalf of the Indonesian people to the US ambassador. For many years, it was displayed at the Battleship *Texas* at the San Jacinto Battlefield Park. When the USS *Houston* (CA-30) Monument was erected in 1995, the bell was placed atop the granite obelisk, where it remains today. (WL.)

Bibliography

Dictionary of American Naval Fighting Ships. Naval History and Heritage Command. www.history.navy.mil/research/histories/ship-histories/danfs.html

Hornfischer, James D. *Ship of Ghosts: The Story of the USS* Houston, *FDR's Legendary Lost Cruiser, and the Epic Saga of her Survivors*. New York, NY: Bantam Books, 2006.

Miller, John Grider. *The Battle to Save the* Houston, *October 1944 to March 1945*. Annapolis, MD: Naval Institute Press, 1986.

Schultz, Duane. *The Last Battle Station: The Story of the USS* Houston. New York, NY: St Martin's Press, 1985.

USS Houston Blue Bonnet Newsletters. University of Houston Libraries, Digital Libraries. digital.lib.uh.edu/collection/p15195coll22.

USS Houston CA-30: The Galloping Ghost of the Java Coast. www.usshouston.org

Winslow, Walter G. "The Galloping Ghost." *United States Naval Institute Proceedings*, February 1949.

———. *The Ghost That Died at Sunda Strait*. Annapolis, MD: Naval Institute Press, 1984.

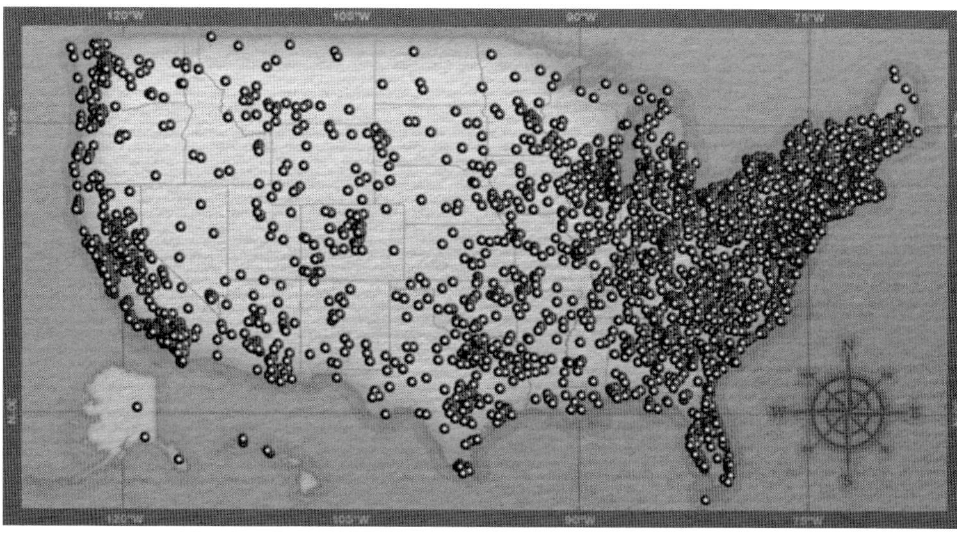

Consistent with our mission to preserve history on a local level, this book was printed in South Carolina on American-made paper and manufactured entirely in the United States. Products carrying the accredited Forest Stewardship Council (FSC) label are printed on 100 percent FSC-certified paper.

MADE IN THE USA